Writing a
Dissertation
FOR
DUMMIES®

Writing a Dissertation FOR DUMMIES®

by Dr Carrie Winstanley

A John Wiley and Sons, Ltd, Publication

Writing a Dissertation For Dummies®

Published by
John Wiley & Sons, Ltd
The Atrium
Southern Gate
Chichester
West Sussex
PO19 8SQ
England

E-mail (for orders and customer service enquires): cs-books@wiley.co.uk

Visit our Home Page on www.wiley.com

Copyright © 2009 John Wiley & Sons, Ltd, Chichester, West Sussex, England

Reprinted with corrections 2010

Published by John Wiley & Sons, Ltd, Chichester, West Sussex

For general information on our other products and services, please contact our Customer Care Department within the U.S. at 877-762-2974, outside the U.S. at 317-572-3993, or fax 317-572-4002.

For technical support, please visit www.wiley.com/techsupport.

Wiley also publishes its books in a variety of electronic formats. Some content that appears in print may not be available in electronic books.

British Library Cataloguing in Publication Data: A catalogue record for this book is available from the British Library

ISBN: 978-0-470-74270-9

Printed and bound in Great Britain by TJ International, Padstow, Cornwall

10 9 8 7

WILEY

About the Author

Dr Carrie Winstanley works with undergraduate and postgraduate students, teaching different aspects of education including psychology, philosophy and history. She also teaches and researches with highly-able children and is especially interested in those who also have learning difficulties, sensory impairments and/or disabilities. She regularly runs workshops with children and adults in museums, galleries and schools, and is fascinated by learning and teaching in formal and non-formal contexts.

Carrie has taught in Higher Education for a decade, following ten years of teaching in schools (in the maintained, independent and international sectors). She is also an educational consultant and writer. Carrie holds higher degrees in social justice and education (PhD, London), psychology of education (MPhil, Cambridge), as well as the philosophy and history of education (MA, Surrey), plus an undergraduate degree in education (BHEd, Kingston, CNAA). She was awarded a National Teaching Fellowship from the Higher Education Academy in 2008.

Dedication

This book is dedicated to the students I have supervised and the tutors who have supervised me.

Acknowledgements

I am grateful to colleagues, both in my immediate workplace and in the wider Higher Education sector, for myriad discussions over the years about supervision and academic writing. Thanks are also due to the many students whose dissertations I have shared and the tutors who supervised my own writing; you have all taught me a great deal.

This project was made possible by Wejdan Ismail and Simon Bell at Wiley, and my heartfelt thanks are due to them and to Colette Holden, Christine Lea and Anne O'Rorke. I appreciate all the support and the perceptive comments that have kept me on track, juggling this book with other projects and with real life too.

I would like to thank Ma, Pa and Suzi for their wonderful ongoing help and support and Missy for some excellent conversations about students and the common mistakes they make. I am also truly grateful to Andy for patience, endless cups of tea at just the right moment and a calming influence.

Publisher's Acknowledgements

We're proud of this book; please send us your comments through our Dummies online registration form located at www.dummies.com/register/.

Some of the people who helped bring this book to market include the following:

Acquisitions, Editorial, and Media Development

Commissioning Editor: Wejdan Ismail

Publishing Assistant: Jennifer Prytherch

Development Editor: Simon Bell

Content Editor: Jo Theedom

Developer: Colette Holden

Copy Editor: Christine Lea

Proofreader: Anne O'Rorke

Technical Reviewer: Jane Wallace

Executive Project Editor: Daniel Mersey

Cover Photos: © Image Source Black/Alamy

Cartoons: Ed McLachlan

Composition Services

Project Coordinator: Lynsey Stanford

Layout and Graphics: Christin Swinford

Proofreader: Jessica Kramer

Indexer: Cheryl Duksta

Contents at a Glance

Table of Contents

Introduction

*I*f you're reading this you're either already a student starting to prepare for your final year project or someone planning to study, and wondering what's entailed. Whatever your motivation, you'll find this book gives you answers to the questions you have and to plenty of questions you didn't realise you wanted to ask. The dissertation is the most significant piece of work most students undertake on their degree course. It's worth more than any other aspect, it has more time assigned to it and it's often the only time when you have the opportunity for sustained one-to-one support from your academic tutor.

You should do all you can to make the most of the possibilities afforded to you in undertaking a dissertation. This book helps you maximise the positive aspects of the experience. You can pick up tips and find out about common pitfalls, as well as having a rich source of help and support for your writing and research.

Before you read further, take a moment to consider that congratulations are in order! If you're writing a social science dissertation, you're probably in the third or final year of your degree course. On most degree courses, a dissertation, or final year project, is obligatory. You can't register for such modules, unless you've successfully completed previous coursework, essays, exams, presentations, portfolios, and many other requirements. You are already a success story!

However, there is still a long way to go. A dissertation is an exciting, challenging, rewarding and often wonderful experience. Simultaneously, it's also likely to be exhausting, frustrating, time-consuming and irritating. You need to maximise the positive and minimise the negative and that's where this book can really help.

About This Book

This book is presented in an accessible way, through straightforward writing and a user-friendly format. To make sense of the book, you don't need to read it from start to finish. In fact you don't even need to read it in order. It's a reference for you to dip into, as and when you need advice or help. It covers the usual empirical dissertations with all you'll need about research methods and analysis, but it also helps you if you're planning a library-based, theoretical thesis.

Conventions Used in This Book

Each chapter covers the basics you'll need and also provides further details and examples that you can skim over if you're pushed for time. I also flag up points in the book where you can cross-reference to different chapters, so that you can read the book thematically with ease.

For ease of navigation, I use the following conventions:

- ✔ *Italic* is used for emphasis, to highlight new words, and terms which the text defines.

- ✔ **Bold** text is used to indicate keywords in bulleted lists.

- ✔ Monofont is used for Internet addresses.

- ✔ Sidebars, the shaded grey boxes you see from time to time, point out information which might come in handy, but doesn't qualify as essential reading.

What You're Not to Read

If you're undertaking an empirical dissertation, you can skip over the sections that deal with non-empirical work and vice-versa. If anything arises where a cross-reference is helpful, I have directed you to it in the text. Here and there I've included anecdotes and examples that are interesting but not in the least bit essential to your dissertation journey. They're presented in grey shaded boxes – sidebars – and you can leave them out without worrying that you've missed something essential.

Foolish Assumptions

I wrote this book with social science students in mind. As I was writing this book I had flashbacks to conversations and supervisions with countless students and colleagues over the years. As I worked on each page, I was thinking about students just like the ones I've supervised over the years, just like those I'm working with now and just like those I'll work with in the future. There's no template for these students: They come from different backgrounds, have varied interests, diverse ideas, unique constellations of skills and their own distinctive approaches to their work. I have made a few basic assumptions about you, though. This book is for you if you:

✔ Are already on a degree course or embarking on one.

✔ Are committed to completing your dissertation.

✔ Have already written some essays.

✔ Are studying some aspect of social science.

✔ Want to improve your grades.

By definition you have to be pretty on the ball to be doing a degree (usually!). This book is for you if you'd just like some help getting to grips with what's expected of you.

How This Book Is Organised

The book has six parts, mostly about the process of the dissertation with a few about broader concerns such as social science in general, or your well-being, along the way. Here's a summary of each section to help you navigate your way around *Writing a Dissertation For Dummies.*

Part 1: Understanding What a Dissertation Is

You need to be clear about which subjects come under the umbrella heading of the 'Social Sciences' and you also need to be sure that you understand the different types of long essays and research projects that are called 'dissertations'. This first part of the book will help you locate your work within the discipline of social science and set you on the path to a useful and realistic research question to form the basis of your dissertation.

Part 11: Getting Set Up for Your Dissertation

In order to get the most out of this project you need to be very clear about exactly what is expected. This part of the book will help you prepare effectively and will save you time and grief once the project is underway. Planning thoroughly means you'll be more organised and won't miss anything vital. This section also gives you strategies for reading and taking notes.

Part III: Getting On with Your Research

Now you are clear about your research question you need to get on with gathering the data to answer your question. This part of the book helps you to get to grips with actually starting to write up your notes. It will also help you gather the required data now that you have a clearer focus and you know what you are looking for both in libraries and through collecting your own experimental data. It also helps you keep an overview of the dissertation process as a whole.

Part IV: Writing and Polishing Your Work

Your data is collected and analysed or your arguments are delineated and your references are stacking up nicely. This part helps you get from piles of ideas to a clear set of arguments, rounded off with a strong conclusion, all fully referenced and neatly presented. There is a glimmer of light at the end of the dissertation tunnel.

Part V: Managing the Overall Experience

Writing a dissertation is an endurance test! You will need stamina to sustain your interest and determination. Giving some attention to your work habits and to your lifestyle will pay dividends when the inevitable rush to the finishing post kicks in, some time down the line.

Part VI: The Part of Tens

The Part of Tens provides you with quick tips and warnings. You'll see how to avoid tripping up on the more commonly found obstacles, reminders about what you need to include and ultimately the definitive list of final advice to ensure you're all done and dusted to the satisfaction of your eagle-eyed examiners.

Icons Used in This Book

The icons you see scattered through the book tell you what you have to know, what you could do with knowing, and what you should steer well clear of.

This icon highlights helpful strategies for your dissertation experience.

Wherever you see this icon there's a point that you should make into a mental or physical note – something to keep in mind.

This book is full of the advice that students really need but don't usually get until after the work is completed. They're priceless alerts to help you avoid mistakes.

Anywhere you see the gradebuster icon you know what you'll have to do in order to get a brilliant mark. Aiming for a first class mark? Look out for these hints and helps.

Where to Go from Here

The typical place to go from here is to the first chapter, but in the case of this book, you should start with what you need. If you're stuck on your questionnaire, head for Chapter 8; if you can't find any journals, it's Chapter 6. If you're just overwhelmed with the whole thing, turn to Chapter 17 and if you're in a panic, start with Part VI to get some perspective on what really needs to be done.

If you're feeling fine and want to just get going on your dissertation, put on the kettle, plump up the sofa cushions and browse through the book until you find something that grabs your eye. Good luck on your dissertation journey.

Part I
Understanding What a Dissertation Is

'I wonder if you could spare a minute to look over my dissertation & just check I've not done <u>too</u> much.'

In this part...

*I*n this part I explain what a dissertation is, how much work it involves, and on what sort of course you can expect to be asked to write one. I also give you the tools to produce a workable and rewarding research question – the question which underpins your dissertation – including how to choose an area which maintains your interest.

Chapter 1

Sorting Out the Basics of a Dissertation

. . . .

In This Chapter

▶ Finding out what a dissertation is

▶ Discovering the different types of dissertation

▶ Sounding out some of the main social science subjects

. . . .

Chances are you've picked up this book because you're embarking on a dissertation, or similar final-year project. This implies that you've successfully completed previous essays and exams and probably even presentations and portfolios as well. So, you're already a successful student and this book will help you build on your strengths whilst identifying ways to improve how you study.

If you're still quite far off from getting to your final year, thinking about it now is a great start - thorough preparation is going to help you succeed.

A dissertation is just an important sounding name for a long essay – based on your own research. Writing a dissertation is an exciting, challenging, rewarding and often wonderful experience. At the same time it can be exhausting, time-consuming, frustrating and exasperating.

Take heart! In this book I set out to tell you the ins and outs of writing a dissertation and give you all the help you need to make sure your dissertation is a success.

What Is Social Science, Exactly?

Broadly, the social sciences look at the state of society and the people that make up societies. By now you're sure to have discovered that the social sciences cover an enormously wide range of subjects. Deciding what counts as social science is an ongoing area for debate – a topic that's great for a dissertation in itself! For clarity in this book I'm going to rely on the Economic and Social Research Council (ESRC) definition of social sciences. The ESRC is the main government funding council for research in social science in England and Wales and so their ideas have currency. In the section 'Pinpointing your field of study' later in the chapter you can find a description of each of the areas the ESRC considers makes up the social sciences.

Here's a mini A–Z rundown of the main social science disciplines; a refresher course that's hopefully going to get your dissertation juices flowing. If the subject you're studying is related to any of the disciplines in the list, with luck the book is going to be spot-on for your dissertation. Throughout this book I use examples from the more commonly studied social science subjects, such as education and sociology, but the ideas apply equally to other sub-disciplines of the social sciences like sociolinguistics, journalism, international relations, criminology and gender studies. These fields usually fall under a broader discipline, so gender studies form part of sociology while international relations constitute part of political science.

Anthropology

Anthropology is the scientific study of human beings and their way of life. The word anthropology comes from the Greek 'anthropos', meaning a 'human being' or 'person'. The main research method in the science of anthropology is *ethnography*, which involves collecting raw data through field work and reviewing the data to get the whole picture of the society being studied and linking the data to other areas such as archaeology, biology, linguistics and the humanities.

Economics

The science of economics analyses and describes how wealth is produced, distributed and consumed. Economists use current thinking backed up by data to find ways of balancing people's economic needs with the way the needs are going to be financed . The word economics comes from the Greek words 'oikos', meaning 'family' or 'household' and 'nomos' meaning 'custom' or 'law'. Generally, economics is split into two branches: the study of individual households, companies, industries, and commodities (microeconomics) and the study of economics on a large scale such as national income and international trade (macroeconomics).

Over the last 20 years, the methods and reasoning underpinning economics are being applied to other social issues. For example, the economic principles of cause and effect, which tries to explain how the economy is affecting people's behaviour in areas such as businesses, families and relationships. Economics also takes in green economics, Marxist ideas, socialism, globalisation, institutional economics and economic sociology. Despite the many different areas that economics embraces, the science is above all concerned with getting value for money by way of human effort, or 'labour'.

Education

Education (also called pedagogy) is the science of teaching and learning. Educational science covers both theoretical and applied research and draws on a multitude of disciplines as well as taking into account other factors affecting learning: emotional, social, psychological, philosophical, historical and the physical setting. Hailing from the Latin verb 'educare', to educate meaning 'to draw out' education concerns acquiring knowledge and skills, and nurturing talents and potential abilities to give the individual the opportunity of leading a full life and making a positive contribution to society.

Much educational research is linked to schooling and the development of children and adolescents, but education isn't just confined to these areas. Educationalists claim that prebirth experiences affect education (and educational opportunity) and studies include a cradle-to-grave approach. Informal education through leisure activities is also getting more attention and educational practice, such as testing and examinations, are continually being questioned, evaluated and explored.

Geography (human)

Geography is made up of three sub-disciplines: human geography (people's relationship with the built environment); physical geography (the natural environment); and environmental geography (the interaction between people and their physical environment). Practical applications of geography include urban planning, transportation and studying the built environment. Geographers use a range of data including aerial photography and statistics in their research. Some geographers consider geography as a pure science, which is why you find that physical geography is separated from human geography in some universities.

History

History is more often thought of as being part of the humanities than of the social sciences. In the UK, history research is funded by the Arts and Humanities Research Council (AHRC). The study of history particularly focuses on both continuity and change and mostly considers the development of humanity as continuous, providing a narrative of past events. Postmodernist theory is challenging the idea of continuity, but for most undergraduate dissertations taking the more traditional approach of continuity still holds good.

The main reason for including the study of history in the social sciences is backed up by the research methods being used when researching history, which includes using primary sources, secondary sources and other evidence. Data comes in the form of documents, public records, images, artefacts and personal memoirs.

Law

Law is all about being governed by established legal systems. The law plays an important and significant part in society, which is why the law is so important to social scientists. Taking a broader view, the law is part of international relations and can be more difficult to enforce. International law is more a study of what's ethically acceptable and of finding ways of using legal systems to work for the good of the majority. The study of law links closely with political science, economics and philosophy, blurring the boundaries between the humanities and the social sciences when it comes to deciding which academic discipline law fits into best.

Linguistics

The science of linguistics deals with language and includes both cognitive and social aspects of the use of language. Linguistics is divided into related subdivisions:

- **Phonetics and phonology:** Deals with pronunciation and speech production.
- **Neurolinguistics:** Explores the role of the brain in language development, and the processing and storage of language in the brain, the investigation of diseases or abnormalities and recovery from injuries and emotional shock.
- **Syntax:** Concerns the rules governing sentence structure.
- **Semantics:** Relates to the meaning of words.

Other social science subjects, such as history and anthropology, include evolution and the origins of language, and psychology looks at emotional and cognitive aspects to understanding and observing human language.

Political science

Political science is the theory and practice of government and politics, which involves exploring and analysing political systems and political behaviour. The study of political science includes international relations and law, foreign policy, comparative politics and studies of superpowers. At national levels political science includes civics, the notion of participation and democracy, political development, public administration and law, justice and public policy.

When studying political science, social science methods are frequently used: surveys, statistical analysis, case studies, and building conceptual models for exploring ideas. Primary sources (historical documents, official records) are used as well as secondary sources, like journal articles and government data.

Psychology (social)

Psychology is the study of the mind and human behaviour and is both a research and an applied discipline. Having knowledge of how people behave is used when treating mental illness and helping people cope with problems occurring in their daily lives. Close links exist between psychology and other fields such as neuroscience, biology and sociology, and specialisms including social psychology, neuropsychology, clinical psychology and educational psychology.

Sociology

Sociologists study the origin, development, structure and functioning of society and are interested in how society is organised, both on micro and macro levels. Sociology is a relatively new academic discipline, only reaching back to the early 19th century. Since then researchers and commentators have created a body of social theory and apply social science research methods to the discipline. Sociology has specialist areas such as: criminology (the study of deviant and criminal behaviour); demography (population studies); gender and race studies and issues to do with socioeconomic status. Sociology provides information about patterns of behaviour across society, influencing policy making.

Social work

Social workers are involved in the public sector, supporting individual people, families, communities and groups and helping people to deal with their social problems. The aim of social work is to make sure that social justice is being applied and to improve the lives of those people less able to make their needs and wishes known. Social workers are committed to enhancing the quality of life for all members of society by applying social theory and research findings to the everyday lives of people at every level of society.

All aspects of social science are included in social work. Social workers build up specialist knowledge from evidence they've collected using social science research methods, such as collecting empirical data through surveys, studying individuals through case-studies and using qualitative information.

Other areas of social science

There are also some other areas of the social sciences that you may like to think about:

- ✓ **Media studies** – involves the analysis of images, sounds and text you get via the media: TV, radio, newspapers and so on.
- ✓ **Development studies** – is about the developing world.
- ✓ **Information science** – looks at systems and methods of storing and retrieving information.
- ✓ **Sociobiology** – attempts to prove that social behaviour has a genetic basis influencing human development.

Pinpointing your field of study

If you didn't come across the subject you're studying in the A–Z list, a useful source for finding your subject is the ESRC website (www.esrcsocietytoday.ac.uk/ESRCInfoCentre/index.aspx) which describes social science in a way that you may find more helpful than a listing of subjects.

Social science is a wide-ranging discipline. For example, the kinds of jobs that social science students go on to do include teaching, policing, business, social work, health care, local government, urban planning, and many more.

Seeing what makes social science a distinct discipline

Although the social sciences include so many different disciplines what they all have in common is that they address the concerns of society and of people. As a result, many of the disciplines adopt similar theories and research methods. The overlap of disciplines can be subtle or overt.

Your reading and your degree course has likely been helping you make sense of the many subject areas in the social sciences and the theories and research methods that are being used. In Table 1-1 you can see a tiny sample of the kinds of social science questions you may meet but which are frequently presented in different forms. I've also noted some of the related theoretical standpoints and a brief summary of the research area.

Table 1-1	Meeting Social Science Questions	
Question	*Theory*	*Summary*
What is knowledge?	Positivist theory	Pursuing scientific method reveals all true knowledge.
How is power constructed?	Conflict theory	Change and order arise from social groups versus individuals struggling to maximise power.
What is society?	Cultural pluralism/ multiculturalism	Coexistence of different cultures within the same area.
How can we decide what is the right course of action?	Utilitarianism	Decisions based on what is best for the greatest number of people.

The more you appreciate and are comfortable with the variety of approaches in the social sciences the easier it's going to be for you to excel in your dissertation. How to improve your knowledge? – by reading, thinking and discussing topics thoroughly with others.

In Table 1-1 you see just a fraction of the theories that abound in the social sciences – research is shifting and developing all the time. For example, you may have already come across critical theory; feminist theory; dialectic theory; materialism; rationalism; postmodernism; pragmatism; structuralism, to name but a few.

Researching social science

No matter which aspect of social science you're studying, you're likely to be faced with a range of research methodologies, some more favoured than others. In Table 1-2 you can see some examples of methods of research that you may meet in your reading.

Table 1-2   Examples of Research Methods

Research Method	Summary
Ethnography	Getting an inside view of a cultural group and trying to understand the group's point of view.
Discourse analysis	Evaluating and analysing communication as a way of uncovering and exposing meaning, viewpoints, understanding and change.
Semiotics	Studying signs, symbols and sign systems to find out how signs and symbols reflect and represent people and communities (and meaning in general).
Hermeneutics (also a theory)	Methods for interpreting texts and examining how the texts link to the interpreter's personal and social context, and so affecting the interpreter's understanding.

You're sure to come across the words *qualitative* and *quantitative* in connection with social science research. Here are the main differences between the two terms together with a brief description of each term:

- **Qualitative data** – usually takes the form of words, pictures and objects, and the data can be subjective because the researcher is personally involved in collecting rich data.

- **Quantitative data** – is numerical data and focuses on classification, statistical models and numerical information that's collected as objectively as possible using research tools.

I've given you a very simple introduction and summary of what social science research involves. You need to read on in this book to get a fuller picture of what social science research involves.

Understanding the Different Types of Dissertation

In social science research, both practical and theoretical considerations are of the utmost importance. In your dissertation, however, you're likely to be taking a practical *or* a theoretical approach. For an undergraduate dissertation, your examiner is going to expect you to choose a largely theoretical or a mainly practical look at your chosen subject. Any useful practical research you carry out requires a sound theoretical basis, and any theoretical study you do needs to link to what's happening in the world around you.

A theoretical study can be mainly abstract with an emphasis on the philosophical, ethical and cultural considerations of the subject, or your subject can be an applied theoretical study with an emphasis on political, social or economic issues, for example. More practical research studies in social science are usually about exploring issues through surveys, action research, observations, case-studies or a review of existing studies.

The type of dissertation you end up writing depends on the topic you're researching. In Table 1-3 I give you a few examples of different ways of approaching a topic just to get you thinking:

Table 1-3   Examples of Practical and Theoretical Approaches to Writing a Dissertation

Concern	Method	Type of Study
Theory/hypothesis	Analysis	Non-empirical
Strategy	Analysis	Non-empirical with examples
Issue	Question people	Empirical
Type of behaviour	Observation	Empirical
Personal viewpoint	Reporting / reflection	Narrative

Empirical dissertations

An empirical dissertation involves collecting data. For example, to gather the views of patients at a GP's surgery, volunteers in a police service, children in a play centre or translators in a refugee centre, you have to find ways of asking the individuals involved what they think, or review what they're doing. You can collect your data in many ways: from questionnaires and observations to interviews and focus groups. Or, you may prefer to collect your data by taking another approach such as looking at and analysing existing data from new angles, making useful comparisons or drawing interesting parallels.

Even if the focus of your dissertation is on using data, don't forget that you're still going to need a sound theoretical basis for your work.

Non-empirical dissertations

Making the choice to do a non-empirical dissertation shouldn't be taken lightly. Sustaining an argument over the length of your whole dissertation is a distinct challenge. If you enjoy spending time in the library, reading, thinking and discussing theory, this is likely to be the right choice for you. If you know that making the university library your home for weeks on end is going to be difficult, you may be better off choosing a more empirical research question to explore.

Key theories in your discipline such as feminism or pragmatism can be the basis of an abstract discussion in your dissertation. Subjects such as sociology have this type of theory at their centre and so it's perfectly valid, for example, to discuss aspects of the theory of pragmatism as your dissertation topic. A dissertation that draws upon major theories, such as in education, more often takes an applied route, but can also be exclusively theoretical, for example, some work in the philosophy of education.

Narrative dissertations

You're more than likely to choose an empirical or a non-empirical dissertation. However, in other disciplines you may come across different methods of producing a dissertation.

Dissertations in many science subjects include or even focus around a laboratory report describing all the aspects of setting up, carrying out and analysing a complex experiment. In physical geography, time is spent somewhere wild and windswept collecting data needed for analysis. Laboratory work and field trips are a key part of the student experience of writing a dissertation. It's possible you may even use a passage from the classics or biography as an illustration or example in your dissertation.

Reading Other Students' Dissertations

A great way of getting a feel for what you're letting yourself in for by doing your dissertation is to look at some examples of previous students' work. Generally, undergraduate dissertations aren't held in the university library so you may have to ask your supervisor if you wish to look at a few undergraduate dissertations. The best way of going about reading the dissertations is to set aside a couple of hours and give yourself plenty of space to spread out. It's a really good idea to try to compare several dissertations at the same time because this gives you a sense of the range of acceptable formats and also discourages you from trying to read each dissertation from cover to cover – yes, you do have better ways of spending your valuable time.

I want to discourage you from the practice of reading large amounts of other students' work (unless your supervisor has specifically told you that there's a dissertation you simply must read) as you've no guarantee of the quality of the student's work – the dissertation may turn out to be a not very inspiring model.

Checking level and course

If the dissertation you're looking at is an MA dissertation, the format is likely to be similar to your undergraduate work, but the work itself is obviously at a higher level, so don't be overwhelmed or worried about what the MA student has achieved. MA dissertations can sometimes be very intimidating!

When you're sure you're looking at an undergraduate dissertation, take some time to check whether the dissertation is from the same programme as the one you're following. Remember that regulations change over the years, and the accepted format for the dissertation you're looking at may no longer be acceptable. In 'Fathoming the format and layout' there are some questions to ask yourself while you're flicking through the dissertations you've selected.

Fathoming format and layout

A well-laid-out dissertation needs to be clear and easy to navigate around, and be manageable in size and weight. Ask yourself:

- ✔ Is the student's name and/or identity number clearly displayed?

- ✔ Is the title obvious?

- ✔ Is the dissertation properly bound?

- ✔ Are the contents pages, appendixes, chapter headings eye-catching and easy to read?

- ✔ Are the abstract, acknowledgements and introduction in the right order?

- ✔ If the dissertation contains charts and graphs, are the charts and graphs clear, and do they make an effective use of colour?

- ✔ Has the student chosen a suitable font that's easy on the eye?

Considering content and argument

You're not going to have time to read the dissertations right through, but you can get a sense of the content by scanning through the chapter headings and subheadings displayed both on the contents pages and in the dissertation itself. If you can find a dissertation that deals with a topic close to your own, jot down some of the chapter headings to see if this dissertation has any links to your own subject. (Don't use the dissertation as your one and only guide, however.)

If you see ideas that you can use in your own dissertation, make a note for future reference. At this stage, you're just getting an overall impression of what an undergraduate dissertation looks like, so concentrating on the introductory section or wherever the student introduces his research question is your best bet. Take note of how the most successful research questions are generally rather narrow, or at least firmly focused. With luck, the student has explained how he narrowed down his ideas from a formless idea to a workable question. Compare a few of the dissertation titles to find out which you think works the best.

You also need to take a good look at the research methodologies. If the student carried out an empirical dissertation using data and practical examples, keep a record of any ideas that strike you as particularly effective. If the dissertation is non-empirical and concerns analysis and interpretation of ideas, look at how the student has structured his chapters. For example, do subheadings relate to theorists or specific ideas, or are the subheadings thematic? If there are no subheadings in chapters, how has the student *signposted* their reader?

If you can find your way around the dissertation effectively, this is a piece of work that has been well signposted. Don't forget that the examiner is likely to have a pile of dissertations to get through, and the easier the dissertation is structured, the more likely that the examiner is going to be in a good mood when he's marking. From leafing through the dissertations, you should now have a good idea of what really works well. If you have any doubts about your judgement, ask your supervisor to check what you think is great is also something that your supervisor considers to be an appropriate model.

Examples of dissertation titles are thoroughly considered in Chapter 2 when you're invited to get to grips with your research question. Take the opportunity for now of jotting down any good (or awful) dissertation titles while you've got the dissertations in front of you.

Decoding bibliographies

Make sure you spend a little time looking at the bibliographies and references in the different dissertations. The way you have to compile your bibliography is set out in the dissertation guidelines, but it's still worth paying attention to the way that students use underlining, italics, spacing, alignment, capital letters, and so on. As you compare the different bibliographies, make a note of which are the best set out and easiest to read – these are the models you want to take on board (as long as the model meets your dissertation guidelines, of course).

Also, look through the chapters, examining how students refer to books, journals, websites, reports and other sources in the body of their dissertations. Again, you're given guidelines to work to but it's a valuable exercise to see different referencing styles in practice.

Criticising constructively

Flicking through a dissertation and pulling it apart, picking on all the errors and focusing on what you think you can do better if the dissertation was your work, is all too easy. Of course the student who's written the dissertation is unlikely to be sitting next to you, waiting for feedback, but don't forget that there are likely to be some good bits in the dissertation (failed ones generally don't make it to the library). Before you get too smug, picking on the bits that need improvement, remember that this student has successfully completed the task that you're about to begin, and he's probably acutely aware of all the things that he could have done better!

Don't spend too long on looking over your fellow students' work – what you're aiming to do is come up with some great ideas for your own dissertation and discover a few things you want to avoid. And that's all.

Chapter 2

Thinking About a Research Question

In This Chapter

▶ Discovering what makes you tick

▶ Finding a suitable topic

▶ Putting your research proposal in order

*F*inding an inspiring research question for your dissertation and coming up with a title that's short, clear and informative can be a long and complex business. In this chapter I help you through the process of finding a research topic that gets you fired up and ready to go. Discovering what intrigues and excites you is an excellent way of selecting a topic to research and for creating a great dissertation proposal.

Discovering What Excites You

As your dissertation develops, the wording of your title may alter, but the basic question(s) that you're researching stay much the same. It's vital that you make a careful choice about what you want to research. Discovering a topic that keeps you interested and motivated is all important. Writing your dissertation is going to take up a lot more time than you normally spend on an essay or other coursework. Most institutions allow one year for dissertations, although some courses allow a little more time, others a little less. At the least, writing your dissertation is going to take a good few months and it can be hard keeping motivated even when you're genuinely interested. Trying to research and write a dissertation that isn't holding your interest can be difficult to manage as well as draining and dispiriting. Some of the questions that I'm asking in the following list may seem trivial, but trust me – if you can tap into areas that arouse your curiosity, you're sure to enjoy the dissertation process a lot more than if you pick a topic based on what you think is expected of you or what you think is going to be easy and manageable.

Jot down your answers to the following questions in your dissertation notebook (yes – new stationery!):

- ✔ What are your favourite TV programmes?
- ✔ What type of music do you like best?
- ✔ What sort of films do you enjoy watching?
- ✔ What kind of books do you read for entertainment?
- ✔ When spending time with friends, what do you like to talk about?
- ✔ What inspired you to go to university?
- ✔ Do you enjoy your own company?
- ✔ Have you a childhood interest that you're still keeping up?
- ✔ What do you do with your free time?
- ✔ Which subjects on your course are you enjoying most?
- ✔ When chatting with other students about what they're studying, which subjects sound appealing and interesting?
- ✔ What sort of impact do you think your career is going to make?

From your answers, try looking for patterns in what you enjoy doing. For example, you may find you enjoy listening to political music, watching documentaries and discussing politics with friends. Or, you have a passion for reading novels set in foreign countries, you like world music and wearing fashions from other cultures. Having highlighted aspects of yourself that make you tick can inspire you to get working on a research topic such as the cost of providing sports facilities in deprived areas or the particular needs of newly arriving immigrants. For example, if you've listed watching soap operas or reading magazines, it seems you're really interested in relationships and people's lives. Think about how your research can focus on people's emotional response to their situation.

Although following your interests is important, be careful not to bring any deeply held personal feelings or hurts into your research. If you select a topic that's upsetting, you may not be doing the subject or yourself any favours. You need to strike a balance, so avoid choosing a topic that's closely linked to a negative personal experience.

Following your interests

One of my students became aware that dance had fascinated her from early childhood, but was viewing dance as just a hobby and not seeing how dance linked in any way with her studies for a degree in education. After realising that her interest in dance was still important to her, she ended up evaluating dance workshops for primary-aged school children, although her original idea was to carry out a theoretical study. She was delighted to be able to research something that she felt passionate about and make it part of her studies. Another student identified an interest in photography and was inspired to carry out a project involving working with preschool children on their perceptions of their day care settings; giving the children digital cameras and analysing the pictures they took of their environment as data for her dissertation.

Picking an idea that interests you

Finding a suitable research question involves building on your previous learning and touching upon issues that you care about. Instead of just thinking 'What would I like to research?' ask yourself which aspects of your field you find fascinating. Some people find that picking the bits they enjoy is easy and end up with more ideas than they can possibly follow through. Others feel that they don't have any specific interests, but in my experience people do have feelings about what they'd rather or rather not read about and research.

Sometimes a student may say that she has no particular interests, but after asking a few probing questions the student gets a clearer picture of what interests her, leading into a possible research topic. Here's a typical conversation between tutor and student – while waiting in the queue for coffee! – about potential dissertation topics:

>**Student:** Actually, I was going to email you because I don't really have a clue about my dissertation topic.
>
>**Tutor:** What are you interested in, generally?
>
>**Student:** You know, just about children and that.
>
>**Tutor:** Any particular age?
>
>**Student:** Yeah, 14- and 15-year-olds. Earlier this year, I helped out at a centre for teenagers who dropped out from school; they were doing some sort of youth scheme.
>
>**Tutor:** Oh, that sounds interesting. What kind of activities did they do?

Student: I was thinking of doing my dissertation on it, but actually it was a bit rubbish. I was really disappointed.

Tutor: In what way?

Student: They had this budget for doing visits, but they were so worried about the teenagers' behaviour that they just didn't even spend it. It seems to me that if you don't trust the teenagers, then you're just making the problem worse. I mean, I know what they were nervous about, but that's the whole point of the scheme, right? Taking people to different places, giving them different chances . . .

Tutor: There's enough material here for a couple of dissertations!

Student: How do you mean?

Tutor: Well, you'd have to be careful how you manage the anonymity of the teenagers, and make sure that any criticism is constructive, but don't you think it would be interesting to see whether there are any studies tackling the problems faced by the centre?

Following this conversation, the student had plenty of ideas on expanding the topic and I only gave a few prompts – to get the student to specify the age group she was interested in, a couple for some more detail, and to encourage her to rethink her initial decision of abandoning studying the centre because her experience there had been negative.

Negative experiences can frequently be rich sources for a research question. Don't dismiss a negative experience too quickly.

After thinking about the range of possible research topics in your field, you're likely to find that some switch you right off, others get you excited and some leave you undecided. Try imagining the topics you've come up with so far as a lucky dip barrel. In your mind, reach in and pull out a topic one by one. Using Table 2-1 assign the topic to one of the three columns listed in the table.

Table 2-1   What Am I Most Interested in Researching?

Possibly Interested	Impossible – Not Interested	Interested

Weigh up the pros and cons of each idea and move the topic from column to column until you have a clear idea which topic you want to choose.

Have a go at doing this exercise more than once and sharing it with friends to encourage discussion. It's useful to put each topic on a Post-it note and, by moving them around the three columns, see which topics have greater appeal and possibilities.

Working out what you don't want to do

If trying to discover what inspires and motivates you isn't working, try focusing on what you *don't* want to research. Start by throwing out all aspects of your field of study that you simply don't want to take further. For example, your field is urban renewal but you have no particular fascination with one aspect of urban renewal over another. Try narrowing down your subject by rejecting the bits that you think are likely to be boring to research in depth. To find where you stand on urban renewal ask yourself:

- ✔ Am I honestly bothered about street furniture?

- ✔ Do I care about community amenities?

- ✔ Do I want to investigate the idea of 'special character' or conservation areas?

- ✔ Am I worried about the design of public buildings?

- ✔ Would I like to know more about how urban projects are funded?

- ✔ Do I want to think about transport?

- ✔ Can I bear to be reading about the gentrification of areas?

- ✔ Do I feel the urge to find out more about compulsory purchase orders?

- ✔ Do I feel strongly about green spaces?

With luck a picture of a possible research question comes into view. This is only the beginning of your journey, however. You need to start doing some initial research to confirm your instinct that this is the topic for you, and thinking it through thoroughly before speaking to your supervisor.

If you've decided on your topic, the section on writing a research proposal will help you put your ideas into practice.

Firing yourself up about ways of working

Despite all your best efforts you may find you come up against a blank wall in choosing a topic to research. If this happens, try going about your search for a topic from a different angle. Try thinking about *how* you'd like to go about a piece of research and *what* research methods you'd like to use and the kind of data your method is going to generate. Considering the following methods of research may help you hit on a research question:

- ✓ **Interviewing** – you enjoy meeting and talking to people.

- ✓ **Case-study** – you're naturally self-confident and are good at building personal relationships without getting too involved.

- ✓ **Reviewing existing data** – focusing your research on the current literature and archival material.

- ✓ **Number-crunching** – you can handle and are fascinated by numbers.

- ✓ **Statistical analysis** – you have an analytical mind.

- ✓ **Qualitative research** – you prefer concentrating on focused samples of research.

- ✓ **Using your own data** – selecting from your own original research and not using empirical data.

If you come to the conclusion that no particular aspect of your field of studies excites you, you still have to find something that you can manage. Even if you aren't completely thrilled to be doing a specific topic, it's not worth worrying about it now. What you have to do is to focus on finding a research question that you can stick to and make sure of finishing your degree studies.

If having looked at research methods as well as subjects, you're still drawing a blank, look back to an essay you've done during your course. You're likely to find that you've already covered some of the reading required for your dissertation.

I'm not suggesting that you simply repeat your previous essays (this isn't allowed), but give some thought to those aspects of your earlier work that are still interesting to you and consider developing the topic for an extended study.

Defining your strengths

Before getting underway with your dissertation and selecting a particular method or approach you need to look honestly at your own strengths and identify areas that may need improvement. You can then choose whether you're prepared to tackle your weaknesses, or stick to what you're comfortable doing.

Think about your whole life, not just your academic experience. Too often you can separate your life into compartments and think of skills as tied to particular activities rather than being tied to you as an individual.

Auditing your skills

UK research councils have produced guidelines for postgraduate students to help them audit their research skills. I've adapted some of the research councils' ideas and added others to make the guidelines relevant to undergraduate students doing dissertations. Think about each question and rate yourself from 1 (little knowledge and experience) to 5 (plenty of knowledge and experience) for each point. After finishing this exercise you're likely to have pinpointed the areas in which you feel confident and areas that need improving. The exercise is useful for helping you choose a suitable research method and talking your method through with your supervisor:

- ✔ **Research skills and techniques:**
    - ❑ I can recognise problems in my field
    - ❑ I can demonstrate original, independent and critical thinking
    - ❑ I have the ability to develop theoretical ideas
    - ❑ I understand relevant research methodologies
    - ❑ I'm able to critically analyse and evaluate research findings
    - ❑ I can summarise, document and report my findings
    - ❑ I can reflect constructively on my progress
- ✔ **Background to research field:**
    - ❑ I've a reasonable grasp of the national and international context in my field
    - ❑ I have some knowledge of recent ideas within my field
    - ❑ I've thought about how people may be affected by my work
    - ❑ I've considered ethical and health and safety concerns from my research project

✔ **Managing research:**

❏ I'm good at setting myself short-term and long-term goals

❏ I can prioritise activities effectively

❏ I'm good at planning ahead

❏ I know where to find appropriate bibliographical sources and archives (in hard copy and electronic format)

❏ I'm confident at using IT to manage my work

✔ **Personal effectiveness:**

❏ I'm keen to learn new techniques

❏ I'm willing to acquire new knowledge

❏ I'm good at finding creative solutions to problems

❏ I'm flexible and open-minded

❏ I have self-awareness

❏ I'm well disciplined

❏ I'm well motivated

❏ I know when to ask for help

❏ I'm an independent worker

✔ **Communication skills:**

❏ My writing is clear and informative

❏ I can write for a target audience

❏ I can construct coherent arguments

Choosing a topic for the wrong reasons

You need to avoid selecting your research topic for the wrong reasons. When attempting to define your research topic, you're aiming to focus on what matters to you and what you find interesting. You need to be ruthless in deleting the subjects you think *should* concern you but which hold no real interest for you. Sometimes, students feel they ought to be studying a certain area because they feel it balances the subjects they cover in their degree course or is going to help them get their dream job. It's usually a bad idea to use these sorts of reasons when choosing a topic for your dissertation.

A voyage of self-discovery

One student I worked with was very shy in class and when it came to her dissertation she needed to interview some teachers but felt awkward and uncomfortable at the prospect. We chatted about what she did for fun outside of university and it came to light that she was involved in amateur dramatics. (No, she wasn't secretly aiming to become a West End star!) It turned out that she did the accounts for the drama company. This required her to present budgets at the executive council meetings and she said she found she wasn't in the least bit nervous about performing her part in front of the organisation.

However, she was clearly lacking in self-assurance in the world of education and theory but highlighting her skills outside of her university course gave her the opportunity to rethink her dissertation research methods and topic area. She was good at juggling figures and presenting from a script, giving her more control over the situation. She decided to use her particular skills for interviewing, which allowed her to think and note down alternative approaches if the discussion headed off in different directions. (Of course, as her tutor, I was keen to address the discrepancy in her university and leisure experiences, but her dissertation is what is relevant here.)

The student came to see that by transferring her skills from one area of her life to another she was sure of carrying out a successful interview with the teachers. She decided that using questionnaires for most of her research and carrying out two scripted interviews was the way forward. By taking this approach the student achieved a great balance; she got to develop her interview skills in a safe way, and through the questionnaires managed to collect enough data for her statistical analysis.

Take a look at job advertisements. Many job ads specify something about academic qualifications but few, if any, mention a particular dissertation theme. Potential employers are far more impressed if you can talk with enthusiasm about what you've studied, even if your studies don't match the job description. You can highlight the skills you've developed through doing your dissertation, showing that you're able to sustain a long-term project. Getting across your ability to get excited about a subject is going to shine through if you're still energised by your dissertation.

Straying off-topic

Sometimes a chosen research topic can take you in directions you didn't expect. If you seem to be straying from your main idea you need to weigh up which direction to take. It may be that your research so far has highlighted an aspect that you'd like to study in more depth but you're unable to follow through at this time in your university career. Leave the topic for now; you can always come back to it in the future. (You've probably just talked yourself into doing an MA!) However, it's possible that your 'off-topic' idea can impact positively on your dissertation and you may need to seriously consider following the idea through, even if that means shifting the direction of your work.

If the idea is a radical departure from your original choice of topic but is honestly what you'd prefer to research, now's the time to review your plans and change the subject of your dissertation. This may seem a ridiculous thing to do after you've put in a lot of planning work, but every day you put off changing the research topic is another day potentially wasted. After making the right shift, you're going to feel a great sense of relief.

Checking Out Your Research Question

In this section I take you through the process of defining your research topic using the following steps:

- ✔ Identifying your interests
- ✔ Generating ideas about your research question
- ✔ Making your initial exploration
- ✔ Refining and narrowing your topic

Identifying your interests

To come up with your research question, you need to know what you want to investigate. In the earlier section 'Discovering What Excites You' I offer you ways of finding out where your passions lie. After getting to grips with your general interests you now need to focus on one particular aspect. Even if your focus is vague and unformed to begin with, make a note of suitable ideas so you can review them systematically to reach a sensible, balanced decision. The process of reviewing each idea involves the refinement of the areas and development of specific questions that form the basis of your dissertation. As I show in Table 2-2, students have good and bad reasons for picking their research questions. Be honest with yourself as you look through the list.

Table 2-2	Good and Bad Reasons for Choosing Research Questions

Good Reasons	*Bad Reasons*
Genuine interest in the area	Seems like an easy option. Often something may look easier than it is. If you see a colleague apparently cruising through her work, it may be that she's really motivated, not that the topic is easy. Talk with your supervisor about what is manageable. Think in terms of 'doable', rather than what is 'easy' or 'hard'.
Familiarity with the field	Not too much theoretical stuff. You can't escape reading when you're undertaking a dissertation. If you want to cut down your reading, choose an area that you've studied a bit in the recent past. Don't choose something that you've written loads of essays on, but pick out an idea that you've touched on before.
Experience of the research methods	Saw a programme on TV. You can draw your inspiration from anything you like but don't assume that you can replicate something from TV. Remember that programmes aren't always thorough or academic and ideas can be simplified or sensationalised to hold audience interest. What you see on TV may not bear much relation to the topic when translated into a dissertation.
Tutor recommended the area	Determined, despite supervisor's advice against. If your tutor is pleading with you to change your topic, it's usually for good reason. She doesn't want to see you embark on an impossible project and she doesn't want to have to pick up the pieces if it all collapses around you. Listen to her; she is there to dispense sound advice.
Prior reading or experience	Can't think of anything else. Desperation is not the best reason to choose a topic. If you're really settling for any old thing because you're worried about time running out, you're likely to regret it later. Go back to your previous courses and re-read your old essays. See if perhaps there's a spark you can build on.
Access to research subjects	My friend is doing the same topic. It's lovely to share, but not a great idea to just go along for a ride with a friend. It's your dissertation, not hers, and you can do similar topics without doing the same thing. It's still possible to share the journey of writing a dissertation without having to write on the same topic.

Generating ideas

Social science is about society, people and the way people live their lives. To help you close in on a research question, think about which topics in the following list interest you most:

- ✔ What is society like?
- ✔ What do people need?
- ✔ How do people behave?
- ✔ What do people think?
- ✔ What do people say?
- ✔ How do people interact?
- ✔ What structures can help people?

Making an initial exploration

Each possible research question you come up with needs to be tested to find out whether it's feasible. There's little point in choosing something very obscure. If you do, you may struggle to find literature or previous research projects in the field. Similarly, you should avoid picking something that doesn't really interest you. Make a note of the following points:

- ✔ **Is your idea central to your field (or at least obviously significant enough to research)?** Find out what and how much research has already been done on your topic. Clearly you don't want to repeat anyone's earlier work, but an undergraduate dissertation is not expected to be highly original and if your topic is close to other recent studies in the field at least you know that what you've chosen has some currency and relevance.

- ✔ **Determine whether your ideas are generally interesting and relevant.** Bounce your ideas off your fellow students and if they don't glaze over and do show interest you can be certain your idea is a winner. Also, ask your supervisor to review your ideas.

- ✔ **Ask yourself whether you're genuinely enthusiastic about the research question.** Make an honest appraisal as to whether you've bothered reading about your subject area and note whether you enjoy explaining to others what you're doing. Ask yourself whether you're really prepared to put yourself out by looking for ideas and comments from experts or experienced practitioners.

✔ **Confirm that your idea is clear**. Explain your research idea in no more than two concise sentences (one is even better). If you can do this effectively, you have a good idea of what you want to investigate.

Getting down to a question you can answer

After coming up with lots of ideas for research topics (see the earlier section 'Generating ideas' and the questions I ask in the section 'Making an initial exploration'), now is the time to take a hard look at your chosen topic. Your idea has to be translated into practical sub-questions. You can do this by coming up with every sub-question that you think you're going to need to answer as part of your broader research question. You need to consider the practicalities of your work and ensure that your project is manageable. These bullet points can help you generate practical question-asking. You need to think of the many 'What?', 'Why?', 'How?', 'Where?' and 'When?' questions.

Think carefully about what new information your readers are going to be learning from your dissertation topic. You need to make the title of your research question clear. For example, does your research question fit one of the following descriptions?

✔ **Critical description:** Building an accurate profile or portrayal.

✔ **Explanation:** Looking at patterns, relationships or phenomena.

✔ **Exploration:** Checking out the details of a situation or taking a snapshot in which you cast a new light on the subject.

Choosing a different starting point

For most students, identifying a broad area for research and then narrowing down to a specific question is the best way of working. For some, however, this can work the other way around, with a specific burning question as the starting point. If you choose this approach, you need to then go on and place your research question into context. Choosing a specific research topic right from the start is more likely to be taken by somebody whose dissertation is based on their workplace because that's where you generally come up against specific practical and pressing questions. (Selecting a specific topic as an action research project is common at MA level, but many undergraduates do also work for a living and this approach can be relevant to them as well.)

Where you're at

Imagine that you're keen to find out about local health care provision. Your research question concerns the role of newly-qualified nurses in managing chronic conditions. By now you've come up with the following sorts of sub-questions: 'What's the experience of novice nurses based in the local hospital compared with those in the GP's surgery?' 'What are "chronic conditions"?' 'What is meant by "community nursing"?' 'To what extent are nurses part of the patient-service consultation process in the local GP's surgery?'

'Why do the experiences of nurses matter?' 'Why do practice and hospital nurses have such different experiences?' 'Why aren't chronic conditions managed in all surgeries?'

'How can I gather information about the role of nurses?' 'Where do I need to go to carry out my research?' 'When is the best time to get in touch and talk to nurses?'

Reviewing the critical description, explanation and exploration gives you more detailed 'What?' sub-questions. Presenting detailed 'Why?' questions tells your reader the reasons for the information being worth knowing. This questioning ensures that your work is relevant to the field.

Showing 'How?' you plan to carry out your research, along with 'Where?' and 'When?' sub-questions highlights the feasibility of your work. When you answer these sub-questions, you need to face up to how realistic your ideas are, review the key factors and the limiting variables, thinking about how you're sure that you're work is valid.

Having considered whether you're interested in explanations, or if you're leaning toward a critical description or maybe an exploration, you need to get down to generating some questions. Now you have a sense of your dissertation, you need to pin down the related questions. You'll find that isolating the methods you need to use to find the answers becomes easier. The next useful step is to group your questions together, eliminating any that are repetitive. You can prioritise your questions with the most appropriate at the top. You can then discard those at the bottom of the heap.

Only choose a research question that you can answer. It's important that you've checked out the available literature and resources on your topic before committing yourself to a particular research question. Think through how you can collect data and evidence, and spend some time exploring your ideas to avoid finding yourself in a dead end.

Posing the perfect question

An excellent research question title takes into account the following:

✔ Avoids jargon and makes the meaning clear

✔ Is straightforward but not simplistic

✔ Is well-structured and steers away from abstractions

✔ Gives some detail, but without wordy clauses and caveats (save these for the dissertation itself)

✔ Is precise, specific and clearly contextualised

✔ Isn't broad or vague

At this point, what you must do is:

✔ Narrow down your area to a small number of areas (four should be the maximum).

✔ Be brutal! Consider which areas you really, fully want to research and eliminate anything about which you're vacillating (such as a topic still in the 'maybe' column).

At this stage you're trying to get the wording right. You may find yourself tweaking your research question as your dissertation progresses. Tweaking is usually allowed but some supervisors prefer the firmest possible research question at this point.

Be absolutely sure that your supervisor has signed off your research question title.

Planning Your Dissertation Proposal

Having to write a dissertation proposal depends upon the university or institution that you're attending. Even if a dissertation proposal isn't a requirement, it's a very useful exercise (and is certainly going to impress your supervisor, especially if it's not part of your assessment). A dissertation proposal is basically a description of the following:

✔ What your dissertation is about

✔ Probable questions that you're going to be examining

✔ Some reference to the theoretical background

- ✔ Research methods you're going to be using (empirical or non-empirical) (refer to Chapter 1)
- ✔ Potential outcomes of the study

Finding out if you need to write a proposal

On some courses the research proposal is assessed and forms part of your final dissertation submission. If this is the case, it's vital that you follow the correct format and submit your work on time. Mostly, a dissertation proposal has a 500 or 1,000 word limit, but you must check what your course specifically requires.

Time spent putting your dissertation proposal together is an investment – you reap rewards because the proposal stops you wasting time and also forms the basis of your dissertation outline. (Head to Chapter 4 for tips on drawing up a great dissertation outline.)

Writing a dissertation proposal, even though it's not a requirement, is still worth doing. You can submit the proposal to your supervisor (with her agreement) and get some valuable feedback.

Exploring the essential parts of a research proposal

The essential parts of a research proposal are generally standard:

- ✔ **Dissertation title (so far):** Aim at making the title short and to the point. (See Chapters 11 and 12.)

- ✔ **Overall objectives**: If you have more than three objectives, your area of research is probably far too broad and needs to be narrowed. (Some university courses may ask you to include a rationale at this stage.)

- ✔ **Literature, context, background:** You can use any of these words as the title of this section, just make sure that you mention key schools of thought or areas of study that are going to provide information about your dissertation. (Some proposals require you to list specific references at this point, others ask for the bibliography at the end. See Chapters 11 and 12 for more on handling the literature.)

✔ **Details of the research:** Here, you can expand the ideas spelt out in your research question. This section is about outlining clearly your area of research.

✔ **Methodologies**: Your work may be empirical (with some sort of study and collection of data such as questionnaires) or non-empirical (no such data, all your research comes from already published writing and projects). If your study is non-empirical, this section is likely to be short; longer if you need to collect or look at the empirical data. If you're allowed to use bullet points in your research proposal, you need do no more than list your intended activities (for example, carrying out interviews, consulting archives or evaluating data. See Chapters 8 and 9 for more on methodology).

✔ **Potential outcomes:** Avoid second-guessing the result of your dissertation. If you knew the outcomes, it would be pretty pointless doing the dissertation! Here, you're summarising the type of outcomes you hope to generate and suggesting a target audience.

✔ **Timeline:** If you're asked to outline how you plan to manage your research, think about including a Gantt chart (go to Chapter 4 for more on Gantt charts) or some kind of concept map. Whatever you do, make your timeline realistic.

✔ **Bibliography**: Check if you're required to provide a list of references and, if so, find out roughly how many references you're expected to list. (See Chapter 14 for more on putting together a good bibliography.)

Adopting the right tone and style

Ask your supervisor for guidance about the tone and style of your research proposal. You need to be flexible and open-minded, showing a willingness to adapt your methods and ideas as your research dictates. Say in your proposal what you intend to do, confidently and adopting a balanced view, suggesting that you've carefully considered the best way of carrying out your study. Be firm but not arrogant; be flexible but not feeble!

Make sure that you follow the rules of grammar in your proposal – be consistent about the tense of your proposal. Most proposals are written using the future tense: 'I will be using questionnaires . . . and so on'. Check with your supervisor for confirmation.

Part II

Getting Set Up for Your Dissertation

In this part...

*P*reparation is all. In this part I take you through the key decisions you need to make on the structure of your dissertation – both the research you have to do and the way the finished item will look and feel.

I also cover the best ways to get started on the project, how to communicate profitably with your supervisor, and how to manage your time effectively. This part goes on to consider how to fine tune your research question, and ends up by letting you in on how to maximise the value of your reading and note-taking.

Chapter 3

Structuring Your Dissertation

*P*resenting a well-structured dissertation is going to make your dissertation a pleasure to read and is a sure way of gaining you marks. In this chapter I give you an overview of how to structure your dissertation and what you need to cover in each part. In Chapters 11 and 12, I guide you through writing each of the parts in more detail and make suggestions for the kinds of subheadings you can use in each chapter of your dissertation. Subheadings are just part of the process – not the final result. However, subheadings are useful tools to keep you on track while you're writing – but once your dissertation is written, you need to delete them from the final draft. (Check, of course, that the text flows coherently without the need for the subheadings.)

Meeting the Main Parts of Your Dissertation

Most dissertations follow the same basic structure and are made up of five parts: an abstract, introduction, methods and discussion, conclusions and references. Although the exact detail of each part can vary (such as the numbers of words allowed in the abstract), the inclusion of each part is standard and fixed. I like to compare the structure of a dissertation with the composition of an orchestral work – broadly your dissertation has a prelude, main movements and a finale. A great musician gets an encore too – and so does a great dissertation.

Before starting your dissertation, find out exactly what is required by your university or institution. For example, there may be particular rules about word length, the fonts you have to use or whether the acknowledgements come before or after your abstract. You must make sure of keeping to the rules and regulations.

Prelude: Your abstract

After the title page and any acknowledgements comes a summary of your dissertation. From your own reading of journal articles and reports, you're likely to be familiar with the purpose of the abstract. In a journal article, the abstract is a summary of the main article, placed directly under the title and usually around 150–250 words long. Sometimes the abstract has a different name such as 'résumé' or 'summary'. In some documents, such as reports, the abstract is usually called the 'executive summary'.

The content of your abstract is important because what you say in your abstract gives the reader the opportunity of judging whether your dissertation is going to be of interest to him. While doing your own research, you're likely to have discarded or pursued different journal articles and reports based purely on the relevance of the abstract and so you know how important it is for giving the reader a feel for what your dissertation covers.

Your abstract is an overview of your whole study: a summary of your research question, methods and results – so you can't write your abstract until you've pretty much finished your dissertation. That day comes – even though right now it may seem unbelievable! When you come to the stage of writing your abstract, it's likely that you're feeling pretty stressed, trying to tie up all the loose ends of your dissertation after a year dedicated to your project. You can imagine how tempting it can be to scribble a short piece as quickly as possible but you can also see that such an approach isn't going to do you any favours or win you marks.

I offer lots of help on writing your abstract in Chapters 11 and 12, but for now be aware that you need to build time into the planning of your dissertation to get the job done effectively.

Prelude: Your introduction

With your introduction you're preparing the ground for the main body of your dissertation. In your introduction you're looking to inspire an interest in your work and explaining something about the background and your reasons for choosing your dissertation topic.

Usually an introduction is around two pages long. Aim to give the reader a clear idea of what to expect to find in the main themes you're presenting and the methods you're using, saying if you've done something experimental and practical, or taken a more theoretical approach. You can hint at the findings and conclusions, but you needn't spell them out as in the abstract. To whet the reader's appetite, try to raise his curiosity as to how the dissertation is going to end.

The introduction is a good place to explain your rationale for the choices you've made. Perhaps say what motivated you to pick this research question, such as an observation you made on a placement, or a course that stimulated your interest. Avoid filling the introduction with too many personal anecdotes. The examiner isn't interested in what you think about that bloke on the telly who made you think about what your lecturer said about that thing that you weren't sure if it was a good thing before but you are now.

 You may be passionate about the area you've chosen to study for your dissertation, but avoid overstating the importance of your work. Without false modesty, you can show that you know that your choice of dissertation subject is relevant and interesting, but you understand that it's not necessarily going to change the world. Shy away from grand claims, but also try not to completely dismiss your work before you've started.

 Even though your introduction is only a short piece of writing, remember to stick to just one point in each paragraph. Using the following subheadings can help you structure your introduction; remembering to delete the subheadings from your final draft:

- ✔ Dissertation aims

- ✔ Background to the dissertation

- ✔ Key question to be explored or issues being scrutinised

- ✔ Brief outline of the structure of the dissertation

Main movements: Your methods and discussion

Whatever topic you're researching in the social sciences, the structure and level of detail in your abstract and introduction are standard. When you reach the main movements of your dissertation – your methods and discussion – you now take an empirical or a non-empirical route (I explain this approach in Chapter 1). The elements required in empirical and non-empirical dissertations are subtly different. To find out more, read the sections 'Examining Empirical Dissertations' and 'Examining Non-Empirical Dissertations' later in this chapter. You need to read up about both approaches just to confirm that you fully understand the method of investigation you're choosing.

Finale: Your conclusion

Every dissertation must have a conclusion – otherwise your research can end up being a pointless interpretation and merely a review of vaguely related ideas. I recall one supervisor listening politely to my grand plan for my dissertation. He looked concerned and sat back in his chair. 'Well, that's very interesting,' he said softly. Leaning forward, he looked at me with an intense expression. 'How are you going to know when you're finished?' he asked. I wasn't sure. I hadn't really thought about the ending of the dissertation.

Think about some of the definitions of the word 'conclusion' – termination, ending, closing, wrapping up, finishing. For your dissertation, however, try to think of the word 'conclusion' as a deduction, inference, supposition or assumption.

You're the one doing the deducing, inferring, supposing or assuming and you're doing this based on the reading, researching, discussing and thinking that you've been doing while carrying out your research. My mistake, as my supervisor made me realise, was that I'd put all my effort into collecting, thinking and researching information, but I hadn't bothered to consider any of the things that I could deduce from my findings. There was no point in the dissertation if I didn't present my conclusions.

A successful dissertation conclusion is short and succinct. Restate the aims of your work and show how your original thoughts have been reinforced or changed through your well-planned and carefully executed research, whether your research is theoretical or practical. You then make a few suggestions on how you can improve or extend your work if you have the opportunity.

Also say something about the importance of your research question to the field you're studying. By emphasising the importance of your research *question*, rather than the importance of your findings, you show that you're aware of the limitations of your work.

In conclusion – avoiding common pitfalls

When it comes to writing up your conclusion there are three main types of conclusions to steer clear of at all costs – 'long and bad' – 'short and bad' – 'bad and fantastic'. The 'long and bad' conclusion is rambling and merely repeats earlier parts of the dissertation without adding anything about what your findings say about the topic being reviewed. The 'short and bad' conclusion is a marginal improvement on the 'long and bad', wasting slightly less of the reader's time and energy. The 'short and bad' is also inclined to repeat facts without coming to a conclusion, but using fewer words and as a result leaving out key points, making any attempt at a conclusion a piece of nonsense .

In the context of your conclusion 'fantastic' means 'unbelievable' and 'implausible' definitely not 'great'! A 'bad and fantastic' conclusion can simply be mind-boggling. Fantastic conclusions often make wild, exaggerated claims, unsupported by your research. These absurd conclusions make far-fetched assertions about how the results of a small-scale study should be adopted by governments or high-level policy makers. If your conclusion is a list of unsubstantiated claims you end up undermining your research findings and losing any credit for all your hard work. Poor conclusions often appear pompous and delusional, always overblown and irritating, frequently unintentionally humorous and sometimes just plain silly. Avoid.

The examiner knows he's marking an undergraduate dissertation. He understands that you don't have access to 5,000 subjects and that you don't have the funds to fly to Australia to carry out your interviews. He expects modest conclusions to your research question and marks the whole piece of work rather than simply checking if your case study is likely to change the field of social anthropology or youth work forever.

Encore! – Your references

I offer guidance on writing references and bibliographies in Chapters 11 and 12. And then, just in case that isn't enough, I devote the whole of Chapter 14 to the surprisingly complex challenge of creating a great bibliography.

For now, just be aware that you need to understand and follow the rules governing references in your field of study and your university or institution when you're presenting your dissertation, even though the system of referencing seems fiddly and fussy. Oh, and remember that formatting and checking your references is 99 per cent certain to take you far longer than you expect (and would like!).

Producing an accurate and complete list of references is such a simple (but tedious) way of gaining valuable marks that you're going to kick yourself if you don't give your references the attention they deserve. Say you only just miss making it into a higher grade classification for your dissertation with the examiner commenting that a few per cent has been deducted for lack of attention to detail and a sloppy approach to referencing. Kick yourself – really hard.

You're going to save a great deal of time, grief and repeat library visits if you have an efficient method for compiling your list of references and bibliography as you go along – for some useful ideas on putting together a list of references, head to Chapters 6 and 14.

Examining Empirical Dissertations

For the full definitions of both empirical and non-empirical dissertations, see Chapter One. Taking the empirical route in researching and writing your dissertation means you can expect the main movements of your dissertation to be straightforward and consistent. The only particularly specific structural decision you're going to need to make concerns how you tackle your data presentation and your analysis of data. Some people devote a chapter to their presentation of data, perhaps including charts and extracts from transcripts, for example. The next chapter is then devoted to discussing findings. Others prefer to integrate the presentation of data with their findings. Whether you choose one or two chapters for data presentation and analysis of findings depends on your supervisor's advice, the nature of your data, the length of your dissertation and personal choice. In this section I tell you about data collection and data analysis to help you make the right choice for your work.

Looking at literature reviews

Supervisors and students often talk about literature reviews without really thinking through what the term means. In the context of your dissertation, 'review' is both a verb and a noun; you review the literature (verb) and produce a review of the literature (noun). Try to think of your review in both ways, to express the process of the review and the final product.

Your aim is to review the literature that tackles the issues raised by your research question. You acknowledge the key writers and ideas in the field as they link to your study by explaining what is being written and said in your field. Usually, during your coursework your tutors have probably been encouraging you to be as analytical as possible, but when you're writing your dissertation you do your analysis when you discuss your results later in your dissertation. When you're discussing your results you refer to your literature review where you've presented your ideas. You can save your fan-club support and violent disagreements for the analysis section of the dissertation.

Do make sure that your literature review is a fair and balanced discussion of the main ideas in your field and you're quoting from the significant writers, presenting what they're actually saying rather than giving your own views of what is being said.

I've listed some possible subheadings that can help you with the draft writing stage of your literature review. They shouldn't appear in the final version, but can help you structure your work effectively. These subheadings are:

- ✔ Significant theories in the field

- ✔ Critiques and differing opinions

- ✔ Rationale for focusing on some theories and leaving out others

- ✔ Where I stand – or with whom I agree and disagree

- ✔ Summary of key issues in the literature

Researching research methodologies

As part of your research methodology, you're asked to explain the methods you're using in your dissertation and also to justify your choices. See Chapter 8 for definitions and explanations of these methods. Some research methodologies you can use include:

- ✔ Interviews

- ✔ Observations

- ✔ Questionnaires

- ✔ Rating scales

- ✔ Standardised tests

- ✔ Surveys

Case studies aren't included in the list of methodologies because a case study isn't a free-standing research method. If you carry out a case study, you're making a close examination of a subject or institution and to do this you have to use one or more of the methods in the list. A case study is a type of research, but a case study makes use of other methods.

As well as reporting on your own experience of using a particular research methodology, you need to refer to the key texts on that research methodology in your field.

Undertaking action research

In the social sciences, researchers at MA or PhD level often do action research projects. Action research just means that the researcher is more involved in the project, planning a change to a group or an individual, putting this into action and then evaluating the outcome. An action research project is usually carried out in a work environment where the researcher is an experienced practitioner, because it's vital to minimise potential problems for the subject(s).

As part of the action research project, the researcher is likely to use some of the research methods I've included in the list above, therefore it's a good idea to have had some experience of using the methods before building them into a longer-term project.

 If your supervisor recommends that you carry out an action research project, he probably feels that you're in a position to do the project effectively. If you have any concerns, check that you fully understand what you're being asked to do and you're sure that you're confident enough to carry out the work.

Staying specific to your field

Each research method has its pros and cons and because of the sheer variety of topics within the social sciences, different fields may need different approaches. For example, in education, if you want to review children in a school setting, many of the plus and minus points concern the effects of the observer on the performance of the subject. If you're studying economics and want to look into people's understanding of the benefits system by interviewing different people, your concerns are more about the subjects feeling uninhibited and your interpretation of their responses.

Make sure that you check with your supervisor to find out the key text for your particular field concerning the specifics about research methodologies as they apply to your subject.

Use the following subheadings to help you write your research methods chapter, and then delete the headings from the final draft.

- ✔ Theoretical backdrop to choice of methods
- ✔ Rationale for selecting methods

✔ Acknowledgement of (some) other methods and reasons for rejection

✔ How I selected my sample

✔ A note about how I'm going to present my data

✔ Statistical and other analytical tools I'm using

✔ Summary of my general feelings about the suitability of my chosen research methods

Dealing with data collection

In the data collection section of your dissertation you talk about the data that you've collected during your research. How you present the data depends on the nature of your data. You can simply give a written description of the data, but providing a visual interpretation of your findings creates more impact. For example, you can use one or more of the following ways of presenting your data:

✔ Graphs

✔ Models or diagrams

✔ Short extracts from transcripts

✔ Pie charts

✔ Tables

✔ Taxonomies (Categories)

See Chapter 12 for more information about these methods.

Avoid using graphs and charts if you have only a few subjects. Presenting a pie chart that shows that three out of four people answered positively to a question is unnecessary and suggests that you're setting too much store by your own research. Also avoid using percentage measures when you've small samples – after all, 50 per cent of two people is only one person.

The word 'data' is a plural term (the singular is datum). When you write about what you plan to do with your data, use the phrase 'What my data show . . .' rather than 'What my data shows . . .' so that the subject and verb agree.

For more on the technicalities of grammar, check out *English Grammar For Dummies* by Lesley J. Ward and Geraldine Woods.

Analysing your data

In the data analysis section of your dissertation, you evaluate the findings you're presenting and show how you develop the ideas to draw conclusions based on your research. Where possible, try to link your analysis to your reading – but avoid merely repeating what you've presented in the literature review. Your data can illustrate ideas from your reading but the focus here is mostly on analysing your findings, breaking down your findings and looking at what they're telling you.

Examining Non-Empirical Dissertations

If you choose to carry out a non-empirical dissertation (head to Chapter 1 to find out the difference between empirical and non-empirical dissertations), you're going to be working in a less structured framework than in an empirical dissertation. The main movements of your dissertation are where you set out your argument. However, you still need to break down your argument into coherent chapters to help your reader navigate to and fro between different ideas that are hopefully beautifully woven into a flowing text.

Deciding whether you need to compile a literature review

Knowing whether to write a literature review in a non-empirical dissertation can be a difficult call, and I suggest you discuss this with your supervisor. Because a non-empirical dissertation is essentially one long argument, you're making references to the literature throughout your argument. Having a separate section where you specify a particular discussion of some literature and leave out other aspects may be unnecessary.

In a non-empirical dissertation, the purpose of a separate literature review is to lay out background literature in a broad, wide-ranging sense as an aid for helping readers find your more specific arguments and criticisms.

The literature review is more a description than an analysis. You're expected to be reasonably objective and to present the authors' ideas factually. For some help in writing your literature review, have a look at my suggested headings in the section 'Looking at literature reviews' earlier in this chapter.

Tackling 'research methodologies' when you don't have any

At first sight it seems irrelevant if you're doing a non-empirical dissertation to write a chapter describing how you managed your research, especially where you're mainly reading, thinking and talking about your work. As I mention in the section 'Looking at literature reviews', reviewing the literature is a 'research methods' and you can explain something of your approach to this task as part of your methodology.

With a non-empirical dissertation, although you're not carrying out interviews or writing questionnaires, you can include some empirical observations to illustrate points you want to make. If you're making an empirical observation, you just need to say where your data comes from and whether you took part in the collecting of the data.

Placing a 'note' at the start of your dissertation saying something like 'The samples throughout this dissertation are copies of quotations from the subjects, collected by their team leader and lent to me as illustrations of their views', does the job. Don't try to fill a whole chapter with methodology when you've hardly anything to say.

Even where you have no empirical data or illustrations, sometimes you may need a short chapter on your research methods explaining how you got hold of your data. You may, for example, want to write about the examples you use from your critical reading of the literature or say a little about the way you chose the theorists referred to in your argument.

Balancing your arguments

In a non-empirical dissertation, trying to balance out your arguments and giving a fair hearing to all sides of the case in question can present difficulties. A one-sided discussion isn't going to be convincing; the more credit you give to the opposing views, the more effective it's going to be when you slay the opposition's opinions with your superior logic and reasoning!

Try using some of the following subheadings to help you write your discussion – remembering to delete the subheadings from your final draft:

- ✔ Laying out the problem
- ✔ Key theory (with which you agree)
- ✔ Main critic

✔ Second theorist (with whom you agree)

✔ Other critics

✔ Your conclusion – after weighing the evidence

Planning your chapters

Presenting a balanced and coherent argument is an important aspect of a non-empirical dissertation and you need to spend some time considering the most useful route through your argument. Your route depends on your chosen research question. In some cases, you can have the most impact if you start from a general discussion and then hone your argument to a firm conclusion. A different tactic is to look at small, specific examples or ideas and then broaden the examples or ideas to draw more general conclusions.

You're going to need to make a decision based on whether you're writing an empirical or non-empirical dissertation, but what is most important is that you avoid a meandering and indistinct ramble through theorists' ideas without really concluding anything of value. Keep in mind that your ideas need to progress logically and lead up to your conclusion. The journey should be full of interesting and relevant aspects, adding something of value to the overall arguments. Go to Chapter 11 to find out more about structuring your argument.

Chapter 4

Getting Started

. . . .

In This Chapter

▶ Starting your research

▶ Getting to know your supervisor

▶ Using your time carefully

▶ Outlining your dissertation

. . . .

*I*f you're itching to get started, this chapter can help you save time. In it, I explain the kinds of careful preparation you should undertake. Much like DIY or cookery, the masking of things you don't want paint on or the greasing of your cake tins feels like an unnecessary delay when what you want to do is get painting, mixing or writing. However, if you don't prepare with care, you can end up wasting precious time. Removing unwanted paint, being unable to extricate your cake from the tin or writing whole passages that turn out to be irrelevant are all pretty irritating. Careful preparation is how to avoid wasting time and turns out to be an investment that pays off at the end.

Finding Your Focus

Well before logging onto your computer or putting pen to paper you need to make sure that you fully understand what doing a dissertation involves. Check out the following list to ensure that you're making the necessary preparations for your dissertation and in the right order:

- ✔ **Selecting your research topic:** If you're still stuck, turn to Chapter 1 for help in selecting a viable topic.

- ✔ **Writing a draft research question:** If you haven't yet prepared your research question, have a look at Chapter 2.

- ✔ **Choosing to do an empirical or non-empirical dissertation:** If you're not sure what the difference is between an empirical and non-empirical dissertation move to Chapter 1 and Chapter 3.

✔ **Opting to do empirical research:** Have you thought about the research methods you're going to be using? Make sure you're clear about what empirical research is by heading to Chapter 3.

Gathering resources

Your university library is now going to be your second home. Students of the social sciences make a lot of use of library resources. In preparation for your dissertation topic you need to source the theoretical background of your chosen topic: even more so if you're planning to base your research on published resources.

Careful and thorough preparation for your dissertation means you won't be reinventing the wheel or spending hours looking for information that you've completely forgotten you already have.

I suggest in Chapter 2 that basing your dissertation on a module, course, or series of lectures that you particularly enjoyed provides a great starting point for finding a research question. Looking back over essays you've done during your course can be a valuable resource for preparing the ground for your dissertation. You may be lucky to discover a great bunch of references and ideas that you didn't have the time or opportunity to pursue – now is your chance to get to grips with these resources. Get all your old notes together and look over them thoroughly. Use your list of references as a basis for your first library visit to prepare for your dissertation.

You may be thinking of doing a dissertation that involves generating your own data through using questionnaires and carrying out interviews. If you're planning on this research method try to remember what led you to making this decision. Also, if there's a particularly great example of the kind of research method you'd like to be using for your dissertation, dig out the reference from your notes to remind yourself what first captured your interest.

Starting your research

After thoroughly preparing the ground for your dissertation by searching the literature for key references on your topic, you can now get on with collecting your data. Having got hold of your references and data means you can start your research.

Your first step is to refine your research question. Chapter 5 gives you practical guidelines on the business of dealing with your research question. Having gathered together all the important references relating to your research question now is the time to get reading and analysing everything on your topic. To make sure that you're reading productively have a look at Chapters 6 and 7, in which I help you get set for effective reading and note-taking.

At this stage you may need to address a number of ethical issues before you start asking people to be subjects for your dissertation. You can find out about the ethics of research in Chapter 5.

Don't go diving into questionnaires, interviews or any other method of research that involves people until your supervisor signs off your research question. As well as wasting your time and other people's by doing the wrong thing, you can end up causing unnecessary offence to people, breaching ethical requirements or breaking the rules and regulations of your university or institution.

Contacting Your Supervisor

You should be allocated a dissertation supervisor at an early stage of your research. The job of your supervisor is to guide you through the different stages of your research project; she's qualified to do this even if your topic is not necessarily her specialist area.

Most courses do their best to allocate a dissertation supervisor at an early stage. (If you don't hear anything after the first few weeks back at university, contact the person leading the course to see if you've missed something or a problem has arisen.) The role of the supervisor is to guide you through the process of your research project. Your supervisor may or may not have taught you before, but what's certain is that she's done a dissertation (or two) before and will be able to help you with yours.

Don't worry if your dissertation supervisor is a specialist in an area that isn't exactly the same as your chosen title. Supervisors successfully guide and examine a range of different subjects that link to their area. I often teach the psychology of education courses at my university for example, but I have postgraduate degrees in history and philosophy of education as well.

Supervisors come in all shapes and sizes and are busy professionals with many competing demands on their time. Your dissertation is probably the biggest thing happening to you in your academic career so far but keep in mind you're one of several students to whom your supervisor has been assigned. You can't expect your supervisor to be chasing you up and keeping you to your timetable. It's important that you make the best use of your supervisor's abilities, experience and time. Before even meeting your supervisor, try to find out where her strengths lie and aim to have your essential preparations well under way, making yourself a pleasure to supervise!

A good supervisor sincerely wants to help you succeed. However, helping you is easier if you're clear about the support you need and if you respond to your supervisor's requests in a timely and polite fashion. Remember that ultimately you need your supervisor more than she needs you – your supervisor already has a degree (maybe even two or three) and at least one successful published dissertation gracing the library shelves.

You're likely to impress your supervisor if you first make contact with her by email or phone, giving an outline of your dissertation or at least offering some kind of work plan. Emphasise that your plan isn't set in stone but that you've thought long and hard about your research question and done some preliminary reading. Providing your supervisor with this information shows initiative, but also shows you still need your supervisor's valuable support.

Understanding the requirements

For many students doing a dissertation is a big learning curve – but also a time for standing on your own two feet. The onus is on you to make sure that you have up-to-date information about what is required for doing a dissertation. If there's an information session, group meeting or introductory lecture for dissertation students, be sure that you go and pick up all the information that's being handed out. You may have access to such information through your university or institution's Intranet – sometimes called a virtual learning environment – read and digest every bit of information with care.

All universities have electronic resources you can access and most of the information you need is there, probably listed under your course's site. These university websites for students (also known as virtual learning environments) are generally very handy so you should get to know yours well. Some are known by the trade name (such as Blackboard or Moodle, for example) and others have local names such as Flexi-Learning Centre, StudyZone, e-learn, Home Study Guide and so on).

Your supervisor can help you unpick any of the trickier aspects of the course requirements – but don't expect your supervisor to check you've read all the information. Your supervisor quite rightly assumes that you know the date for submitting your dissertation, the code number of your module and other essential details.

Considering communication

Universities have different rules, guidelines and expectations for how supervisors and students work together. From your experience at school or college you're likely to have some idea of how things run at your institution. A few things to sort out include:

- ✔ Checking whether your tutors have drop-in times or whether you need to make an appointment to see your supervisor.

- ✔ Making yourself known to your course administrators, who can help you to get in touch with your supervisor if she doesn't get back to you after a long wait.

- ✔ Finding out about what support systems are available for students with dyslexia and other disabilities.

- ✔ Getting in touch with your supervisor – find out from your course administrator whether your supervisor prefers phone or email contact.

If you aren't familiar with the way your university or institution operates for meeting with your supervisor and other tutors, find out right now, preferably from fellow students or from support staff. It's your responsibility to be clear about how your university works on a day-to-day basis.

Making the first move to meet your supervisor is up to you. Your best way is by email. Don't expect an instant response. When term is under way academic staff can get 50 to 100 emails a day. I try to respond to email messages in a reasonable time, but with the best will in the world it isn't always possible for a tutor or supervisor to give you a speedy reply. Some weeks your supervisor may be working off campus or just extremely busy and it's reasonable to wait about a week for your supervisor to respond. If you still don't get a response, resend your email and ask politely for a meeting.

Make sure that you begin on the right foot. If you've never met your supervisor up to now, err on the side of caution and start off fairly formally. Your supervisor is soon going to make it clear how she prefers to be addressed. A professor is likely to be irritated by too casual an address, but no one is likely to be offended if you use a formal title on your first email, phone call or face-to-face meeting.

Write your emails in proper English, using full sentences and capital letters, and avoiding text-speak at all costs. Say what you have to say concisely and as briefly as possible. Don't bombard your supervisor with lots of attachments or really long messages, but do remember to say that you've been getting on with some research, or preparation, and that you're familiar with the course requirements.

Asking sensible questions

If you need to get answers to questions about your dissertation, most of them are likely to be found in the guidelines you've already picked up (see the section 'Understanding the requirements for your dissertation'). If you can't find the answer in the guidelines, you can then ask your supervisor for help. Although there's no such thing as a stupid question when setting out into the unknown that is your dissertation, you certainly shouldn't ask your supervisor unnecessary, irritating and exasperating questions that only serve to wind up your supervisor and give you a poor image. For example, asking about the length of your bibliography is a reasonable question to ask your supervisor, because your bibliography is key to your project. But asking what the hand-in date is, or whether you need to put the course on the title page of your dissertation is, unsurprisingly, likely to annoy your supervisor. When asking questions the general rule is to try to find the answer to your question in the rules and regulations first. Ask your supervisor about the practical issues relating to your dissertation only if you've exhausted all other avenues. Make your questions specific, to show that you've been thinking about what to do.

Your supervisor is there to give you specific and useful commentary on your writing and ideas, and you need to note your supervisor's suggestions and act upon them. A supervisor isn't there to do your work for you. Following your supervisor's comments and advice is likely to improve your dissertation. You can expect your grades to rise by 5 to 10 per cent if you do what your supervisor suggests – a more dramatic improvement is unrealistic (although possible of course).

Making the most of supervisions

In the section 'Making Contact with Your Supervisor' I point out that a supervisor's time is usually quite limited and so you need to get the best out of the precious time you have with your supervisor. Try to think about what you can do before, during and after your supervision to capitalise on the time spent with your supervisor.

Before a supervision

You have the appointment fixed up and you're planning what you need to do. Use this checklist of practical tips before seeing your supervisor:

❏ Check the time and location of your supervision – don't be late.

❏ Email or send a hard copy of any particular questions or concerns you may have that you think your supervisor would appreciate knowing before the session.

❏ Bring along some of the work you've been doing to show your supervisor if you're asked.

❏ Make sure that your papers, books and other resources are in order so you don't waste time searching for a vital item during your supervision time.

❏ Make sure that you have a pen (that works!).

❏ Switch off your mobile phone before going into the room.

❏ Write a clear list of questions and issues that you want to ask at the end of your supervision session.

So now you're thoroughly prepared. Good. Unless you have a very comfortable relationship with your supervisor already, meetings can sometimes be a bit like going to the doctor. You can be so anxious that everything goes well that you forget to take notes and as soon as you leave the meeting you realise you've forgotten half of what your supervisor has been saying.

During a supervision

You've prepared carefully and you're all set. Here's how to get the most out of the meeting with your supervisor:

✔ When going into the room and greeting your supervisor, politely ask how long your supervision session is likely to last so that you can make sure that you have time to get through what you need to do.

✔ If the meeting is steering away from the questions that you want to bring up, be sure to let your supervisor know that you've got issues that you want to tackle as well.

✔ If you find note-taking difficult, politely ask your supervisor if you can record the supervision, but don't get upset if she declines; just ask your supervisor to allow you a little extra time to get down all her pearls of wisdom.

✔ Pay attention to what's being said and try not to get distracted, because later you may regret not having listened more carefully.

✔ If you don't understand something your supervisor is saying (or any notes she writes for you), ask her to explain.

✔ Be realistic about any agreement you make with your supervisor about handing in future work.

✔ Get a clear date for any work your supervisor asks you to send in or future meetings so that you know exactly what to do.

✔ Be honest if you're stuck or struggling – your supervisor can only help you if she knows there's a problem.

After the supervision

Your supervision is over – phew! If you have the time, find a quiet corner in the cafeteria or library to go over what's just been discussed and make sure that you know exactly what to do next.

✔ Run through your supervision notes and make sure that everything is legible and in logical order – you may need to write a few things out again, just for clarity.

✔ If your supervisor gave you any notes during the session, check through the notes again to be sure that you understand everything.

✔ Make a list of any queries resulting from the supervision – you can email your supervisor after checking carefully through your questions.

✔ Get out your diary and plan in any work you need to do, highlighting your deadline but also making a note a few days before the deadline to finish the draft of whatever you're being asked to hand in to your supervisor.

If you need to ask any further questions after the session with your supervisor, this is best done by email: be polite, clear and to the point. Stick to any agreed deadlines.

Building a positive relationship

Putting in a bit of effort in building rapport with your supervisor is going to make working on your dissertation a much more pleasant and enjoyable experience. Remember, just like you, your supervisor is trying to balance work, family and play. Getting along well with your supervisor is good for your spirits and helps in keeping you motivated in seeing your dissertation through right to the end.

Aim at always being polite and considerate when you're with your supervisor. Don't try to be too familiar – better to err on the side of formality until you've had a few meetings and got to know the way she works. Politeness goes a long way, as does enthusiasm! Put yourself in your supervisor's place and imagine the effect your positive attitude has over a negative one.

Even if things aren't going too well for you and your dissertation, try to avoid just moaning and whining. Supervisors are generally keen to help and your supervisor isn't going to be able to do anything for you unless you explain clearly that you have some problems. General dissatisfaction, feeling that things just aren't working out, non-specific misery and being irritated are understandable, but you need to put your supervisor in a position to be able to help you. Analyse what's not working before your next session with your supervisor. No one expects you to solve your problems on your own. Again, try some empathy – your supervisor is going to be more eager to help if you present her with all the facts in a calm and reasoned manner.

Getting work to your supervisor

Your supervisor is always sure to have a heavy workload so if you need your supervisor to correct a piece of your work, you need to arrange this with her well in advance. Allow your supervisor enough time to turn the work around – normally at least a week, depending on how much work you want your supervisor to read. Ask your supervisor whether she prefers a printout or sending a Word file by email. If you're sending a Word file find out if she wants you to use Track Changes, or some other Word feature. Make sure, when sending a hard copy, that you know where to send your copy and how you're going to get it back.

If you'd like your supervisor to post your work back, it's helpful to include an addressed envelope with your copy. Universities usually pay for the postage but a self-addressed envelope saves your supervisor hassle and makes sure that your work gets back to you in double-quick time. You should also add your phone number and email address to the work in case your tutor would like to contact you directly about what you've written.

Most supervisors have heard every excuse under the sun for work being late! Be honest: if you know you're going to miss the deadline, let your supervisor know in good time. It can be very irritating for a supervisor who, after making time to pop into the university purely to collect a student's work, finds that the work isn't there. You need to keep your supervisor happy, so always try to be cooperative and helpful. Letting your supervisor know that you're going to be late with some work, in a polite fashion, is better than pretending that the work isn't yet due. Be aware that a supervisor may not be allowed to mark late work, and you need to accept this, especially as you're the person missing the deadline.

From your supervisor's standpoint, knowing what work is coming in allows her to organise her schedule. If you miss the slot that your supervisor has assigned to marking your draft, you can't expect her to create a new slot just for you (unless your circumstances are very serious, in which case your supervisor, like most academics, is likely to do whatever she can to help). Just occasionally (but don't count on it!) missing a deadline isn't held against you – and works in your supervisor's favour – she being inundated with work and therefore quite relieved you're missing your slot and happy to accept your work on another date.

Coping when things go wrong

Usually most supervisor–student relationships proceed without problems and need little attention. However, from time to time, relationships break down. If you find yourself in this situation, you need to face up to the problem and deal with it. Ignoring the problem means you're in danger of losing out on passing your dissertation as well as feeling pretty miserable in the process. You're inevitably going to regret getting into such a situation – so start acting now to find a solution to your difficulty. How you go about solving your difficulty depends quite a bit on the nature of the problem itself.

You get no response from your supervisor

You've tried contacting your supervisor but she simply isn't available. Your next step is to go to one of your tutors or a member of the support staff who knows you well and explain that you can't get in touch with your supervisor. Keep copies of any emails, perhaps printing out the emails to show that you've made several attempts to contact your supervisor. Give your supervisor ample time to get in touch with you, but when this stretches to a few weeks I suggest you take some action.

Your supervisor doesn't mark your draft work

If you arrange with your supervisor for her to make comments on a piece of your draft work but she fails to complete the work as arranged, your first step is to contact your supervisor directly. If you get no response after about a week, contact your supervisor again. Take copies of any emails you have from your supervisor about marking your draft work and then arrange to see a different tutor or a member of the support staff. Explain the situation calmly and ask the tutor or support staff what they think you should do. Take a copy of your draft work because it's possible that another member of staff is able to comment on your work in place of your supervisor.

Don't destroy your relationship with your supervisor by accusing her of doing or not doing something that she had no idea she was supposed to do, or not do. Contact her before you march off to the office to file an irate complaint.

Managing Your Time

Writing a dissertation is likely to be the biggest piece of work you're going to tackle on your university course. To do your dissertation justice means spending a lot of your time and energy on your dissertation – and sometimes tears. It need come as no surprise that you're expected to write a dissertation as part of your course, having been given all the information about your course when you first started. So there's no reason for waiting until the first day of your last year to start thinking about it!

Most universities allow one academic year for students to complete their dissertation, but some university courses require a longer or shorter project. Whatever the timescale of your university or institution, a year stretching ahead of you can seem an age. Anyone who's done a dissertation tells you with glee that this is merely an illusion and that you need to do some careful planning to make the best use of your time. Time has a way of evaporating like thin air – and all too soon the submission date is hanging over you like a dark cloud.

 Checking your submission date is your responsibility. You're a final-year undergraduate student, and it's likely that first-year students look up to you with respect, even a little awe – so, no excuses, it's your responsibility.

Knowing your strengths

Do you have a strategy for managing deadlines? If you're well organised and rarely miss a deadline, you're now just going to have to expand your methods to manage a larger piece of work. (By the way – you're in the minority, but I'd like to say well done and congratulations! Meeting deadlines is no mean feat.)

For most people who are writing to a deadline time gets tighter and tighter as the deadline approaches. You find yourself struggling to get finished, leaving little or even no time for final checks and proofreading. If you're one of those people, you need to plan the time allowed for your dissertation with great care to make sure that the quality of your research and writing is kept up to the mark.

If meeting a deadline is a disaster area for you, having a plan in place for checking your progress is a must. Your plan is also going to help you to think about why you're always late with your work. Being busy and having lots of pressures obviously goes some way to explaining the problem, but you well know that other people have similar difficulties and still meet their deadlines. What can you learn from another person's approach?

Think about the following statements and decide (honestly) which matches you best. Read everything else in this chapter with your own responses in mind. Your responses to the statements are likely to help you develop patterns of work to suit your own style. Also check out Chapter 10 to see how you're progressing, Chapter 16 to discover more about your work habits, and Chapter 17 to focus on your physical and emotional wellbeing:

- ❑ I'm a lark – I like getting up early, functioning best in the morning.

- ❑ I'm a night owl – I take ages to get going, but love burning the midnight oil.

- ❑ I like to have several projects on the go at the same time – having lots to do keeps me interested.

- ❑ I can focus on only one thing at a time, otherwise I get in a muddle.

- ❑ I like to have everything planned to the last detail.

- ❑ I need to go with the flow and find schedules suffocating.

- ❑ I prefer to get the simple tasks done first and then get down to the tough stuff and so have a sense of achievement.

- ❑ The difficult tasks really worry me – I like to get them out of the way as soon as I can.

Being realistic

Right – time for a reality check. How long is a year? 'Twelve months' I hear you say. 'Nope, the year I'm talking about is four months long!' I reply. 'How so?' you protest. 'Well, it's like this.'

Usually you have one academic year to write your dissertation. I say 'academic year' because an academic year is shorter than a calendar year. You probably start the academic year sometime between the middle of September and the middle of October, and you have to submit your finished dissertation (polished and perfect, completed and bound) in the following May or June. That's actually about seven months in total.

Take out a few weeks for sickness, holidays and trips to the pub, and you have about six months. Now deduct the time you need for your other course work: essays, presentations and attending lectures. Also take off the hours a week you spend doing paid part-time work. On top of this subtract the time you need for keeping up with your family and friends, and the many groups you're involved in that make inroads on the time you have for your dissertation.

Oh, and don't forget – you also have to spend time eating and sleeping. Now – how long is a year?

Rather scarily, your 'year' may seem a lot less time than it first appeared. This doesn't have to be a problem, however. What you need to do is plan your time effectively and then manage your time well. The best way of managing your time is by having a timeline.

Creating a timeline

A timeline is a schedule of events or a plan and it is presented chronologically. Your approach to your dissertation timeline depends on a number of factors such as your work space and whether you prefer ideas, for example, to be presented in a visual map or a linear list. A way of working out what is best for you is to think about how you like taking notes – straight prose, lists and numbered information, or using more organic lists with coloured diagrams, linked together with arrows?

You may like to create a table with overlapping lines called a Gantt chart, showing the different tasks you've set yourself and how the tasks run alongside one another. You can see an example of a Gantt chart in Figure 4-1.

Making contingency plans

Sometimes you find your careful plans for managing your dissertation going pear-shaped. You need to be able to cope with setbacks and salvage what you can. Aim to complete each task as early on as possible so that you have time to make any necessary changes. You can help yourself by building enough time into your dissertation timetable to allow for mini disasters and keeping ahead of the game so that any crises don't slow you up too much.

The plans you make when crises occur differ depending on what you need to change or develop. In Chapters 16 and 17 I give you ideas for dealing with difficulties and in Chapter 10 you can find suggestions for you to review as you go.

	Summer	Sept	Oct	Nov	Dec	Jan	Feb	Mar	Apr	May	Jun
Background reading	⊢———	——	—⊣								
Proposal/initial meetings		⊢——	—⊣								
Literature review		⊢——	——	——	——	—⊣					
Research methods planning			⊢——	—⊣							
Data collection					⊢——	—⊣					
Check on progress / Data analysis						⊢⊣	⊢——	—⊣			
Submit some draft work	⊢——	——	—⊣		⊢——	—⊣					
Discuss conclusions							⊢—⊣	⊢—⊣			
Further drafts							⊢——	—⊣			
Final meeting									⊢—⊣		
Final draft									⊢——	—⊣	

Figure 4-1: An example of a Gantt chart.

At this stage, you can think about what you'd most like to get done, but also think of an alternative if you run into difficulties. For example, you may prefer to distribute your questionnaire to 50 students at your university but your contingency plan would be to add up all the friends and acquaintances you have from the classes and clubs you attend and see if that would be a reasonable sample. You may try asking a tutor if you can give out your questionnaire during a taught session. It would mean reducing your ideal number from 50 to, say, 25, but at least you have some data you can use.

Creating a Dissertation Outline

Outlining your dissertation involves two main aspects: a practical list of what you need to do and a sketch of what you want to say.

First, in the section 'Trying out to-do lists' I offer you a list of 31 items that you can use as the basis of your own to-do list. Writing your to-do list is the easiest part of your dissertation, being just a list of tasks. I've arranged the tasks roughly in the order that you're likely to do them, although some of the tasks overlap.

Second, the outline of your dissertation needs to say clearly what thoughts and ideas you're going to include in each section of your dissertation. Sketching out what you need to say and structuring the presentation of your thoughts and ideas can be done in a number of ways but the two most popular methods are linear planning and concept planning (sometimes known as 'mind-mapping'). People often have strong feelings about which style they prefer; each method has pros and cons. I talk about linear planning in the section 'Looking at linear planning' and about concept planning in the section 'Considering concept and mind-mapping'.

If you find creating the outline a useful part of your planning strategy, it's a good idea to use the same outline style for each chapter. This helps you to write a dissertation with a clear, tight structure and avoid repetition and confusion. A well-structured outline leads to a coherent dissertation.

 Never think about your dissertation plan as set in stone – a good dissertation develops as you're working on it and you've no need to be afraid of moving slightly away from your original plans. If you're going wildly off track, however, seek support from your supervisor as soon as possible.

Looking at linear planning

When using linear planning for your dissertation outline, list your tasks in order of doing them, starting with your first dissertation task through to the end. Linear planning makes for a very clear outline, but it's more difficult to make changes as you go along than with a concept map. For your linear plan you can use the chapter headings I give you in Chapter 3 (or headings recommended by your supervisor) or the headings in the following list:

1. **Introduction and rationale:**

   'Why on earth am I doing this?' 'What led me to this topic?'

2. **Research question:**

   Explain all the terms in the research question so that they're clear.

3. **Outline of the literature:**

   'Who are the key thinkers?' 'What are the key texts?' 'What is the underlying theoretical idea?'

   Now choose the **4a** or the **4b** heading.

    4a. Empirical research methodologies:

        Pros and cons of different methods, for example question-naire, interview, observation

        Presentation of data – what I've found out

        Analysis of data/Discussion of data

    4b. Non-empirical main theorists and supporters:

        Counter-arguments and supporters

        My own view of the argument (and supporting theorists)

    5. Conclusions and suggestions for further research:

        What I have found in relation to the research question

        Ideas for developing the dissertation topic

    6. Appendixes and bibliography:

        Additional material that would interrupt the flow of writing

        All the references and materials used

Considering concept-mapping

If you prefer a more visual approach to your outline plan of your dissertation, a concept or mind-map may suit you better. The disadvantage of the concept map is that you still have to write your dissertation in the traditional linear format, and so you're going to have to convert your concept map into another form.

A key advantage of a concept map is that you can modify your listed tasks as you go along without having to completely rewrite your map each time. In Figure 4-2 you can see an example of a concept map for a linguistics dissertation looking at how children speak.

Trying out to-do lists

You need to be aware of the danger of making a to-do list: you can spend more time creating the list than you spend working on your dissertation. However, a comprehensive to-do list has some useful purposes:

✔ Keeping in front of you an overview of your work.

✔ Providing a clear record of your progress so that you know what's left to do.

✔ Helping build a sense of satisfaction as you tick things off.

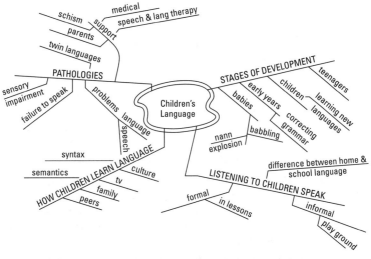

Figure 4-2: An example of a concept map.

When you're creating your own to-do list, your list is tailored to your dissertation, but many of the following suggestions are likely to be elements of your list. Use this 'To-do list' as a basis for creating your own.

1. Choose a subject and carry out some initial investigations.

2. Have a look through dissertations written by other students.

3. Write a proposal/finalise your research question.

4. Ask your supervisor to sign off your research topic.

5. Decide what type of dissertation you're going to write, empirical or non-empirical.

6. If you've chosen an empirical study, think through your research methodologies and check your decisions with your supervisor.

7. Spend some time organising how you're going to keep your notes in order.

8. Read, read, read! Take notes of the literature as you go.

9. Read about the pros and cons of the different research methodologies and take notes as you go.

10. Start writing up the essential parts of your literature review and research methodologies – this is an ongoing process and the notes from your reading form part of your dissertation.

11. Plan the overall structure of your dissertation – create outlines for each chapter.

12. If your writing is not flowing by this stage, have a go at starting your introduction/rationale just to get some words on paper.

13. Arrange for your supervisor to look at some of your draft work.

14. Make sure that you're all set for carrying out empirical work. For example, have you had ethical clearance? Have you sought permissions from subjects?

15. Sketch out the general arguments (for and against) for your dissertation. If your work is empirical, you're looking for ideas to support your findings and provide a backdrop to your work. If your work is non-empirical, this to-do list item should be tackled in detail.

16. Empirical only: carry out your empirical work.

17. Empirical only: organise the data you collect and make a note of any difficulties (these notes are going to be very helpful for discussion when you come to finish writing your research methodologies).

18. Empirical only: analyse your data and discuss your conclusions with your supervisor.

19. Non-empirical only: discuss the key thinkers and detractors of your topic with your supervisor, checking that you've understood their ideas and that you haven't left out any key thinkers.

20. Write up your findings/thoughts.

21. Write (or redraft) your introduction and conclusion.

22. Check over diagrams, charts and so on, and make decisions about what you're going to put in the appendixes.

23. Arrange for your supervisor to look at some more of your draft work.

24. Pull together everything you've done so far checking that you've covered all the elements required – this is your first full draft.

25. Make a new to-do list for filling in any gaps and be sure that you've covered everything.

26. Write up your final version, by editing your existing work and completing any outstanding items.

27. As you complete chapters, ask a friend to proofread carefully.

28. Keep in touch with your supervisor, checking that she has enough time for you if you need extra help.

29. Be sure that you know the rules for binding your dissertation and check how long binding takes.

30. Keep the submission date for your dissertation right in front of you and be sure of submitting your dissertation on time.

31. Relax!

Chapter 5

Finalising Your Research Question and Considering Ethics

. . . .

In This Chapter

▶ Underpinning theories for your research

▶ Deciding when you do and don't need empirical data

▶ Sorting out ethical concerns

. . . .

oming up with your research question makes you feel good. Now you're going to focus on your approach to the issues or themes you're going to be discussing in your dissertation and think carefully about the type of dissertation you're writing.

This chapter helps you specify your theoretical underpinning and shows you some different theoretical positions. The chapter also helps you decide if you need to collect data beyond the usual reading and research you do for essays. You may be thinking you need to conduct an interview or questionnaire and this chapter helps you decide if you do or you don't.

And importantly, before going a step further, you need to make sure of fulfilling any ethical obligations linked to the research topic and research methodology you're carrying out. This chapter tells you what you need to know to ensure that your work meets the requirements.

Looking at How You View the World

How you view the world is going to have a bearing on all aspects of your dissertation – from deciding on your research question, to selecting your methodologies and to interpreting relevant theories. Whether or not you focus your dissertation on theory, you're going to need to get to grips with theoretical ideas about your topic and have a clear understanding of your own philosophical standpoint.

Theoretical viewpoints for undergraduate social science dissertations generally fall at a point on a spectrum. Your ideas are likely to be somewhere between a fixed, positive view of the world or a more fluid, flexible view. Your way of looking at the world determines how you approach your dissertation – an issue I consider in the following sections.

Deciding whether you're a positivist or a relativist

Whatever your research question, you're likely to have an opinion on how the world *should* work and how the world actually *does* work: your philosophical standpoint. Every aspect of your dissertation is going to be based on your philosophical approach – you need to be clear where you stand and how your philosophical opinions are likely to affect your study.

The most common and extreme viewpoints in the social sciences are positivism and relativism. I explain the ideas in the sections 'Positivism' and 'Relativism', but you're already probably familiar with the ideas of positivism and relativism, even though the terminology may seem a bit foreign to you.

I've only space in this book to offer you a simplified explanation of positivism and relativism. If you want to find out more you need to discuss with your supervisor the best texts to explore positivism and relativism in more depth.

Positivism and relativism aren't the only philosophies of course, but are a useful example, because positivism and relativism sit at the outermost ends of a range of ideas underpinning social science subjects. Where *you* sit is going to affect your approach and conclusions as your research develops.

How does my viewpoint influence my dissertation?

Here's an easy way of illustrating how your philosophical standpoint influences your dissertation. Imagine you're interested in victims of crime giving testimony in court. You're focusing on measuring and reviewing how the process is run, perhaps comparing different systems in different areas of the country, looking at procedure, or considering how society is changing. These issues are likely to be well served using methods that are generally found in positivist studies. For example, collecting data about how many people attend hearings or the gender breakdown of victims. What you're looking for is data you can evaluate showing what happens in court.

Taking a relativist standpoint means that you're more interested in the experience of being in court and giving evidence. Immediately you can see that the relativist approach is likely to be coloured by the way that people express their feelings about what they've been through or observed.

Rather than collecting bald facts as with a positivist stance, you're going to need a set of different approaches such as analysing transcriptions to review the sort of language people use when expressing themselves, or preferably, interviewing police or support officers who can help you understand victims' experiences (approaching the victims directly would be an ethical minefield). Seeing and hearing what people say, how they say it and how they behave helps you to understand what people are experiencing.

Neither a positivist nor a relativist approach is 'right' or 'wrong' in itself. But you do need to be sure where you sit and make your methodologies and analysis consistent with your position.

You may find your philosophical ideas shifting as you go along. Changing your philosophical ideas isn't a problem; in fact looking at your research question from another angle can be an advantage because you now have more to discuss. Even though you may find taking a different viewpoint disconcerting, you need to explain any fundamental changes to your outlook because your philosophy is going to affect your dissertation in many ways.

 With the positivist and relativist approaches, and all the philosophical approaches in between, you're making choices about what you want to find out and the best way of doing so. No one philosophical approach is going to be completely objective, but if you plump for a positivist stance, you're aiming for an impartial detached perspective, whereas a relativist stance is more personal

Positivism

Positivism is about reason and objectivity. Positivists argue that knowledge is identified by an unbiased, impartial observer who looks closely and measures the situation in a detached and unemotional way. Taking the positivist approach assumes that people live in a shared reality and that what is being observed can be checked out by other witnesses who can reproduce the experiments and so generate the same results. This view claims that positivist research is general, reliable, verifiable and replicable, and that generally agreed theories and understandings are created through taking the positivist approach.

You're a positivist if you believe that:

✔ The world has an inherent order

✔ There's one shared reality

✔ You get the true picture through using the human senses and intellect

Relativism

From the relativist position the ideas underpinning research are differently conceived. The idea of one external reality is challenged. In the place of one shared reality, relativists put forward the idea that an individual has his own personal reality shaped by his unique viewpoint. Everyone has a way of looking at the world, formed by individual emotions, experiences and understandings.

Relativists appreciate that people do have shared understandings: for example, how people communicate, but relativists focus on different interpretations and how words are being used and also body language. Different responses to situations show a wide range of personal realities. Analysing the way people communicate (or *discourse*) can be tricky, but taking a relativist approach helps researchers understand different views and hence the nature of our world. Relativists avoid generalising because this can mean ignoring personal views. Similarly, relying merely on the senses and the memory (as with positivism) is a tactic that relativists question.

You're a relativist if you believe that:

✔ Order in the world is created by people and societies

✔ Making general statements about the world, societies and communities is unacceptable

✔ People themselves shape the world as views and opinions shift and change

A middle way: Reconciliation

Some theorists call the balance between the two extremes of positivism and relativism *reconciliation*. A researcher taking the reconciliation stance believes that some facts and information can be known with certainty, but that other knowledge is dependent on human and social issues. Reconciliation takes into account that some knowledge is far less predictable and is affected by different interpretations.

According to the reconciliationist's view, physics, biology, chemistry and some features of geography are the least affected by the whims of a researcher's interpretation. Scientific facts are known and proved, the facts having a predictability and logic that help to explain them.

Knowledge in the social sciences is subject to the physical laws of the world and the universe, but different language and methods, different ways of reviewing and understanding the knowledge need to be used to explain what is happening. The interrelationships and complexities of the human world need to be interpreted through the systems in which they exist. It's also necessary to view human systems and experiences through the eyes of the people involved in what is being studied.

Note that your philosophical views are unlikely to fit neatly into 'just positivism' or 'just relativism'. Give thought to where you think you stand, but don't be surprised if your ideas shift as you research your dissertation.

Giving a lot of thought to your philosophical outlook is going to support and shine through your dissertation topic. Most people spend not nearly enough time addressing the stance that underpins their work. Knowing which way your philosophical stance leans is going to determine which way your research takes you, as well as showing how well your philosophical thinking is developing owing to your degree studies.

Working out whether you need to deal with theory

You may think of yourself as being a very philosophical person; or having no philosophical views of any sort; or choosing your area of study specifically to avoid dealing with philosophical ideas. Try not to be put off by the philosophical thinking I raise in this chapter. How you view the world is just an expression of your way of thinking. When your supervisor asks you for your views about an aspect of your research question he's partly talking about whether you have a positivist or relativist stance, even if he doesn't use the specific language I'm using here.

For example: you're researching a particular aspect of day care for preschool children. There are many ways of approaching the topic and your personal view affects which direction you choose in carrying out your research.

In an empirical dissertation, a *moderately positivist* approach involves gathering data about the number of children who are attending for day care and the ratio of children to qualified staff and other care workers. You think about available resources and the funds directed to the centre. Your methodologies may include an analysis of relevant statistics and data, and perhaps a comparison with other such centres with a different or similar demographic.

As a *moderate relativist*, you're keen to carry out your research within the social context, focusing on people's viewpoints and personal stories. You're likely to be using interviews and perhaps taking part as an observer at the day-care centre. You're probably conducting a focus group or holding interviews, concentrating on the views of children and staff in the day-care centre, to confirm the facts you've unearthed.

Both the positivist and relativist approaches require data, but the ways of collecting data are different. You notice that the positivist approach is designed so that the study can be repeated by another researcher, whereas the relativist approach is more personal and tied to the researcher and the specific social context he's looking at.

When it comes to analysing the data, there are more differences. The positivist researcher is looking for objective facts, making connections and looking at patterns, while the relativist researcher is more interested in how the children and carers are interacting, what the children and carers are experiencing and what results can be taken from the observations. A researcher taking a reconciliatory standpoint is likely to focus on general principles that can be supported by clear factual evidence and then illustrated by examples.

Applying your philosophical position to a predominantly theoretical dissertation

If you're working exclusively on theory and not really trying to apply ideas to practical situations, you may be wondering how the idea of different philosophical views fits with the theories you're planning to explore. Although you may not see an obvious connection, how you interpret the theories you're exploring is going to be coloured by your position on the positivist-relativist spectrum.

Using the moderately positivist and moderately relativist examples from the section 'Working out whether you need to deal with theory', and carrying out non-empirical research, you're still going to come up with different interpretations depending on your philosophical stance. You may be considering how other studies recommend different types of provision and evaluating the methods such studies use and the conclusions the studies draw.

For example, you're looking at the pros and cons of an informal approach to child care against a strictly structured day-care setting. You may be looking closely at the principles without necessarily mentioning any of the practical problems or issues. However, a theoretical study still involves thinking about your underlying philosophical stance – what you think are the most important aspects of education is part of your world view and fits somewhere along the positivist-relativist spectrum. You're going to need to know where you stand to help explain your analysis of the competing theories you're reviewing.

Many students have a moderate approach and most examiners aren't surprised to see a mix of quantitative and qualitative methods. For example, an examiner isn't going to be surprised by a mainly positivist approach with a nod towards relativist ideas. What the examiner wants is evidence that the student has thought carefully and chosen a stance and methods that truly help to give answers to the research question.

Although some research methods seem to match a positivist or relativist philosophical stance, no one research method is fixed in stone. All the research methods can be harnessed in different ways, as I explain in Chapter 8.

Picking out the important theories

You're likely to find that there are some theories and theorists who are fundamental to your research question, and leaving them out of your dissertation would be a terrible sin. Such theories and theorists cover ideas and issues that have a forceful influence on the subject. The theorists and theories are familiar and recognisable – well-known and well-established names frequently recurring on your degree course.

Ideas transforming a field of study (and their originators) are important because the ideas shape all the understandings that follow. The theories and theorists often change the language being used in the subject area and challenge previous thinking. As a theory develops, there are inevitably detractors who criticise and adapt the original ideas, maybe ultimately reducing the worth of the initial key theory. Even if ideas are under attack, any long-lasting influence on the subject has to be acknowledged in your dissertation.

Beware of thinking that you won't need to mention very important theorists whose ideas are now being challenged and thought to be outdated. Your examiner may not see such omissions as your sophisticated, thoughtful approach. All your examiner sees is that you haven't bothered to mention the main thinkers relating to your research question.

You can recognise the key theorists and theories because they're the ones you've already been introduced to and whose ideas are repeatedly referred to by more than one tutor on your degree course. If your course favours a particular version of key theories (a specific text or writer) and where the key thinker's ideas relate to your dissertation, you definitely need to include them in your work – the examiner is expecting to see the key theorists and theories mentioned.

I can't give you a definitive list of key theorists because this book covers too many different specialist fields, but a good way of finding out who and what counts as 'key' is to look at a few decent (and recent) textbooks on your subject. Run your eye over the contents pages taking note of the main headings; it's likely that textbooks have the same type of content (broadly speaking). If the same theory arises in three core textbooks, it's a safe bet that you need to know about it!

Some key thinkers are so familiar that your field of study takes their ideas as the norm. You need to decide how to reference a key thinker showing you're aware of their importance without misleading the examiner about the sources you've been using. If you haven't looked at what a key thinker has written since your first term of your first year, don't claim to have reread their famous 1874 publication in the original Flemish. If there's an accepted modern interpretation, translation or straightforward explanation of the theory, make sure that you reference that text.

Always use and reference the texts recommended on your course, especially if the texts have been highlighted by more than one tutor.

If you're stuck on how to reference a key thinker who has a strong presence in your research, you need to speak to your supervisor. Make a list of several alternative suggestions and give a clear example of where and how the theorist surfaces in your dissertation. This information shows that you're thinking about your query carefully and allows your supervisor to make positive suggestions.

Choosing which theories to include

Choosing which theories to include in your dissertation is crucial. You've a limited word count and you won't be able to do justice to every theory and theorist you meet in your reading. It's important to take your lead from your supervisor and other tutors.

Ask your supervisor to help you decide which theories you need to include and which you can safely leave out. In addition, try scanning your lecture notes and making a list of suggestions based on what you've been taught during your degree course.

Discovering new theories

Through your independent study you're likely to have come across ideas and thinkers that are new to you and you need to check out their worth. If you're finding them interesting, that suggests the ideas and thinkers are relevant, but you still need to know something about the suitability and soundness of the theory to your field of study. One way of finding out is to look at the source of the reference. You can find out more in Chapter 6, but for now, bear in mind the following simple rules:

- ✔ If the theory appears in a recommended academic journal or book, the idea is probably sound.

- ✔ If the theory is referenced in a book or article by your supervisor, you're onto a winner.

- ✔ If the theory comes from a popular tabloid, on an unreferenced or 'wiki' Internet site, it's potentially problematic.

- ✔ Always do some carefully detailed quality control before relying on what you've found – especially if the theory is from a questionable source.

Citing the 'right' number of references

One of the most common questions that students ask their tutor or supervisor is 'How many references do I cite in an essay or dissertation?' I know that my students are often suspicious of my apparently vague response to this question, but it isn't vagueness, it's an honest reply.

Although for an average essay of 2500 words, citing just three references is probably way too thin, and 50 is over the top, it's impossible to suggest a fail-safe formula, such as 'four references for each 1,000 words' because the number of references needing to be cited is geared to your subject. For example, if you're writing about the effects of social housing policy in a city, you're going to be quoting a lot of local and national government statistics and listing websites. Or, if you're engaged in a criticism of a key theorist's influential idea about how communities are affected by their social housing project, you're more likely to be focusing on that one theorist and on his detractors and supporters: this sort of essay may need far fewer references. The number of references you need to cite depends very much on your subject matter and the sort of essay you're writing.

Whys and Wherefores of Using Empirical Data

Many students doing a social science dissertation include empirical data (what you've found out) in their dissertation; some students analyse existing data; and a significant minority of students write theoretical papers, like an extended essay.

Don't take it for granted that you need to generate your own data to earn top marks for your dissertation. An effective analysis of an existing study is far preferable to a less rigorous study of new data.

Deciding what kind of question to ask

You may have an idea of what you want to research and a sense of the viewpoint you're coming from, but now you need more specific questions to answer. This section suggests ways to narrow down your study and get to grips with exact and precise questions.

The sort of data you need to gather is closely linked to the type of question you're asking:

✔ **A case study?** If your study is about a specific case or a person's particular experience, you're going to need data about the case or the person's views and ideas.

✔ **A general phenomenon?** If your study is about what's happening generally, you're going to be making a survey and needing statistics or centrally produced information covering a wide range of people.

✔ **A policy?** If your study involves examining a policy: this is an evaluation. You're going to need evidence of the policy in practice or at least the views of experts in the area of study to find out if the policy is successful.

✔ **A comparison?** Are you trying to decide which of two methods is better suited to a specific problem? Your data is going to be around the results of each approach and perhaps the underlying principles.

Whatever type of topic you're researching you need data of some description, but a particular topic may require more specific data than others. The policy question, for example, can be answered by a non-empirical library-based study. The other topics need empirical data to answer the research question.

Getting your answers from secondary data

Secondary data is data that's already been collected and recorded by another researcher. It's up to you to dig out, compare, relate and interpret the data for your dissertation topic. The census is an example of data that's collected nationally and if you make use of data from the census in your dissertation that's a review of secondary data.

Any journal or newspaper article you read is an example of secondary data. But you need to be discerning about what you read, hear and see – if you're not reading critically you can end up with some dodgy 'facts'. The key with secondary data is to be scrupulous about the sources. Go to Chapter 7 for assessing the validity of secondary data sources.

If you're planning to carry out any of the following, you're going to be evaluating secondary data (this is a tiny selection of the kinds of projects – but you get the idea):

✔ Reviewing policy documents

✔ Analysing statistical data

✔ Looking for patterns within national data

✔ Evaluating major research project or initiatives

✔ Interpreting survey results

✔ Comparing national or international concerns

Meeting the methods that help you find your answers

In Chapter 8 you find out about collecting and generating empirical data and the various research methods you can use. Before starting to collect any empirical data, you need to have an idea of the kinds of information you may require so that you can decide if your research question is feasible. If you suddenly realise that your question requires you to post 250 letters asking for information, you're quickly going to find that the postage costs are prohibitive and you may need to find another research topic.

For now, be aware of the following commonly used methods for collecting information (this list is just a guide):

✔ Questionnaires

✔ Interviews

✔ Observations

✔ Measuring or recording something

✔ Diaries or reflective journals

✔ Taking part in an event or activity

The data you collect from using the methods in the list is called primary data (data you've collected yourself). In everyday life, what you're experiencing through your senses is primary data, but when you're doing research you need to record what you find so that you can carry out your analysis; so your primary data consists of documents, observations, measurements and summaries.

Settling for an empirical or non-empirical dissertation

Collecting your own data means using empirical methods. You're going to be designing surveys or some method of observation. If you choose to do an empirical dissertation, you're likely to be analysing secondary empirical data (involving no collecting of primary data).

If you're choosing to do a non-empirical dissertation, you're conducting an argument (or series of arguments) sustained over the length of the dissertation. Check out Chapters 1 and 2 for the main differences between empirical and non-empirical dissertations.

Whether you're choosing to do an empirical or non-empirical dissertation, your choice needs to match the research question – your research question governs your method of research.

Make sure that you're absolutely clear about the nature of your research question and the data you're going to need so that you know where to look for help and how to plan and carry out your work.

I've separated empirical and non-empirical dissertations quite starkly in order to explain them as clearly as possible. For some students, this division may be rather forced, because it's likely you come across overlap and connections between different research techniques (just as you're going to find that your methodology and analysis don't always fit neatly into a positivist or relativist category).

Finalising your research question

After thinking through your philosophical standpoint and the kinds of data you're going to need, you now have a clear understanding of what your research question involves. Your research question defines your project and marks the boundaries of your work, driving your data collection and data analysis and giving your data a clear purpose.

Fusing positivist and relativist viewpoints

One student I was supervising managed to make use of positivist and relativist standpoints in her dissertation. Her work was fundamentally positivist – she designed a questionnaire focusing on gathering facts objectively. But she also asked for people's views in the questionnaire and so her data was both quantitative and qualitative – built around the idea of discovering the truth about the quality of provision that she considered could be measured objectively.

But the student felt that her study was a bit sterile. She wanted to include in her dissertation something about how the children saw their day-care setting and so introducing a more personal and emotional dimension to her research. To gather the views of the young children, many of whom had limited language skills, she gave each child a disposable camera asking them to take snaps of the areas, activities and people at the day-care centre they liked best. The photos, although often blurred, taken from some rather unusual angles, and sometimes strange, were very telling and of course quite charming. The data the children provided added another dimension to her study, pulling her study along the philosophical spectrum towards a more relativist standpoint. The student's methodology proved to be just right for her dissertation: brought to life by addressing the topic through the children's eyes. The photos in no way detracted from what she was saying, even helping to get across the points she was making more powerfully.

The Internet provides a valuable source for checklists for assessing the suitability of your research question. Some of the best include 'The Research Room' from Empire State College, New York (www.esc.edu/esconline/across_esc/writerscomplex.nsf/wholeshortlinks2/Research+Room+Menu?opendocument) and the 'Companion for Undergraduate Dissertations', from the Higher Education Academy (www.socscidiss.bham.ac.uk/s7.html).

I've created a checklist here that can also be helpful, but remember that you and your supervisor are really the best judges of a topic that's suitable and realistic for you to research. Go through the following checklist, considering each point and hopefully ticking each of the boxes:

✔ **Your question and the field of study:**

❑ You've chosen an area that's significant in your field

❑ A reasonable body of literature exists forming a context for your work

❑ Your supervisor and fellow students can see the value and relevance of your ideas

❑ The area is worth making the effort to research

✔ **Your question is clearly expressed:**

❑ You haven't made any assumptions

❑ Your research terms are clearly defined

❑ There's no ambiguity

❑ You've been as specific as possible

❑ The research question is reasonably clear and concise

❑ You've avoided using loaded language

✔ **Your question is manageable:**

❑ You have access to subjects that make the data collection feasible

❑ The scale of the project is right for your level

❑ You can obtain the necessary ethical clearance

❑ It's within your area of knowledge (or at least you've enough background to help you out – your material isn't all brand new)

❑ You don't need expensive equipment or a budget for travel to carry out your research

❑ You can easily get the results you need within the timescale

✔ **Your question genuinely interests you – but you're not obsessive:**

❑ You're going to stay motivated about your topic during the time you're spending on your dissertation (or you think it more likely than not)

❑ You're genuinely interested in your research question but not to the exclusion of other areas of your life (so you don't end up getting too involved)

❑ You're not so involved that you can't stay objective

In the list that follows you can see examples of dissertation research questions that I've collected from students over the years. I make comments and where appropriate reframe the student's original research question making doing the research feasible. Using the criteria from the checklist, consider which questions in this list are sensible and can actually be addressed, and which are rather too wide-ranging, or are impossible or inappropriate.

All the research questions (except for Example 9) are best answered by gathering empirical data. Example 9 is likely to be answered through mainly library-based research, using the non-empirical approach.

1. How gifted children aren't having their needs met in schools.

2. Preschool children on gallery visits: which workshop pedagogies best help them engage with artworks at Tate Britain?

3. A review of support for children with dyslexia in schools in the UK.

4. A review of the Son-Rise and Lovaas methods for helping children with autism: which is most effective for encouraging verbal communication with a small group of seven-year-olds?

5. Learning in museums: how well is it done?

6. How well do school children manage their dyslexia in maintained primary schools? A case study of a Key Stage 2 boy.

7. An investigation into the problems of children whose mothers work full-time.

8. An investigation of how twins communicate in general.

9. Free for all? A review of the effects of recent policy developments on museums and galleries.

10. What teachers think about the Gifted and Talented strategy for primary pupils: an investigation into the policy and practice of a school.

Examples 1 and 7 make assumptions, the outcomes of which have already been decided. They therefore need to be reframed more objectively. Something like this would be better: 'A review of evidence for the claim that highly able children would benefit from more targeted attention in primary schools', or 'A survey of the effects of working parents on young children'. Although these are still unsatisfactory, they're an improvement on the first versions.

Several of the questions are far too broadly conceived. Example 3 is too ambitious (*All* schools in the UK? *All* age phases? How is this measured?), and examples 5 and 8 are too vague to be put into practice (What kind of learning in what kind of museums? Who is doing the learning? Children? Adults? Tourists? What is meant by 'how well'? / Communicate with whom? Each other? Their families? What age are these twins? and so on). The questions lack clear definitions and parameters.

Numbers 2 and 4 are better; nicely limited and clear. Both cite specific instances to be reviewed and the claims they make from their results can be easily related to similar scenarios. They don't need to be grandiose and don't claim influence beyond their particular situations.

6 and 10 are case studies with rather precise descriptions of what is to be undertaken. They may seem rather narrow (as do 2 and 4) but they're clearly based on feasible, accessible situations and if the students provide a thoroughly researched context and rationale, their conclusions can provide a useful support or refutation of current practice.

Question 9 is rather more theoretical and has carefully avoided subjectivity in the title. I'd expect that the student may conclude that recent policy has been good, bad or mixed in terms of supporting the aims of museums and galleries, but I've no inkling of any bias in the title which is a positive start.

Keeping Things Ethical

Social science studies are about individuals, communities and societies. Even if you're not carrying out a case study, questionnaire or interview when doing your research for your dissertation, you're bound to be looking at an issue that involves people – and before starting off you need to sort out any ethical matters connected with your research.

You have to make sure that the interests and rights of anyone affected by your work are safeguarded and you must ensure that you keep to the following:

- Obeying the legislation on human rights and data protection
- Maintaining good-quality research (data collection, storage analysis, dissemination of information)
- Gaining the informed consent of your subjects
- Thinking through the consequences of your work

Most undergraduate dissertations are fairly straightforward because the sample group you're researching is usually fairly small and the context is known to the supervisor and the student. I recommend this scenario (of knowing your subjects and there being minimal risk and concern) because it makes the whole process manageable and more feasible in the timescale that you're given for your dissertation.

If your research causes you to fall into any of the following categories, you need to ask your supervisor for advice on what you should do:

✔ Your study involves vulnerable participants and/or those unable to give informed consent (such as children or people with learning difficulties or disabilities).

✔ Some of your subjects may be feeling under pressure to take part (friends, colleagues, family members).

✔ Your research means discussing issues that may upset people or cause stress, such as health matters, personal experiences or something the person knows to be illegal, such as drug use.

✔ Your study involves communicating with a 'gatekeeper' in order for you to have access to the subjects (for example, you need to obtain the agreement of the teacher to access the children in her class).

✔ Your participants may be taking part without their knowledge (for example, carrying out observation of children in a playground).

✔ You may be at risk when carrying out observations or interviews. (Chapter 8 gives you guidelines on this topic.)

Checking you're complying with the university regulations

Universities have specific regulations about getting ethical clearance for any part of a study that may breach ethical guidelines. You're going to have to comply with particular permissions if you're carrying out observations or interviews. In Chapter 8 you can find a template on the ethical issues of collecting empirical data.

Your university may ask you to complete a form to get ethical clearance for your research. This is the norm for higher level studies and research projects but less common for undergraduate dissertations. If you do need to fill in a form addressing ethical concerns, the questions you're likely to be asked are:

✔ Aim of study.

✔ Background (naming some of the literature and other studies in a similar area).

✔ Research methodologies and methods.

✔ Potential problems for subjects (such as discussing sensitive issues).

✔ Potential problems for the researcher (such as travel following interviews carried out in the evening).

✔ Methods of recruiting subjects (including declaration of inducements – that is, whether or not you paid them).

✔ Evidence of having informed consent.

✔ Data protection (including the security of your data storage and anonymity of subjects).

Look through the list and have an answer in mind for each question in case ethical concerns and obligations come up during supervision.

To be on the safe side, complete a form with all these questions answered anyway – the worst your supervisor can do is accuse you of working really hard!

Gaining informed consent

You must have the consent of people taking part in your research. In most cases you're required to have written consent and your course tutor or department may well have a standard form for you to use. Consent forms are designed to comply with Government requirements, which exist to protect vulnerable people from any poor research practices. One example of this is the Criminal Records Bureau (CRB) check that you're going to need if your research involves children.

Your responsibility to your subjects doesn't end once you've collected the data. It's up to you to be frank and honest when interpreting your subjects' words and actions. You're not allowed to twist words or alter what people have said or done.

Respecting other people's ideas and views

When you're doing interviews and carrying out questionnaires, it's important to keep your thoughts to yourself. Hiding your feelings can be hard, but if you disagree violently with someone you can end up stopping the person from expressing his views for fear of 'getting something wrong'.

Don't be a robot though – you can express mild surprise if someone says something really strange (you may find some subjects are after a reaction, so you sometimes need to oblige), but try not to let other people's views faze you. After all, you're asking for the person's opinion, so you need to let him express his opinion without feeling stupid.

Knowing what's appropriate

A group of first-year undergraduate students were interested in looking at teen-agers' views about how sexual content is used to boost sales of magazines. The students put together an interview schedule for a focus group but didn't run the questions by a tutor first. Using university headed notepaper so that the questions looked official the students presented the group of 13- and 14-year-olds with the questions. The first question asked: 'Have you had sex?' and the questions moved onto others including 'Do you think that all your friends are sexually active?' and 'How does it feel to be the only one in your group of friends who's still a virgin?' Clearly these questions wouldn't have been approved by the tutor, but the students were genuinely surprised when the university staff expressed their shock.

Strike the right balance between modesty and arrogance. Don't be so self-deprecating that people think that your research is a waste of time: 'Oh, it's just a little project, it's not that interesting, it's not a big deal'. Also avoid sounding self-important as this is equally off-putting: 'Yes, I'm dealing with some really vital issues here – I want to expose the problems and find a solution to these continual low standards.'

Keeping your subjects' anonymity

When you're writing about the people in your research project, you need to disguise the person's real identity, making sure that the person can't be identified and traced. Some of your subjects may say that you don't need to hide their identity, but although that can seem like a good idea at the time, you don't yet know where your research is going to take you and you may later regret choosing that option.

A parent (not just the institution where the child is living, studying, or staying) must agree on behalf of a child.

Speak to your dissertation tutor about the legal aspects of your work. Generally a 'child' is 16 years old or under, but if someone is 17 and still studying in school, for example, you need to follow different guidelines than if you were asking your college peers who are over 18, or a 17-year-old with a full-time job.

The onus is on you to check the legality of what you want to pursue. Consult your tutor if in doubt.

Changing the names of your research subjects when you're writing about them is a good idea, but you need to do this with care and make it clear that you've changed the person's names to preserve their privacy by simply saying: 'In this dissertation, the names of subjects have been changed to preserve their anonymity'.

Give some thought to what the alternative names are going to be. Changing 'Kelly' to 'Kerry' or 'Ian' to 'Iain' isn't going to do a good job of hiding anything much, and also be sure that you don't change genders by mistake.

Although it can be a good idea to find a name that reflects the cultural background of your research subjects, if this is relevant to the study – take care here that you don't slip into stereotype.

Researchers often refer to their subjects as 'Child X' or 'Mrs Y' and this does the job perfectly well. I'm not keen on reading dissertations that use this method because it seems very impersonal and makes for a jerky read. If I'm marking a large number of dissertations that use the same convention, like other examiners, I tend to forget which 'Child A' is which because there's no personality linked to a person labelled by an initial letter of the alphabet (except for 'Mr T' of course).

Your rule of thumb is to use recognisable names that aren't too outlandish and that are distinct from one another (don't call your three subjects 'Emily', 'Emma' and 'Emmie' for example). Remember to be consistent throughout your dissertation.

Keep the real and 'code' names of your subjects in your dissertation notebook so that you don't get confused.

Also remember to hide the names of schools, hospitals, specific departments or organisations you've been allowed to review where there are any potentially sensitive issues. Don't try to anonymise organisations such as governments or government departments, even if you're being critical.

In your appendixes and additional material you have to make sure that you anonymise any letter headings, delete logos from policy documents and change names or delete them from personal reports. It's a fairly common error in dissertations to find that students give away their subjects' identities in the additional material and I suspect it's because students leave dealing with the appendixes and additional material until the last moment.

When you've finished writing up your dissertation, do a Word 'Find' search through the text, looking for the real names of your subjects in case you've slipped up somewhere.

Avoiding plagiarism

Plagiarism is stealing another person's ideas or writings and passing them off as your own. It's unethical for you to use another person's work without correctly acknowledging the person in your original sources.

I give you detailed information about avoiding plagiarism in Chapter 7 on researching and in Chapter 13 on writing.

 Your best way of insuring against plagiarism is to be scrupulous with your note-taking so that you always have the necessary details to hand to use for acknowledging the original sources of your information. (See Chapter 6 for a more in-depth discussion of plagiarism.)

Acknowledging the people who help you

In several different chapters (Chapters 11, 12 and 15), I explain in detail about writing your acknowledgements. Your acknowledgements are more about courtesy than being a fixed requirement in your dissertation, but it's good manners to acknowledge people who've helped you by being subjects in your research, or by making it easy for you to find your subjects.

For example, if you've interviewed budget holders about how they forecast their annual spend and your gatekeeper contact at the department was a research officer or someone in human resources, be sure to thank your contact as well as the subjects you interviewed.

You can make your acknowledgements without revealing the person's identity. Use the person's job title and if they evenutally see a copy of your dissertation they're going to know who they are and recognise and appreciate your gratitude. All you need to say is: 'With sincere thanks to all those people who helped me by giving up their valuable time and sharing their considered views'.

Chapter 6

Reading and Note-Taking Efficiently

*T*he thing that's most likely to guarantee that your dissertation is top-notch is reading, reading and yet more reading. Getting to know a broad range of writers in your field of study and the many different types of material available means you're acquiring a vast amount of information – and being introduced to a wide variety of styles and quality of writing. As well as using your reading for sharpening your thinking, you have a great opportunity for discovering ways of refining your own reading and writing skills.

Your supervisor may be moved to show you a piece of work by a previous student, for you to get a feel for the kind of writing tutors expect to read. Although you may find reading another student's work useful, never allow such writing to replace writing published by experts in your field. Remember that a supervisor may be offering you an example of weak writing simply to show you what kind of work to avoid handing in. Always read critically!

Making the Most of Your Reading

Using the appropriate reading techniques can make your reading so much more pleasurable and pain free. You need to match your reading style to what you're reading, but having trouble with reading is a common problem for students because being taught reading techniques is rare. Most people are pretty good at adjusting their way of speaking to suit the occasion – for example, avoiding using swear words in front of very young children and grandma, and of course, the budgerigar.

Reading is much the same. When your favourite magazine comes out, you don't necessarily read it from front to back, or give an equal amount of time and attention to each article. It's okay to skip over the advertisements, editorial and news sections, cutting straight to the gossip and horoscopes, if that's why you bought the magazine in the first place. Reading a novel by a favourite author is another story. The joy of savouring each passage is the point of reading the novel – if you just wanted the storyline, you get hold of a review or synopsis. Reading a recipe is different again; you glance at the recipe to see if it appeals, then you review the cooking techniques. Then you flick back and forth from ingredients to method to timings, passing lightly over some sections of the recipe and reading other parts with extreme care.

Investing energy and effort into improving your approach to your reading is going to prove a bonus – saving you time overall and avoiding trouble and frustration.

I can't emphasise enough how important it is to read widely and deeply if you're aiming high. Discuss further readings with your supervisor, but only when you've thoroughly got to grips with the essentials of reading fruitfully and productively.

Skimming: Using the contents page, chapter headings and indexes

Skimming a book or article involves skipping through it in order to decide how relevant the content is to your study. Your aim is to get a general sense of the suitability of the text for your dissertation topic as well as the readability and style.

The title is the key

When you're initially searching for books and articles for your dissertation, make sure that you read the full title of the work. The title often gives you an important clue as to the attitude or approach that the author has taken to the subject of the book or article. Very often academic texts have 'It does what it says on the tin' titles and when a text has a punchier, more memorable title, this is usually followed (after a colon) by a more detailed explanatory subheading. You find *Social Work from 1870–1980* and think 'Bingo – a book on the history of social work – just what I need for my study on the effects of social work on the lives of children!'. Now take a closer look at the full title and check out how useful the text is likely to be to your studies. The book's called: *Social Work from 1870–1980: A Biographical Review of the Impact of Training on Retired Social Workers' Self-Concept.* Probably a good read – but only marginally relevant for the purposes of your research!

Skimming involves reading through the contents page, exploring the index and looking for the key terms you're using in your research and any related ideas that grab your attention. If you don't immediately reject the book after your initial inspection, go on to look at the start and finish of each chapter. Most academic books have an introduction and conclusion to each chapter and some have outlines of ideas, summaries and lists of key points. Sometimes you can get the information you need by taking notes from the opening and closing paragraphs of each chapter. If the text looks as if it's well worth reading all through – then get hold of the book by hook or by crook.

If your dissertation lends itself to presenting data visually, flicking through the book and skimming the models, tables, charts and diagrams can also give you a feeling for the text's relevance.

Journal articles are generally easier to skim as they're short and include abstracts and conclusions summarising the subject being discussed. For both journal articles and books, it's also useful to be conscious of the style of writing to help you decide whether to put in more time for a closer reading. Don't expect every text you pick up to be instantly understandable; academic work contains a lot of jargon and the way ideas are expressed can be off-putting. However, you may need to put in a bit of effort to fully understand what the book is saying, so don't reject a book immediately because you've read a few sentences that you didn't quite get the meaning of first time round.

Scanning: Scouring for what you really need

Scanning is a precise and systematic activity. You're focusing on searching for a particular piece of information. For example: you're scanning the index of a book with a useful-looking title. Run your finger down the pages of the index looking out for key terms, author or ideas, hunting for synonyms, but not getting distracted by vaguely related ideas or topics. To avoid being sidetracked, you need to scan in an orderly and systematic fashion. To do this, you should start at the first page of the index and work through to the end rather than jumping from place to place.

You may find that the index lists a lot of different page references for the particular term you're searching for – this is where Post-it notes come in handy. Irritatingly, some indexes list a page reference where you find nothing more than a tantalising mention of the idea you're after but no useful information. You can end up flipping backwards and forwards through the book, losing your page and getting muddled, especially with hardback books that refuse to lie flat. As you're combing the index, jot down your key word and then list the page references on your Post-it notes. Keep going through the index and when you've finished all (or a significant chunk) go through the pages where you stuck your Post-it notes removing the irrelevant references, crossing out all those you won't be following up and circling the terms that are significant.

 As journal articles don't have indexes, you may find it harder to scan them. They're shorter of course so you may not need to scan. However, if you'd like to, one tip would be to run an electronic 'search' or 'find' on an electronic copy, which highlights the key words.

Deep reading

Reading in depth, or *close reading*, means keeping your mind on the job and paying attention to detail. After finding the perfect text for your research by skimming and scanning (see 'Skimming: Using the contents page, chapter headings and indexes' and 'Scanning: Scouring for what you really need), your next step is to deep read the text itself.

Reading for instructions

From taking exams you know that reading the instructions is vitally important to make sure that you're answering the question being asked. Likewise, you need to do deep reading of your university dissertation guidelines, making certain you know what you have to do in order to pass.

Working out how to apply different statistical analyses or carry out research methods also demands a thorough scrutiny of any instructions. Such directional writing is short and clear, so keeping your mind on the job isn't too tricky. Grasping and interpreting the instructions boils down to you being confident that you can do what's set down.

Reading for meaning

Deep reading a full-length book or journal article is a different skill from reading for instructions. To understand what a book or journal article is about, you need to read the text word by word, letting the meaning sink in thoroughly. If the language is familiar this can be a straightforward exercise, and taking notes helps you crystallise your interpretation of what you're reading – how to interpret what you're reading is explained in the section 'Testing your understanding thoroughly' later in this chapter. Sometimes, no matter how much effort you put into concentrating on the text, the meaning escapes you. Nothing sticks in your mind; the harder you try, the worse it gets.

You must be honest with yourself – are you grasping enough of the meaning of what you're reading to be able to explain what's being said to someone who's unfamiliar with the topic? I'm not suggesting you need to know the text by heart, but you do need to be sure that you're getting a clear understanding of the ideas being put forward.

A good way of checking how much you're understanding is to verbalise what you're trying to master. You can verbalise out loud (if you're working at home on your own) or mentally (a better option if you're reading on the bus!). Imagine you're talking someone through the passage of text, trying to get across to the person the main points. If you can put the ideas into different words that explain the ideas, you've got the point of verbalising.

Having a dictionary to hand is an essential tool for deep reading. Relying on your dictionary may seem an old-fashioned idea, but you'll be surprised how many words that come up when the words you're reading are familiar but you can't actually pin down the meaning. Try giving the meaning of the words in the following list. They're all words that students I've worked with have vaguely understood, but when pressed haven't been able to give a specific definition. The answers are in the sidebar at the end of the chapter.

- ✔ **Obsequious** (adjective)
- ✔ **Mordant** (adjective)
- ✔ **Generic** (adjective)
- ✔ **Concomitant** (adjective)
- ✔ **Paradox** (noun)

Like my students, I'm sure that you've heard the words in the list, may have used them yourself and can pronounce them correctly. But can you define them? Honestly? (Good for you if you can, by the way.) Often the context is a good clue to the meaning of a word, but if the meaning doesn't leap out at you, you need to look the word up – the correct meaning of the word may be critical to your research. When you're reading for pleasure, or just to get the gist of something, it's not necessary to be so meticulous, but for deep reading you need to be clear about what the author's saying.

Looking words up every few minutes can disrupt your reading of the text and so you need to assess the texts you pick up and weed out those that look too complex and hard going. There's no shame in failing to get the meaning of everything that may be relevant; many academic texts are littered with jargon, some are densely written and others aim squarely at a very specific audience with an advanced experience of a topic.

If you find that core texts recommended by your supervisor are way too difficult for you, ask for help from your supervisor or from the support staff at your university. At degree level you need to have a certain level of understanding and if you find yourself struggling with that level, you may benefit from some help.

Here's a simple way of assessing whether a text is too hard for you. When I was teaching in primary schools, I used this method with the children on our library visits, but I think that the method's also quite suitable for degree-level students. With the children, I call the method the 'five-finger test'. Open your book at a random page of text. Start reading. Every time you come across a word to which you can't give a clear meaning (be honest), put your finger on the word. Read on and keep one finger on each word that you don't know or can't be sure that you fully understand. If you run out of fingers before the end of the page, the book is too hard and you should give it up (or at least know that you need to determinedly use a dictionary as you're reading). You *don't need* to use your fingers of course, but you get the idea!

Beware of giving up too soon. It's worth trying to read a few more random pages – your first selected page may have just been bad luck, or you may have stumbled on a long obscure quotation. However, abandoning a text because it's too difficult isn't giving up; it's being realistic. Just because that book or article doesn't suit you now, doesn't mean that you're never going to be able to make sense of it in the future. It's likely that there are many alternative titles you can use – why battle on with an impenetrable book if there's a title to hand that suits you better?

Testing your understanding thoroughly

Knowing what the words are saying isn't the whole story. Reading for meaning also requires an appreciation of what the passage is telling you when taken as a whole. You may remember doing reading comprehension exercises at school. A structured questioning of a text can definitely help you find out how much you're understanding what you're reading. Take a passage from a book you're reading for your research and ask yourself the following questions:

- ✔ What are the main three points of the passage?
- ✔ Say why you agree/disagree with the author.
- ✔ Find an example from your experience illustrating one or more of the points being raised.
- ✔ Think of an alternative title for the passage that sums up the meaning.

✔ Find one word or phrase that can be a suitable subheading for each paragraph.

✔ Make a note of any unfamiliar words where you've worked out the meaning from the context or looked up in your trusty dictionary.

Working with fellow students while doing the exercise can be very helpful, especially if you're all working with the same core text, or main chapters and articles that link to all your topics. If you plan on setting your own questions to a text, you first need a thorough understanding of the text and answering the questions involves discussing what a correct answer looks like. The aim of the exercise is not to get your comprehension questions right, but to focus your attention on the detail of the passage. If you're working on your own, your supervisor may be willing to check over your understanding of the text if you present your findings in a clear and helpful way (having made an appointment beforehand, of course). If you're working with fellow students, try to arrange a discussion and debate about meanings, ideas and conclusions. Either way, working along-side someone else is a great strategy for tackling a thorny passage.

Speed reading

You can dramatically increase the number of texts you want to read by learning to speed read. Speed reading isn't about taking the easy option and may even be unsuitable for some people. Speed reading is an assortment of reading methods that are designed to step up your reading pace while storing the information you pick up as you move along. There's nothing magical about speed reading – it's just a more efficient way of reading than 'normal' reading, training you to use smooth and steady eye movements while cutting out time-wasting habits like skipping back and forth along a page or rereading passages and mentally vocalising each word.

 If you have a specific reading difficulty, such as dyslexia, or a speech problem (aphasia) or visual impairment, speed reading may not work for you. Other options exist, such as placing coloured plastic filters on the page or screen, or text-to-speech conversion software that can 'read' words from a monitor. As you're no doubt well aware, professional support workers are best placed to give you individual suggestions on building up your reading skills.

Generally, speed reading techniques are far easier to apply to a printed text than to a computer screen, but some speed reading practitioners claim that using a computer is equally successful. In speed reading you can use a combination of tactics to sharpen reading skills.

I am told that on a VDU, you can use a cursor if you're an adept mouse controller or slick at scrolling, but I find the following two practical actions help me to speed read:

Two practical methods of speed reading are:

✔ **Using a paper guide:** You may need to be more experienced, adept or confident for this to work well the first few times you try. You use the paper or card as a line guide, covering the text you've just been reading. As you read you move the paper or card down the page, hiding the text as you go. Most of us are used to reading down a page and uncovering the text as we go, but in this case what you're covering up is the bit you've just read. This prevents you constantly stopping and skipping back to words or phrases you've just read. Most people do this unconsciously, assuming they need to reread in order to understand the meaning, but it's an unnecessary habit. Move the paper or card down the page with a steady hand and slightly faster than feels comfortable (you need to stretch your hands to make the action work). Start your speed reading at a *slowish* pace, increasing your speed bit by bit – practice makes perfect in speed reading.

✔ **Using your hand along the text:** You can use your hand instead of using a paper guide, but this time you're not obscuring the text you've just read and so you need to have a bit of experience of speed reading to make this method work well for you. As with the paper method, make sure that you're using a smooth, even movement when running your hand down the page, just a little faster than you think you can manage. The way that both the paper guide and the hand methods work is by using the natural tendency of the eye to follow a moving object. Without any effort, your eyes are drawn to motion and you can boost the efficiency of your eyes by keeping them moving continuously forward, and using your hand as a guide.

When you're speed reading you drop the typical habit of saying the words to yourself, called *sub vocalisation*. Going back to when you first learned to read silently, you were probably moving your lips, forming the words without making the sounds. Some adults continue to sound the words under their breath while reading, but most people say each word they're reading in their heads. You're likely to be doing that right now, as you're reading this book.

Sub vocalisation slows down your reading. It's a common technique used when learning to read but also a habit. If you're keen on learning to speed read, you have to look at your reading habits. Being conscious of your sub vocalisation is likely to help you to break the habit. First, you can simply try to stop. Second, try hopping (seamlessly) from key word to key word, ignoring 'joining words' such as 'and', 'then' and 'to', and so on.

Another way of stopping yourself from sub vocalising is by using your mouth to make a different noise, such as humming or quiet singing (but best not do this in a crowded library). If you find yourself mouthing words as you're reading, try putting your hand on your mouth to stop your tongue moving, or at least to heighten your awareness of when you're mouthing, and therefore sub vocalising.

Unlearning the word-for-word reading technique you were probably taught as a child is another way of improving your speed reading technique. Being able to *chunk* text saves you having to read each word and chunking clearly increases the speed of your reading. To chunk text you need to take words in groups of three or four, looking at phrases and using punctuation to break paragraphs down into sections. Using the paper or card guide or your hand is helpful for when you're chunking.

Taking a course on speed reading is a good way of getting started. Some of the short-cut suggestions I make are frowned upon by the 'experts' who think that learning a little about speed reading can get in the way of developing the 'genuine' techniques offered by speed reading workshops and seminars or using specific materials (guess what – speed reading courses aren't free!). Other speed readers say that the methods I describe in this chapter are sound introductory methods. With application, the tactics I tell you about do work and can really help. Be wary of expensive speed reading courses, especially those that guarantee you to develop a photographic memory. Despite claims, no reliable, empirical studies exist proving that 'anyone can develop a photographic memory'.

You can tell from what I've said here that I'm sceptical about the claims that you get from speed reading 'gurus' and their pricey seminars and magical materials. For that reason, I'm not going to wholeheartedly recommend any courses or resources. However, one very successful writer, Tony Buzan, has done some useful work for students on different aspects of study skills and his books have reliable tips and ideas in them as a rule. He has written a book
specifically for students on speed reading – *The Speed Reading Book* (Student Edition), published by BBC Publications.

Whether speed reading is worth the effort depends on you and what you want to achieve. You need to think about balancing speed with comprehension. Only you can know how well speed reading works for you when reading a text for meaning and understanding. I found that speed reading was tremendously useful for studying, but it ruined the experience of reading novels. I just couldn't get out of the speed reading habit for a while. Years on, I speed read less, but the skill of speed reading is there for times when I'm under pressure to get through a great deal of reading matter. If you're already a fast reader, speed reading may well be for you.

Recognising great writing styles

To get the most out of your reading, you need to make sure that you're reading actively, looking at style as well as meaning. Recognising the writing style may require you to repeat your reading of the text, because on your first reading you're mainly concerned with working out what is being said, but a second reading can help you appreciate how what is said is being expressed. When you find a passage that you feel is particularly well written, you need to reread the passage with care, thinking about the following:

- ✔ How does the writer make it clear that she has a specific audience in mind?

- ✔ What does the writer do to get your attention from the start of the passage?

- ✔ Is the writer using particular words that make the work interesting to read?

- ✔ How has the writer organised her text? (For example, has she used subheadings?)

- ✔ How does the writer reference other people's ideas? How do the references help the text to flow, rather than being interruptions?

- ✔ Does the writer use a conclusion, or a summary? What makes the ending of the passage memorable, rather than just repetitive?

Go back over some of your essays you've done during your degree course and look at comments from tutors about your writing style – both the good and the bad. Noting your tutor's comments is likely to give you a good idea of your writing strengths and the areas that may need improvement.

Honing Your Note-Taking Skills

Developing an efficient method of note-taking is vital for keeping an accurate record of your research. You generate a great deal of information while doing your reading and research and you need ready access to your notes when you're writing your main chapters (and your literature review in particular). You may already have a method of taking notes that works well for you, but now is a good time to review your system and perfect your current techniques.

When you're reading a library book, stop yourself from jotting down notes in the margins or anywhere else in the book. You probably know how annoying it is to pick up a book that someone else has covered with graffiti notes. Writing notes in library books makes the book unreadable for other people and is also an act of vandalism. If you want to scrawl all over a text, you must buy your own copy or make photocopies.

Taking notes serves a range of purposes. When you're recording a direct quotation, you need to be scrupulous in getting the quotation down accurately, word for word. When you're noting a main point, you can get away with jotting down the point by using keywords, and leaving out any unnecessary details.

Having a system in place for keeping track of your notes that makes them easily and readily accessible is essential. Whichever style you use, you're need to ensure that you get down the information you need and that you distinguish clearly between your words and those of the author you're reading.

If you try one method and it's not working for you, don't be afraid of trying a different method that may be better. What you need is a method that works.

Choosing between handwritten and electronic notes

Most students record their notes in electronic format or by keeping a file on paper. In Table 6-1 you can see a list of the advantages and disadvantages of both methods.

Table 6-1	Recording Your Notes: Using Paper or Electronic Format	
Paper – Advantages	**Paper – Disadvantages**
Easier to use while you're on the bus or train, or on the move.	If you lose your notebook (and have no back-up copy), it's a disaster.
You avoid introducing unforced errors that come from cutting and pasting when keeping your notes in electronic format.	You may have to type up your notes to make sure that they're readable.
You only have to keep watch over your notebook – no need to keep backing up for fear of electronic meltdown.	Reading your writing can be hard if it's not always legible!
Electronic Format – Advantages	**Electronic Format – Disadvantages**
While you're recording your notes, you're creating a file ready for writing up your dissertation.	You always need to carry your laptop or your electronic notebook around with you.
You can cut and paste rather than rewrite.	You must remember to make regular back-ups of your file.
If your memory stick crashes, you still have the disk version or the copy on the Intranet to fall back on.	You need to keep batteries charged, or lug your power cable round with you wherever you go.

Keeping notes on paper or in electronic format seem to have about equal plusses and minuses. Having a two-way approach may be your best option allowing you the flexibility of having access to your notes whether you're at home or away.

Personally, I prefer taking notes on paper but then systematically transferring them onto my computer. This method of keeping notes is especially useful for keeping accurate and up-to-date bibliographic details – which can prove a godsend when producing your bibliography in the final stages of your dissertation.

Getting down the gist of a text or passage

When you're taking notes, the idea is to capture the general meaning and ideas of the text or passage. What you're after is a way of representing the key ideas, so you leave out examples and detailed explanations. You need to develop a form of shorthand to help you get your ideas down quickly while still capturing the meaning of the passage concisely and accurately. Being concise helps you later on when you're scanning through your notes and picking out what you need for your writing.

Table 6-2 shows some simple shorthand codes that education students have found helpful over the years (the codes are much like text speak).

Table 6-2 Using Shorthand Codes for Note-Taking	
Word	*Shorthand*
the	x
with	w.
children	chn
education	ed
schools	schs
therefore	∴
teacher	tchr
learning	lrng
pupil	pup
government	govt
classrooms	clrm
because	Invert of therefore

Don't try creating a shorthand code for words like *but* and *not*, because such words can change the meaning of the sentence and you can end up saying the opposite of what the author first meant.

Before you start writing your notes, read through the passage to make sure that you're not going to be wasting time by making notes on parts that are made clear or explained better a bit later on in the passage. Earlier in this chapter in the sections 'Scanning: Scouring for what you need to know' and 'Skimming: Using the contents page, chapter headings and indexes', I talk about different types of reading such as skimming and scanning. When you're taking notes, you need to make use of these techniques to see exactly what's worth noting down.

Photocopying a portion of the chapter and using a highlighter pen to pick out the main points can sometimes be a useful strategy. You may not need the whole passage for your dissertation, but you have a copy of the passage to hand in case you want to reread that section to get a better understanding.

Distinguishing between summaries and commentaries

When you're note-taking, you need to be able to distinguish between the facts that are presented to you (summaries) and your own views and opinions (commentaries). While you take notes, make it clear which is which so that you don't assign your views and opinions to the author (commentaries) and you don't forget your own brilliant insights (summaries).

In Table 6-3 you can see a form I've designed to help you in recording your summaries and commentaries from reading journal articles. I use the form (or a variation of it) when reviewing and sharing journal articles with my students. Some students have used the form just once or twice, whereas other students make photocopies or an electronic version, and some students use the form for most of their note-taking.

Table 6-3	Form for Recording Your Summaries and Commentaries of Journal Articles
Author(s)	
Title of article	
Name of journal	
Date, volume, edition	
Page numbers	
Main Points of Article	
1.	
2.	
3.	
4.	

Critical Analysis of Article

What I agreed with most

What I disagreed with most

Useful ideas

Drawbacks (style of writing, subjective ideas, no relation to practice)

Links to Dissertation

How article fits with what I want to say

How article links to other authors

My dissertation chapters where article will be helpful

 You can adapt this form for use with Internet or other sources and you may want to add a note to yourself about where you found the information in case you need to back track to check something later.

 The form I've designed in Table 6-3 only gives you the opportunity of recording your reading of journal articles in a brief and concise format. The way you're recording information on this form isn't nearly detailed enough for getting you a first-class degree. If you're aiming for a top grade, you need to go into far greater detail, capturing and recording all the nuances and subtleties of the arguments in the article.

Presenting quotations and references

There are a number of ways of presenting quotations in your dissertation (check out your dissertation guidelines). Here are some tips for making sure that you present your quotations properly and they stand out in the text:

- ✔ **Word-for-word quotation as part of one of your paragraphs –** the quotation is enclosed in quotation marks ('. . .') and is less than 12 words long.

- ✔ **A quotation of between 12 and 40 words –** the text is indented, and separated from your own words by blank lines (usually you don't need quotation marks for this style of quotation).

- ✔ **A paragraph or sentence that is related to a text, but not quoted from a text.** Here you may have a couple of words in quotation marks within your own words that summarise a long piece into a short interpretation.

Chapter 14 gives you all the information you need to get referencing, but for now make sure that your quotations are recorded in your notes meticulously, guaranteeing that you have every word correct and all the reference details completely accurate.

You can forget about a first-class degree if you make errors in your references. Making errors in references is as foolhardy as speeding on your driving test – get your references right, or keep to the speed limit.

Stamping out plagiarism

Using an author's ideas for inspiration, support and illustration is an expected part of your dissertation. However, trying to pass off another person's ideas and words as your own is totally unacceptable. When you take the work of others (published or not) and present it as your own, without acknowledging the author, you've stolen the author's work and this is plagiarism. Plagiarism is cheating. Every university in Britain (in fact, in the world) has rules guarding against plagiarism and the kinds of penalties awarded to anyone who breaks the rules. Penalties can range from a simple verbal warning, through a more serious formal written warning, to the point where the person may be dismissed from the university for repeat offences of plagiarism. What is certain for students is that grades are cut for work where tutors identify plagiarism.

In the academic world, plagiarism is treated extremely seriously. In my experience, very few students set out to deliberately deceive their tutors (although some do). Most students slip into plagiarism through poor note-taking skills, weak time management and a lack of understanding and/or attention to referencing. Unfortunately for disorganised students, such *explanations* for plagiarism don't *excuse* plagiarising. Weak work is given a suitably weak grade. The onus is on you, the student, to improve your note-taking skills, time management and referencing. You mustn't get drawn into plagiarising because of poor referencing. In Chapter 14 you find specific details of how to include references and quotations into your written work.

Plagiarism can result in you being forced to leave your university. Make sure that you're absolutely clued up on the rules governing plagiarism at your university.

Really, really stupid plagiarising

Almost every tutor I've spoken to in higher education has a personal experience of plagiarism. Often it's a case where a student has plagiarised from the tutor's work and then handed in the essay for the tutor to mark. It may just be a sentence or two, or part of a paragraph, but if it's work the tutor has agonised over in order to get exactly the right phrasing or to make sure that she's getting the correct meaning across– the chances are that she recognises her own work. If the essay has been set by the tutor and is in a rather narrow, specialised area, it's highly likely that the student is going to quote from the tutor. How stupid can you be not to acknowledge the person who's going to be marking the essay?

What's even more stupid about this type of plagiarising is that academics in general are rather flattered when students quote from their work, especially when the piece is obscure and it means that at least somebody is reading it! Students plagiarising from their own tutors are making the double error of failing to flatter and succeeding to irritate!

Methods for detecting plagiarism are becoming more and more sophisticated and most universities require you to upload an electronic version of your dissertation to a website which automatically cross-checks what you've written with a vast database of other student essays, books, journals, websites and other sources. Supervisors usually allow students to upload their work sometime before the deadline for their dissertation. If this is an option for you, you need to take advantage of the opportunity and check any questionable references that your dissertation contains. If the database highlighted passages of text that you haven't identified as quotations (by using quotation marks) or if the database picked up parts of your writing that haven't been properly referenced, now is the time to make corrections.

The best way of avoiding plagiarism is to keep very careful notes at the outset so that you're not tempted to fudge or slightly massage any of the ideas or references you've picked up. Taking the trouble to note down and record the full and precise details of references is essential for keeping on the right side of the law.

Undoubtedly, many students manage to get away with plagiarising the odd sentence or paragraph here and there, and in some cases may escape detection even if they're plagiarising a slightly longer piece. It's not worth taking the risk, however. Just because one tutor has failed to pick up on the plagiarism, doesn't mean that the work is going to get through the moderating process.

Answers

The meanings of the words you 'sort of know', are from *Collins English Dictionary: Millennium Edition*, (1998):

- ✔ Obsequious (adj): obedient or attentive in an ingratiating or servile manner; submissive or compliant.

- ✔ Mordant (adj): sarcastic or caustic; pungent.

- ✔ Generic (adj): applicable or referring to a whole class or group; relating to a 'genus' (biology).

- ✔ Concomitant (adj): existing or occurring together; associative.

- ✔ Paradox (n): seemingly absurd or self-contradictory statement that is or may be true; a self-contradictory proposition, such as I always tell lies.

Just because you got away with plagiarising once doesn't mean you're going to get away with it again. Your dissertation is probably the single most important piece of work that you're ever going to write. Falling into the trap of plagiarising just isn't worth the risk of losing out.

Part III
Getting On with Your Research

'I've come to collect the books I ordered
the other day.'

In this part...

A great dissertation needs a solid grounding in well-researched information. This part focuses on pulling together the data you need: I cover how to collect it, evaluate it and begin to shape it into the finished item.

This is also the section to come to if you want to know how to generate your own data through interviews, questionnaires or observation, and how to handle that data once you've got it. I finish up the part with a range of handy tips on how to review your progress – and how to keep plugging away.

Chapter 7

Collecting Information and Researching

- -

In This Chapter

▶ Looking into the online catalogue and different libraries

▶ Dealing with databases and journals

▶ Using the Internet and other sources

- -

*Y*ou've settled on your research topic – well done! Now you need to turn detective – searching for and gathering all the information you can to support and prove your theories. Now is the time for collecting together and examining the literature in your field of study; information from far and wide – as well as on your doorstep.

Getting to grips with the bewildering range of resources is quite a task in itself. In this chapter I tell you about the different kinds of information available and show you where to go to find the information you need – from hotfooting it to your university library to going online and surfing the World Wide Web.

Making the Most of Your Library

Embarking on a dissertation is a great opportunity for getting to grips with your university library. You may already know your university library well, but if you've been avoiding the library until now, perhaps feeling it intimidating, now is your chance of making the library your biggest friend and resource by putting it to work for you. Generally, at the start of the academic year the library holds lots of induction courses to help you get to know your library and the library staff who are there, eager and willing, to guide you and give you any help you need. Asking a professional librarian to advise and direct you to the information you're searching for is likely to get you off to a flying start.

If you discover that the university library doesn't have a brilliant collection for your particular subject, find out from your librarian if there are other libraries that have special collections relating to your subject that you can use. Also ask about any schemes available for students doing dissertations to use other university libraries for free, especially during vacations.

Registering with your library

Before you can start using your university library you need to register with the library, proving that you're a fully paid-up student of the university. The library computer has a record of any previous transactions made by you at the library and if it happens you've got overdue books you need to clear your account of fines and unreturned books, there and then, however painful! Coming clean about lost or damaged items is your best policy – having the support of the librarians during your dissertation is worth ten minutes of embarrassment at the checkout.

You may also need to register for a password or identity number for using online databases, word processing facilities or photocopying services. Make sure that you have current information about opening times before setting off on a three-hour round trip on a day when the library is closed for staff training.

Searching library catalogues

University libraries have online catalogues that can generally be accessed off-site by logging onto to the Internet on your PC as well as through terminals in the library (most libraries have online catalogues on each floor). Before logging onto the library catalogue be sure to have at least the name of the author or the full title of the item you're looking for. It can be very frustrating and time-wasting if you only have partial information. If this happens, don't immediately give up; try a bit of lateral thinking. For example, you enter the author's name 'Paul Torrance' into the *Author* search option and the catalogue comes up with nil. You know that the author exists so try another tactic. In the *Keyword* option just put in 'Torrance'. Bingo, you discover from the list of 'Torrances' that the online catalogue throws up that your author is actually indexed under 'E. P. Torrance'; you've found your man.

Another approach if you get a nil return on an author search, knowing full well that the author exists, is to search for the name on the Internet to see if the author is listed differently from the reference you've been given. A lot of tutors refer to people in their field in a different way from the author's official name. Your tutor or supervisor may be so familiar with the author that he quite forgets to point out that the author is indexed on the library catalogue under a set of initials that your tutor hardly ever thinks to use.

Doing a bit of homework on your subject before using the *Keyword* search option can pay dividends. It's a good idea to arm yourself with a range of alternative words for your subject that you've already looked up in a thesaurus. For example, *wealth* can also be searched for under 'riches', 'affluence', 'prosperity', 'luxury' or even 'moneybags'.

Sometimes the word or words used to describe a condition or subject can vary according to different cultural attitudes. Try to find out via the Internet or through your tutor or supervisor whether the term you're using is expressed differently in other areas of the English-speaking world. For example, in the UK, the description 'handicapped' is thought of as derogatory, and using the term 'people with disabilities' is much preferred. The word 'handicapped' is far more commonly used in the US, however, and some of the important works in the field of disability published in the US use 'handicapped' regularly in titles of books and articles. If you're unaware of cultural differences, you may find yourself missing some potentially useful literature in your subject area by limiting yourself to what is politically correct in the UK.

Keep in mind that fashions change and that as a field of study develops the language and terms being used change as well to get across the latest thinking, and older terms and descriptions can fall out of favour. For example, you may think of those feisty individuals in your suffragette study as 'women', but there are likely to be a lot of references to them in the literature as 'girls' or 'ladies'. Don't let your nice thinking hinder you from carrying out a thorough search for relevant texts.

Using the *Keyword* search option is great for browsing. While you're browsing you're likely of course to turn up titles that are totally irrelevant, but keyword searching can also bring up all sorts of references and ideas that you may not have thought of up to now. Perhaps you're looking, for example, for books about autism, from the legal perspective of child protection – you discover a load of publications on the medical and educational aspects of autism that can add a vital dimension to your dissertation.

When you find titles of books and other items that are going to be useful for your dissertation, make sure that you note the details accurately, especially the subject number of the book and its location in the library. (Chapter 6 tells you more about note-taking.) It's all too easy to jot down the references in a jumble and then find yourself at a loss when facing endless rows of shelves. Relying on your short-term memory can turn out to be a mini-disaster; you may have a rough idea of the title but when you see three or four titles with very similar wording you can find yourself having to trek back to the online catalogue to double-check. While searching the online catalogue, note down the reference information with as much care as if you're putting together a reference for your bibliography – taking the author and title and the classification number of the item (a lot of university libraries use the Dewey number system). It's also a good idea to jot down the date as there may be more than one edition. Taking down accurate details of the reference at this point is going to be enormously valuable and a great time-saver when you come to compiling your bibliography.

Trying different media, specialist libraries and archives

Your university library houses far more materials than just books and journals; you can find DVDs, videos, CD-ROMs, music manuscripts, newspapers, maps, games and toys (usually for use by teacher education students), sets of play scripts, slides of artworks and much more. The online catalogue offers you the option of searching for other types of material other than just books and journals. (In the section 'Exploring Journals and Databases' later in the chapter I talk about journals and searching databases, which are also important aspects of your research.) Depending on your dissertation topic, searching for information from newspapers, DVDs and videos, for example, can be a valuable way of shedding new light on your subject.

 Be aware when logging onto the online catalogue that the system usually defaults to searching for books. Check you're searching on the appropriate media option, for example, *Videos*. Most libraries still have large video collections and provide viewing suites or dedicated terminals for viewing, especially when the material is reference only and can't be checked out of the library. Make use of the media if it's relevant to your dissertation; looking at your subject from another angle can be reinvigorating and refreshing, especially if you're feeling weary and a bit jaded.

Your university library online catalogue offers you access to a vast amount of information. But many specialist libraries up and down the country are computerising their collections, giving access to other users as well as their own members. However, you need to take into account that some of the collections you discover belong to small organisations with limited funds and are less likely to have full electronic access. In Table 7-1 you can see a list of different types of specialist libraries, together with examples.

Don't miss the boat!

I was once working with a student who literally missed the boat by failing to broaden her search options. The student was writing about teaching the controversial issue of war and was looking for material she wanted to recommend to history teachers working with very able Year 11 pupils. She found some great books, but until she broadened her search options to include videos and DVDs, she had missed out on some great movies, such as *Das Boot* ('The Boat'). This excellent film directed by Wolfgang Peterson (1981) speaks explicitly about the claustrophobia of being in a submarine and has been widely acclaimed for meticulously capturing the nature of war.

Table 7-1	Specialist Libraries as a Resource
Type	*Example*
University Departmental Libraries	Senate House Library (University of London)
National and International	The British Library
	National Library of Wales
	National Library of Scotland
	The Library of Congress (US)
Professional Bodies	Royal College of Nursing Library
Archives	Froebel Archives (Roehampton University Library)
Community Libraries	Peckham Library and Media Centre (one of the new 'super-libraries')
Voluntary Organisations	The Oxfam Library (Oxford Business Park)
Museums and Galleries	The Museum of Garden History library
Research Organisations	The Research Evidence in Education Library (REEL)
Public Records	Kew Public Records Office

Specialist libraries and archives are treasure troves of exciting, in-depth resources and if you're genuinely interested in your topic, they can be exciting places to study. Specialist libraries are also mysteriously brilliant at stealing time – what feels like an hour of absorbing research in an archive can turn out to be three or four hours of your actual life! You think you can pop in to make just a few notes, but you can so easily get sidetracked into reading all manner of fascinating materials. Be ruthless (unless you've unlimited time for your dissertation, though that's highly unlikely). You need to set yourself specific tasks for each visit and set the alarm on your mobile phone or watch (on silent vibrate of course) so that you're not losing track of time.

Searching the shelves

Shelf searches can be remarkably productive although not very systematic. You go to the section of the library holding the core texts on the subject you're researching. While browsing you can find interesting and sometimes obscure books you didn't hit on when searching the online catalogue; prowling around your favourite stacks can sometimes offer a spark of inspiration when you're flagging. You may find books that have weird titles that didn't pop up through a keyword search, or got missed off the online catalogue during the cataloguing process.

Don't forget to look at the top shelves and the bottom shelves – most people only focus at eye level and sometimes when you've lost hope, you spot the exact book you're after in an odd place. The same goes for books in the oversize section; people often forget to check this area of the stock, where books are shelved because they're too large to fit in the normal sequence. This is particularly useful to remember if you've left things late and you're finding that many of the titles you wanted have been checked out by keen and organised fellow students!

 Shelf searches alone aren't going to give you all the information you need for your research topic – a shelf search, though useful, isn't systematic and you can miss out on important information that is available in other sections of the library.

Exploring Journals and Databases

Hunting down information in journals and knowing how best to use online databases for searching the literature is vital to your dissertation. In this section I help you find out more about the different types of journals, what journals offer and how to get hold of key articles relating to your dissertation.

Millions of journal articles exist – tracking down suitable articles is made easy by searching a database geared to your field of study.

Understanding the basics of journals

Although most of your research is likely to come from books, journal articles (also known as *papers*) are important because journals contain current research and report on recent happenings in the field. By the time a book reaches the bookshops or library shelves inevitably some of the information in the book may well be out of date or being challenged by newer ideas that you can find published in journals.

Journal articles are usually around 3,000 to 7,000 words long and obviously quicker to read than a full-length book. Some journals are aimed squarely at an academic audience whereas other types of journals are aimed at practitioners in a particular profession, having a more hands-on and vocational slant. Publication of academic journals is usually weekly, fortnightly or monthly whereas professional journals are more likely to be published on a monthly basis.

Appreciating academic journals

Your own supervisor and other university staff you know probably contribute regularly to an academic journal – being experts in their fields. Each journal has its own clear focus; presenting a variety of writings: research reports, discussion of conceptual issues, challenges to another person's arguments and ideas, critical reviews of literature, identification of phenomena and patterns of behaviour, new ideas about the field, commentaries on policy and personal accounts of academic experiences.

Academic journals can vary in format, most journals having their own particular guidelines for contributors, such as listing bibliographies and presenting references in the text. Most journals contain an abstract and most include an introductory section and a conclusion. If you're trying to save time by skimming (refer to Chapter 6), you can read the abstract, introduction and conclusion and then decide whether it's worth reading the whole article.

To follow an argument on a particular subject, academic journals sometimes use the device of the academic dialogue to keep the discussion going on the subject over several issues. First, an academic states his position, another criticises, the first academic rebuffs, another academic wades in for the attack or another academic for the defence, and so on. You need to dig around to find these trails in a journal – they can look something like the following:

> ✔ *Freeing the police: How the service functions better without helmets,* by E. Morse, Law and Order (Spring, 2001)
>
> ✔ *The vital role of the helmet in empowering the police,* by G. Dixon, Law and Order, (Summer, 2001)
>
> ✔ *Restating the redundancy of formal headwear in criminal justice: A response to Dixon,* by E. Morse, Law and Order (Autumn, 2001)
>
> ✔ *Evidence to support Dixon's thesis on the necessity of uniform,* by J. Taggart, Law and Order (Winter, 2001)
>
> ✔ *Headgear and the law: A post-structuralist solution,* by R. Lewis and J. Hathaway, Law and Order (Spring, 2002)
>
> . . . and so on.

A student writing a non-empirical dissertation may find academic disputes particularly useful. A few great things about academic disputes are worth sharing (other than the fun of seeing academics having a bun fight in public – without shedding blood):

> ✔ **Presenting a sustained argument:** You have an exemplary model of seeing experienced scholars dealing with an argument.
>
> ✔ **Counter argument:** You get to see how the scholar's detractors put forward their objections.
>
> ✔ **Current thinking:** You have an excellent opportunity of picking up the latest thinking and ideas before they reach book form.

If you're basing your ideas in your dissertation on a core text, try finding the journal articles that came out before the book was published (often the articles are listed in the book's bibliography). You can pick up handy articles where academics point out the weaknesses in the argument. You can then go on to build on your criticism of the ideas in the core text using arguments from the journal articles.

Perusing professional journals

Professional journals target an audience that's actively involved in a particular profession. The articles offer ideas, suggestions and comments that reflect the first-hand experience of the authors, or the views of people who have a significant number of years working in the area and can give a valuable overview of general developments. A professional journal sometimes has articles on applying theory to practical situations, but you find much less discussion of theories compared with academic journals. Bear in mind that the conclusions drawn in a professional journal don't always carry the weight of conclusions in academic journals. Although professional journal articles can be helpful in your dissertation when looking at how a theory works in practice, you need to be cautious about making professional opinion central to your study.

Articles in professional journals don't ordinarily have abstracts and are often quite short, sometimes having no references or bibliography. Annoyingly, professional journals are often much easier and more entertaining to read! They use less jargon and it's easy to see how the issues being raised can have an impact on the readers who work in that particular profession. Don't let this more practical approach blur your vision about the merit of the argument however – remember that the opinions being presented are the subjective views of one individual and the ideas are less likely to have been rigorously reviewed.

Exploring peer review and journal audiences

Academic journals, like professional journals, present the views of individuals and groups, but before an article is published in an academic journal the article goes through a (more or less) robust system of checks and balances. A great part of an academic's job involves criticism – and new ideas are set upon, sometimes quite viciously. An academic needs to back up his argument with evidence (usually empirical or theoretical) and to have survived the process of being evaluated by other experts in the field before the article gets to publication. This process is called 'peer review' and all academic journal articles are subject to such scrutiny, although to different degrees.

Unless your dissertation topic centres around professional practice, your tutor or supervisor is likely to be talking about academic journals when he's imploring you to 'read more journals'. The front pages of an academic journal clearly state the journal's aims and if you're not sure whether the one you're looking over is for the right audience, photocopy or print out the description and check with your tutor who can say at once if the articles in the journal are relevant or worth reading.

Using databases for finding relevant journal articles

Searching for journal articles using electronic databases and also databases in hard copy can be a very satisfying activity. Tracking down and collecting recent articles on your topic is best done online in order to navigate around the enormous range of journal articles that are published regularly. You access the databases using CD-ROMs and through networks including the Internet and also Intranets, such as your university library search facility. You're almost certainly going to need what's called an *ATHENS* password, which is free, to log onto the databases. All you need to do is sign up at your library. I recommend that you go to one of the training courses your university library runs on learning how to structure your searches to get the best results. Treat database training as part of your dissertation research; you're likely to come away from the training session with some actual references on your dissertation topic, so the session isn't just an exercise, it's productive.

Sometimes you find the perfect journal article for your research topic after carrying out a database search, only to find that your library doesn't subscribe to the journal containing the article. If you believe that the article is really important to you, ask your university library to get the article for you on inter-library loan through the British Library Inter-Library Loans service. However, there's likely to be a charge for this service.

What's available to you

A vast number of journals are published in Britain and worldwide covering every subject under the sun. Your university can only afford to subscribe and house just a selection of what's available. The journals and subject databases that your university takes reflect the main specialisms at the university. If you happen to be the only social scientist at the National University of Pure Science and Theoretical Oceanography and you're researching 'The Social Aspects of Eating Red Meat', you may find you're having difficulty finding suitable articles because your library doesn't subscribe to a relevant social science database, such as ASSIA. If this is the case, ask your tutor or supervisor for advice on which other libraries in the area are likely to have material relating to your subject. In the section 'Making the Most of Your Library' earlier in this chapter, I suggest some other libraries and archives that may hold the information you're looking for – never give up, because there's no shortage of information available if you know where to look.

Databases vary in the type of information they hold. Some databases are dedicated to supplying only *citations*, which just gives the author, title of the article, name of the journal and the date of publication. A citation database works by naming a key article from the past and then listing all the papers citing the original paper since that date. This can be a useful way of following an argument on a particular topic. Other databases, as well as giving the author, title of the article, journal name and date of publication, include an *abstract* of the article summarising the contents of an article, including the conclusions. If you decide from the citation or abstract that you'd like to read the whole paper, you check the journal title on the library catalogue and, if found, you can get a photocopy of the article or sometimes access the article online.

Some databases have the full text of the article, usually as a PDF file. (With a PDF you can't get into the file to make changes or cut and paste any parts of the article into your dissertation, which helps to prevent plagiarism), (refer to Chapter 6.) Whether you've just a citation, abstract or the full text of an article, be sure of making a careful record of all the bibliographical details of the article for your bibliography.

To make life easier and to save precious time, open up a Word file for storing your references as you go. Your Word file then forms the basis of your bibliography. Don't forget that the references in your Word file are going to need formatting following your dissertation guidelines, but the basic typing is done for you when copying and pasting the reference from the database. It's best to store your Word file on a memory stick, but if your university system doesn't allow you to use memory sticks (because of virus risks) store your file on your space on the Intranet and download your file when you get home. Ask the computer helpdesk staff if you have any problems importing or downloading the file.

Here's a list of social science databases that are invaluable for doing literature searches in the area of social science:

- British Education Index (BEI)
- Education Resources Information Centre (ERIC)
- Australian Education Index (AEI)
- Social Science Citation Index (SSCI)
- Applied Social Sciences Index and Abstracts (ASSIA)
- British Education Index (BEI)
- PsycINFO and PsycARTICLES
- British Library's Electronic Table of Contents (ZETOC)
- International Biography of the Social Sciences (IBSS)

Meeting microfiche

You may find that your university library stores some material on a microfiche, such as copies of original documents or old newspapers. Many specialist and smaller libraries may also have their library catalogues and databases in microfiche format. A microfiche is a small piece of plastic film containing data that's too tiny to read with the naked eye. You insert the microfiche into a microfiche reader that magnifies the text making the document easily readable on the screen. Using microfiche makes you feel like a real detective from one of those American psychological thrillers (the detective scanning the microfiche in a darkened library at night, hunting for vital clues), and you coming up with that piece of information so essential to your research.

As well as using the electronic databases, there may be times when you have to use a paper copy of the database. A lot of databases have only been in electronic format since the mid-1980s or later, and if you're searching for older information, you may need to go back and consult the hard copy versions.

Deciding whether you need the whole article

Going through and reading the abstracts of the set of articles you found from your database search is a good way of picking out those articles that are going to be really useful for your research. You can get through about 20 or 30 abstracts quite quickly, helping you narrow down your search for the relevant information. Scanning the abstracts also means you're saving yourself time and money from unnecessarily photocopying articles you aren't going to need after all.

Having gathered together a list of useful-looking journal articles your next move is to get hold of the full articles – hopefully your library has the journals in stock. However, for some of the articles, printing out just the abstracts may give you the information you need such as showing the names of people who are writing in your field of research. Deciding whether to get hold of a photocopy of an article may also depend on the format of the article. Databases offering you full text articles, rather than just references, direct you to using software such as Adobe to open the document and read the article as a PDF file (PDF stands for 'portable document format'). You can save the PDF file to your memory stick or hard drive (remembering it's forbidden to try to alter a PDF file, so it may be just as useful to get hold of a photocopy of the article anyway).

You may even find that making notes from reading the abstract on screen is all that you need from some articles; mark the rest of the references for printing out and reading later. Make sure that your notes are meaningful though (go to Chapter 6). If you decide later that your notes from the abstract make the article worth reading in full, you can always come back to the article (providing you've got the reference clearly recorded).

Nosing in newspapers and magazines

Newspapers bring you the most up-to-date stories and information and provide a useful way of catching up on the latest views and opinions on a particular topic. You need to bear in mind that different newspapers have different political leanings and therefore bias. For example, *The Daily Telegraph* and *The Guardian* are at different ends of the political spectrum. But what about *The Times of India*? – it has one of the widest circulations of any broadsheet in the world (if not the widest) – and the *New York Times*, the *Herald Tribune* or the *Washington Post*? And don't forget you can also make use of magazines such as *The Economist*, *Newsweek* and *Time*.

Most foreign newspapers are printed in the official language of the country but the international scene is also dominated by English-speaking papers now frequently being issued in digital format. If you want to see what a particular newspaper is making of a news story, try logging into www.newspapers.com where you can access the world's newspapers.

The newspapers I mention in this section are all written in English – but if you're fluent in another language such as French or Spanish there's a good reason for using the article in *Le Monde* or *El Pais* for your research if the article's relevant. However, if you're quoting from a foreign language article in your dissertation you need to provide a translation for your supervisor or the person marking your work.

Databases index newspaper and magazines articles in the same way as journal articles and your database search can turn up a reference or the full version of the article. You can hunt down older newspaper articles by checking out the paper version of the database you're using, where you often find the article printed in full from which you can then make a photocopy.

Newspapers aim to be controversial and present stories from the newspaper's own viewpoint. This means that you're reading the opinions of the editor and his fellow journalists. This isn't necessarily a problem, but it's important that you're aware that the facts of the story may be biased and that you need to check out the key information.

Searching the Internet and Other Sources

The Internet is both the best and the worst resource available to you for researching your dissertation. What's great about the Internet, as well as being time-consuming, is the incredible array of information. What's worst about the Internet is that there's no system in place for monitoring or testing if the information is reliable. It's up to you to judge the information you're being presented with for relevance, usefulness, quality writing, or if the information is just plain wrong.

Finding academic info online

If your dissertation topic links to a module or course you've already taken, your tutor or supervisor very likely recommended Internet sites that have been tried and tested by the academic staff. The databases I describe in the section 'Using databases for finding relevant journal articles' earlier in the chapter (such as the SSCI and ERIC), are generally reliable, because the material is under peer review. Unfortunately, Internet sites aren't all created equal, and some are more suitable for academic research than others. Google, for example has a related site, called Google Scholar (http://scholar.google.co.uk/) that restricts websites to academic sites rather than to commercial sites. The quality of the information on the academic sites isn't guaranteed, but Google Scholar reduces the amount of dross you trawl through and cuts out irritating irrelevancies such as price comparison and auction sites. Intute is another useful website (www.intute.ac.uk/) and other websites exist that are specific to different fields, see (http://bubl.ac.uk/) for directions to these other sites. Before starting to use a website for your research, ask your university librarian and supervisor for advice on the usefulness of the site.

Improving your online searches

Carrying out a properly structured online search is essential for hitting on relevant information. You can systematically narrow down, widen or cut out irrelevant references by linking the words AND, OR, NOT to your initial set of references that you come up with. Here are some practical ways of structuring your search:

- ✔ Specifying the years you're searching (for example, 2002–2007)

- ✔ Using a dictionary or thesaurus to ensure that you're covering all the search terms

- ✔ Making use of keyword searches (or 'scope notes') for topics that use popular rather than academic terminolgy

To help you widen the scope of your search, try adding an asterisk (*) to the stem of your word. For example, if you input politic*, the search finds all words with that stem, bringing up references with politics, politician, political in the title of the article and in the abstract. You can also use asterisks for covering different ways of spelling, for example, for finding both 'systemize' and 'systemise' if you input systemi*e, which throws up titles and abstracts using both spellings.

- ✔ Narrowing your search by using AND: for example, 'cities AND planning' so you don't get thousands of results for each word, but only results for both.

- ✔ Avoiding completely superfluous and potentially enormous sets of useless references by using NOT: for example, 'phrases and utterances, NOT speech'.

- ✔ Using OR for widening your search, by putting your search terms in round brackets, for example, '(dreams OR trances)'.

- ✔ Limiting your set of references to English-language articles only – (unless of course you happen to be fluent in Chinese or other languages, in which case you're well away).

Judging the quality of a website

Weighing up whether a website is reliable and likely to be useful in your research can be tricky. Take a look at the following organisations to judge if the information they handle is likely to help you in your research:

✔ **Government department websites:** Useful for hard facts, not so great on analysis.

The different government department websites display a great deal of data, statistics, and other information, presented in a way that tries to be objective. But you also need to remember that the Government is trying to present a positive image and is unlikely to indulge in significant criticism of its own policies. Government sites are extremely useful for up-to-date information about current strategies but not very useful when it comes to evaluating initiatives.

✔ **University websites:** Cutting-edge or at least up to date, but may be rather too narrow in focus.

Just about all universities have research centres specialising in particular academic fields. Some aspects of university research programmes are available to the public through the Internet, whereas other research programmes are only open to members of the university. Most of the material on a university website is reliable, having been scrutinised by other experts in the field.

✔ **Non-governmental organisation (NGOs) websites:** Offer useful analysis and criticism of government policies but you need to be clear about an NGO's agenda.

✔ **Independent organisations' websites:** Particularly useful for evaluating government strategy and policies in general. Beware! Some organisations have a particular axe to grind and so criticism can lack balance or fairness. You may have already been given a list of relevant independent organisations useful for your research by your tutor or supervisor, or you've come across independent organisations in your reading.

✔ **Single-authored websites:** Can be brilliant, can be dire!

The quality of a site where there's a single author is entirely dependent on that author. If the author is a known expert in your field, you're likely to be onto a good thing. However, if you've never heard of the person before, how do you know that the author has any more knowledge than you?

✔ **News reports (newspapers and TV) websites:** Watch out for bias. Never rely on a news report being accurate. You need to check out what you've found with other academic research that's being done. If, however, you just want to summarise popular opinion, or show examples of bias, websites reporting the news are perfect for these purposes.

Wikiworlds, or everyone can't be wrong, can they?

Wiki websites, written by non-experts, grow daily in number. I'm not anti wiki websites or against the democratisation of information that allows everyone to have their say – but like many academics I'm concerned about the number of inaccuracies on so many Internet sites. Because a lot of Internet sites escape any sort of monitoring, errors slip through unchecked and undetected – something that's never allowed to happen when journals and books are being prepared for publication.

A few years ago, a colleague and I met for our moderation meeting where we swap work with one another to check that we're being fair with our grades. A significant number of students had made the same curious error about a key figure in developmental psychology (Jean Piaget) who they described as German rather than Swiss. The error about Jean Piaget's nationality wasn't important for the students' essay, but all the students had made the same mistake. My colleague and I were both starting to question what we thought we knew, that Jean Piaget was Swiss – the students couldn't all be wrong could they? Had we simply been giving out the wrong information? We inspected our notes and they were fine. When we checked further on the Internet, however, we found that Wikipedia stated that Piaget had been born in Germany. Other more important errors were also included in the entry on Piaget and those students who hadn't used any further sources ended up turning in very weak essays, many of which failed. I'm glad to say the Wikipedia 'Piaget' entry is pretty good today, at the time of writing – but I can't make any guarantees about the accuracy of the facts on Wikipedia concerning Piaget at the time that you're reading this book!

Using the Internet wisely

Restricting your Internet searches to websites that are likely to be of reasonable quality (rather than any old website) is a good start, but it's up to you to test if what you're reading on the Internet is reliable enough for your research. You need information that's presented neutrally from a dependable source that can stand up under scrutiny. When you're looking at website, ask yourself:

- ✔ How credible is the source? Do you recognise the organisation, authors, background or other particulars?

- ✔ How neutral is the source? If the information isn't completely objective, is the subjectivity presented in a transparent or clear manner? Is there a reasonable explanation for the information being subjective?

✔ How up-to-date is the website and when was it last updated? Are the links on the web page still functioning?

✔ How applicable is the information? Is the website too general or too specific? The website may be designed to meet a very different need from yours, such as a particular case study that's only relevant in a small number of cases.

✔ What claims does the website make? If the suggestions are entirely bizarre and eccentric, are they going to be relevant to your research? A website that makes reference to similar authors and ideas and doesn't leap out at you as being seriously peculiar may prove useful.

When you're viewing a website, remember to keep your critical wits about you!

Investigating Other Sources

Official government publications contain a mine of information for filling in the essential details as well as providing hard facts about what's happening in the UK. Your university library is likely to subscribe to the online UK Official Publications database (UKOP) where you can do keyword searches for statistical and other information on topics from births and deaths to popular culture such as film and TV.

Radio and TV programmes can also be valuable sources of information, especially news programmes such as the *Today* programme and *Newsnight*. Chapter 14 tackles how to reference material taken from TV and radio, but take care in your research that you're not portraying a producer's view as objective fact when it's more likely the opinion of the producer himself.

There's a whole range of writing available called *grey literature*, which includes any publications or unpublished work carried out by academics, but which doesn't have an ISBN (International Standard Book Number) or an ISSN (International Standard Serial Number). Papers presented at conferences, dissertations, theses, pamphlets, booklets, all come under the heading of grey literature. If you come across a reference that doesn't have an ISBN or ISSN that you think may be relevant and can't track it down on the online catalogue, ask the library staff for help in locating the item.

Chapter 8

Generating Your Own Empirical Data

· ·

In This Chapter

▶ Making effective use of questionnaires and sampling

▶ Investigating interviewing

▶ Focusing on people's behaviour

▶ Taking account of case studies

· ·

*E*mpirical data is all about creating your own evidence from your observations and experience of a particular situation or event. In this chapter, you find out about producing home-grown information by using a range of different methods to provide the data you need for your dissertation. I only have space here to give you an introduction to the basics of collecting empirical data and highlighting the key points. If you're keen to go into the subject in more depth, there are lots of books available for you to delve into for more information.

Different research areas use their own tried-and-tested methods for collecting data suited to the subject (for example, psychology uses precisely defined observation, whereas in education a more impressionistic approach is generally taken). Make sure that you're sticking to what's expected and accepted in your subject area.

In this chapter I show you the key methods of data collection in the social sciences, and explain the differences between qualitative and quantitative data. Bear in mind that some methods of data collection are better suited to producing qualitative data than quantitative data, and vice versa.

No one method of collecting data guarantees reliable data by itself. You need to plan and prepare your method of collecting data thoroughly and efficiently.

While you're thinking about the sort of research methods you're going to be using, think ahead to how you're going to be analysing your data as you design your research. Generally, grouping your data into themes is known as *coding*. It's a way of marking the bits that cover the same points or relate to the same overall topic, grouping your questions and data into related areas, rather than dotting them about randomly. Whatever method you use, you can build some ideas for coding into the collection design. (Chapter 9 tells you about data analysis.)

Code your data groups into themes and issues so you can collate all the evidence for the points you want to make. If you're looking to increase your potential grade, you can build more sophisticated coding such as assigning numerical values to answers. For example, include adding a [1] for primary teacher and [2] for secondary teacher or having all 'Yes' responses coded with a number.

You can find myriad resources for helping you understand how to develop empirical data in books and on websites. A few good ones include:

- ✔ King's College, London: www.kcl.ac.uk/schools/ humanities/depts/elc/kings/thesis
- ✔ The Web Center for Social Research Methods (USA): www.socialresearchmethods.net/tutorial/tutorial.htm
- ✔ Middlesex University: www.mdx.ac.uk/www/study/ research.htm
- ✔ Punch, K.F. (2005) Introduction to Social Research: Quantitative and Qualitative Approaches London: Sage.

Querying with Questionnaires and Surveys

Surveys usually refer to broad areas of research, whilst questionnaires are more specific and often on a smaller scale. Bear in mind that the word 'survey' is a verb and a noun. The verb refers to the process of collecting ideas, and the noun refers to the information that you collect. Both terms relate to the enquiry process carried out with a range of different people to whom the same questions are posed.

Different types of survey and questionnaire exist, with various purposes such as description or explanation. You can carry out surveys and questionnaires face to face, or by email, post or telephone.

A survey is the name that's usually applied to a comprehensive study of a large population. For an undergraduate dissertation, the more common choices for collecting data are by conducting a questionnaire and carrying out sampling.

Constructing a questionnaire

A questionnaire is a request for information, opinions and/or ideas using a written format. Before starting to design your questionnaire, you need to know what you're trying to achieve and how your objectives are going to influence the type of question you choose for your questionnaire, for example, by asking a range of different questions that bring out different responses:

- ✔ Closed questions with a single answer

- ✔ Closed questions with multiple choices

- ✔ Questions answered by rating or a ranking

- ✔ Open-ended simple questions (short answer)

- ✔ Open-ended complex questions (long answer)

Closed questions limit respondents' answers to being able to select from existing answers. People can agree or disagree with a statement or can choose from given options. *Open questions* don't offer any choices and respondents are required to generate their own answers with different degrees of elaboration as appropriate.

If you're looking for mainly *quantitative* responses (that you can count, or quantify), you're going to be asking the first three questions in the bulleted list; and if you're looking for qualitative responses (probably in flowing text), you're going to be asking the last two questions in the list.

In practice, it's common for questionnaires to begin with limited or closed questions and to end by giving people the opportunity to express their opinion in their own way.

Using a combination of different types of questions leaves you with a mixture of quantitative and qualitative data; generally the ideal mix for the validity of your questions and possibilities for repeating the exercise, together with some richer data for illustrating your research.

You're unlikely to be in a position of being able to carry out a practice run of your questionnaire, so you need to be sure of looking carefully at the questions you're asking to avoid any confusion.

Designing an engaging questionnaire

You've probably filled in loads of questionnaires, so you may be familiar with different kinds of questionnaire formats and know too well how irritating and frustrating it can be when trying to answer questions that are badly put together.

Think back to questionnaires you've filled in – what design features make a questionnaire successful? Which layouts are easy to complete? Which styles of questionnaires are plain irritating? Use your own experience to construct the perfect questionnaire.

You want your questionnaire to be designed so that it draws respondents in and is easy to complete, engaging rather than off-putting. Try looking at the questionnaire from your respondents' points of view, asking the following:

✔ Is the questionnaire well spaced?

✔ Is the questionnaire clearly formatted?

✔ Are the questions contained and not split over pages?

✔ Are you using a font that's easy to read and a reasonable size?

✔ Are the response boxes and lines positioned so that it's clear where you're supposed to place your ticks or write?

✔ Is the questionnaire a reasonable length (definitely not too long)?

When you're sending out your questionnaire, it's useful to include a covering letter and also clear instructions (sometimes called a *rubric*) to go with your questionnaire. Your covering letter needs to include:

✔ Why you're carrying out the study.

✔ Details of your course and university to give context.

✔ Guarantees that all responses are going to be treated as confidential.

✔ Your contact details.

✔ Any instructions on filling in the questionnaire such as where to use crosses or ticks, and so on.

✔ In your covering letter or at the end of the questionnaire, thank your respondents for their time and effort.

✔ Information on how and where to return the questionnaire.

✔ A deadline for return (as politely worded as possible).

Take care to find out something of the background of your respondents, for example, levels of literacy and intellectual understanding. If English isn't the person's first language or your respondents are elderly or have learning problems, have you made sure that the respondents know what they need to do? You don't want to scare anyone off.

Asking good questions

Your questions need to be straightforward, avoiding complexity that can make your later analysis tricky. If you need to ask multiple choice questions, try limiting the number otherwise the question is going to get too complicated. Keep in mind though that a binomial option (only two choices), though easy to review, limits the number of answers you're going to get.

Make sure that your questions are:

✔ Short and succinct – by cutting out unnecessary words.

✔ Straightforward and free of jargon – by using plain English.

✔ Clear – by replacing vague words like 'generally' with specific words such as 'weekly'.

✔ Phrased so that you get the answers you need – ask 'In your view, what three measures can the Government take to try to reduce alcohol-related youth crime?' rather than 'What's the real solution to youth crime in the world?'

Think about dividing your questionnaire into sections so that when people are filling in the questionnaire their experience is broken up into chunks. Building a breather into answering the questions is likely to keep your respondents motivated and interested.

 Closed questions are useful when you know that you have alternative limited and clearly delineated replies. More complex issues need open questions.

 Use some simple and easy questions to help people get started. Ask them their job title, or age and gender (if appropriate). But don't leave all the key questions until the end in case your respondents never get there!

When you're offering ratings and rankings in your questionnaire, give respondents the opportunity of not having to answer just 'Yes' and 'No' questions and so letting people show they can think for themselves. The most common formula for doing this (called a five-level Likert scale) includes a 'don't know' option allowing respondents to take a neutral position.

1. Strongly disagree

2. Disagree

3. Neither agree nor disagree

4. Agree

5. Strongly agree

Having just four options (by deleting the third choice from the list) is a *forced choice* method, which makes people side one way or the other and can put people off. However, you aren't going to get much out of a questionnaire with 15 'don't know' responses and nothing else.

The solution (however many choices you're giving) is to balance your questions throughout and to use a variety of language. In place of 'agree/disagree' you can insert 'important' (ranging from extremely important to not at all important). You need to allow your respondent space to balance what they've said with at least one open question. If they've ticked all the negative boxes in the questionnaire, they may like to say 'although I am unhappy with x and y, I should mention that p and q are brilliant and it makes it worthwhile working here as a result.' Having an equal number of 'Yes' and 'No' options allows your respondents to say what position they're taking without feeling overly positive or negative or, for example, reporting that their work place is 'all good' or 'all bad'.

Avoiding questionnaire pitfalls

Try avoiding the most common pitfall in questionnaire design – asking ambiguous questions. If you have the chance, test out your questions on a few friends and definitely show your questionnaire to your supervisor to make sure that your questions are clearly focused and unambiguous. The smallest, simplest error can result in failing to generate any useful responses at all.

Questions to ask yourself in order to pinpoint the strengths and weaknesses of a questionnaire include:

✔ Is the purpose of the questionnaire clear and easily apparent?

✔ Is the questionnaire simple to administer?

✔ Is the data produced from the questionnaire going to be easy to interpret?

✔ Are the questions clear and unambiguous?

✔ Is the questionnaire valid? Does the questionnaire actually measure what it sets out to measure?

✔ Is the questionnaire reliable? If the questionnaire is going to be used with a similar group, is the questionnaire going to generate comparable results?

Be aware that you may run into problems as listed below. Follow the advice in this chapter to avoid them in the first place.

✔ Low response rate

✔ Long wait for responses to be returned despite reminders

✔ No real control over who actually fills in the questionnaire or how seriously the questionnaire's being taken

✔ No way of getting back to a respondent who has a query

✔ Your questionnaires come back incomplete

✔ Subjects with literacy or language problems you didn't know about

✔ People change their answers – respondents aren't necessarily giving spontaneous answers

A way of having control over administering your questionnaire is by handing out your questionnaire at the end (or start) of a class or meeting rather than emailing or posting it to your subjects (and so helping to avoid a low response rate, and so on). However, other problems can come up, such as people not having enough time to fill in the questionnaire and feeling inhibited by being surrounded by other people in the class or meeting. A happy medium may be to give the questionnaire out and ask for it back at the next class or meeting.

What you *do* have complete control over is the design of your questionnaire. Try avoiding the following common mistakes – at all costs:

✔ **Double negatives** – 'Do you think that a lack of holiday pay is not a bad thing?'

✔ **Ambiguity** – Avoid words with more than one meaning or possible misinterpretations (if you want to know about someone's first salaried professional role, don't ask about the person's 'first job' because she may tell you about her paper round).

- ✔ **No brainers** – 'Do you think that children who use wheelchairs should be banned from school trips?'

- ✔ **Offensive** – 'Why do you think that people with dyslexia tend to be failures at school?'

- ✔ **Over-reliance on memory** – 'Are the children in your nursery class happier than your own classmates when you were at school?'

- ✔ **Assumed knowledge or experience** – 'When you visit a museum, do you prefer exhibits you build yourself and then take apart or discovery learning exhibits?' or 'How long have you been a cyclist?'

- ✔ **Leading questions** – 'Do you agree that Berrylands has a better train station than New Malden?'

- ✔ **Loaded questions** – 'Is it reasonable to deprive children of fresh air and healthy exercise by punishing them through playtime detentions?'

- ✔ **Double-barrelled questions** – Avoid presenting more than one issue at a time (so don't use 'and'), 'Do you swim in the mornings and at the weekends?'

Sussing out sampling

Sampling is about examining and analysing data taken from a random group to find out what's going on in the population as a whole. For example, professional researchers use sampling to explore *populations* (in research terms this means a group of people, objects, organisations or events that fit the particular case being surveyed). For an undergraduate dissertation, you're also going to be looking at people (for example, student nurses), objects (such as art galleries), organisations (like environmental volunteer workers) or events (a school inspection, or a museum workshop).

Because it's not possible to speak to every single member of a particular 'population', you select a sample from the population and run your survey or questionnaire with that group. The responses you get from the sample group effectively represent the views you're likely to find among the larger population.

The size of your sample *is* important, but you're not expected to carry out anything like the scale of research done by professionals looking at an enormous population. Who you select for your sample is more important than the actual numbers and so you need to think carefully about choosing the subjects that you're going to be investigating.

You can select your sample in many different ways, but for the purposes of an undergraduate dissertation, there are two main ways of selecting samples: randomly (in a haphazard fashion), and non-randomly (where samples are selected using a strategy). Both ways have pros and cons:

- ✔ **Randomly.** Selecting a random sample is like taking part in a lottery. If you have an enormous population and a sizeable sample, it's a great way of getting a reliable representation of the views of the entire population under scrutiny. You may find though that random sampling results in an uneven set of views, or you sometimes can't get hold of individuals in the sample, or maybe some individuals just refuse to be part of the survey.

- ✔ **Non-randomly.** Selecting a sample non-randomly cuts down on the generalisability (general principles) of your findings. However, it may be that you're not focusing on generalisability but are more concerned with representation of a typical sample (called *purposive sampling*). You may also be looking for a quota, where you select equal numbers from different groups (for example, newly qualified police officers in urban, suburban and rural settings).

Making a choice about selecting your sample group randomly or non-randomly depends on the type of data you're interested in finding and the character of your population. For an undergraduate dissertation, students often end up with *accidental* or *convenience* sampling. Accidental or convenience sampling is non-random, and you're taking your sample from a population where you're sure of having easy access. There's limited generalisability from accidental or convenience sampling, but there's a greater chance that you're going to get a pleasing return rate for your questionnaire.

Understanding validity, transferability, replicability and generalisability

A number of aspects of a research question need to be taken into account if the research is to be taken seriously – undergraduate or professional alike. Some of the aspects have implications for your choice of population and how sampling is carried out. Your investigation needs to be:

- ✔ **Valid:** Well-founded, convincing and justifiable, demonstrated through using consistent and objective research methods.

- ✔ **Transferable:** The principles you talk about can be translated to different contexts.

✔ **Replicable:** If someone follows your methods, they can recreate your work.

✔ **Generalisable:** You can draw general principles from your specific investigation.

Selecting the sample size

Asking 'How big is a sample' is a bit like asking 'How long is a piece of string?' It's difficult to give a simple answer about the size of a sample, because the sample size depends on how you select the sample and whether the population is unchanging, or patchy and inconsistent. You also need to be realistic about how much time and money you have to run your survey. Practicalities like postage costs, printing, addressing envelopes and time for interpreting results all need to be taken into consideration.

Having the largest sample you can manage is going to give you the most reliable data for drawing your conclusions. However, if what you're aiming for is gathering as much data as you can from a particular sample, you're going to need to take a slightly different approach. Either way, you have to take on board what sampling involves to show that you've thought through the choices you made before beginning your research topic.

If your population is made up of very different individuals, it's more important to represent the views of each individual than simply to draw a general conclusion – non-randomly selecting your population is likely to help improve the validity of your research.

Querying qualitative and quantitative data

Quantitative data from questionnaires comes from the simpler questions usually found at the start of the questionnaire, designed to ease the respondent into the process of answering the questions that follow. Quantitative data covers questions about people's ages, work positions, gender, income, and so on.

Further on into the questionnaire, questions usually become more involved, generating more qualitative information concerning opinions, attitudes and ideas.

Interviewing People

A great way of getting the data you need for your research question is by interviewing people. You can approach interviewing in a number of ways; the methods you choose depend on what you're trying to find out. The kinds of methods you can choose include:

- Life history
- Paired
- Formal
- In-depth
- Narrative
- Racial or cultural groups

However, the most common interview methods used for undergraduate dissertations are one-to-one, semi-structured or structured methods and I'm focusing on these methods in the following sections.

Before deciding on using interviewing as a way of generating empirical data, you need to think about the advantages and disadvantages of conducting interviews:

- **Advantages:** The flexibility that interviewing allows. You can change the direction of discussion in an interview and capitalise on ideas that come up that you didn't expect.

- **Disadvantages:** The biggest problem with interviews is the amount of preparation you have to put in and the amount of follow-up time needed (plus the time taken on the interview itself).

The quality of an interview depends on both the interviewer and the person being interviewed. You only have control over how well you carry out the interview and no matter how carefully you choose your subject, you can't predict the worth of her responses.

 Whether you choose a semi-structured or structured method of interviewing, your main task is to listen. The interview is about the person you're interviewing, and not about you. Keep your comments on the answers you're given to a minimum.

To help you decide who you want to interview and which method of interviewing to use, you need to think about exactly what kind of data you want to collect. Start by making a list of the sort of facts you're trying to discover.

You can choose to interview individuals or small groups. When you conduct an interview with a group, it's usually known as running a focus group, which just means that there's more than one subject and you're focusing on a particular issue or concern. The points in this section about interviewing are directed mainly at one-on-one interviews, but are also relevant to focus groups. (See the section 'Running group interviews' later in this chapter.)

Preparation is key. Work out what you need to do to make sure that your interview is worthwhile and that you go into the interview with everything planned and organised.

Here are some practical steps to take before carrying out an interview:

1. Discuss your plans with your tutor or supervisor and get your plans agreed before you go further.

2. Contact the person you want to interview (by phone, email or letter) and after introducing yourself set out what you're trying to achieve by doing the interview.

3. Make an appointment with the person you want to interview at a time to suit her.

4. If appropriate, make sure that you get permission from your subject to record the interview.

5. Discuss the timing of the interview with the person you're interviewing making sure you're both clear how long the interview is going to take and that you have somewhere suitable to carry out the interview.

6. Make sure that you're thoroughly prepared – that you've clearly noted your list of questions in the order you're going to ask them and check that you have pens, pencils, batteries and any other equipment you may need.

7. Be sure to give yourself enough time for getting to your interview destination; having made certain that you're expected.

Picking subjects and questions

Choosing the right person to interview is all important. To avoid wasting the interviewee's time and yours, make sure that you've picked someone with the background and knowledge that matches the data you need for your research question. Once you've found the right person and she's happy to be interviewed, you need to decide what you're going to talk about.

Deciding what you want from the interview is also very important. You need to consider whether the answers that you're after lean more towards quantitative or qualitative data, and then ask open or closed questions accordingly. You may well be after facts rather than opinion, which is going to influence your questioning. If you're looking for:

✔ **Hard facts and figures** – ask precise questions; send the questions to the person you're interviewing ahead of time so that she has time to gather the data you're asking for. Don't ask for facts that you can readily find in your university library or that are available to the general public – come to the interview armed with those facts in advance.

✔ **General opinion** – ask open questions that allow the interviewee to give a full answer. The person stops talking when she feels she's said enough. An open question often starts with 'What', 'How' or 'Why'.

✔ **Expert opinion** – ask open-ended questions, but the questions need to be pointed so that the issues you want to explore are considered; 'I'm interested in your take on the idea of *x*' or 'What's your view on *y*?'

✔ **Information** – ask closed questions, which generally start with 'Who', 'Where' or 'When' and limit the questions further by asking the person being interviewed to choose from a list such as 'Yes', 'No' or 'Maybe'.

Many interviewers use a combination of the questions in the list, starting with a few questions asking for basic information before moving onto opinion. Starting your interview with this formula is likely to help put the interviewee at her ease.

A good interview is made up of a balance of questions allowing the person being interviewed to share her knowledge and ideas, as well as feeling drawn into the interview by your thoughtful and well-structured questions.

Always avoid frustrating the person you're interviewing, for example by cutting the person off during her answers, or preventing her from getting her points across.

Comparing different sorts of interview

How your interview goes depends on whether the interview is structured, semi-structured or unstructured. Which method you choose depends on what you want to find out, who you're talking to and your own personal style. In Table 8-1 you can see some of the features and some of the advantages and disadvantages of the different approaches to interviewing.

Table 8-1	Features of Different Kinds of Interviews	
Structured	*Semi-structured*	*Unstructured*
Uses direct and specific questions only	Some key questions planned, with allowance for other issues to be raised	Free-flowing discussion; no fixed agenda
Specific order of questions	Indicative order of questions, but okay to depart from the order	No specific order for questions
The focus is on how many people make the same points rather than individual views	Supplementary questions are offered to collate people's different viewpoints, but all are expected to answer the main questions	The interviewer is seeking depth of response and follows the interests of the interviewee
Must follow fixed schedule	Can leave out some questions as appropriate	Difficult to replicate as follows interests of interviewee and these will differ from person to person
Rather rigid style	Relaxed style	Conversational

When you're deciding which of the interview styles is best for you, you also need to take into account whether the style of interview is going to affect your note-taking or transcribing when you're doing your data analysis after the interview. It's possible that an unstructured interview wanders so widely that it's going to be more difficult to analyse. Or a highly structured interview, although giving you the necessary data, may not allow for illustrative examples or richness of response.

Recording the interview

As part of the interview process, you need to think about the pros and cons of the different methods for capturing data during the interview so that, after the interview, you can easily analyse the responses you've obtained. This section looks at the pros and cons of different methods and gives you detailed practical tips on how to run an interview:

✔ **Written notes:** Taking notes during the interview means that you can start analysing your data immediately after the interview from your notes (even better if you're inputting your notes straight into your laptop during the interview). However, it's difficult to take full notes while you're actually interviewing. You can ask somebody else to come in and take notes for you but a third person may not be knowledgeable about your research and may not quite capture all the issues. Having an extra person at the interview can also change the dynamic of the interview, which can be a problem if the interview is confidential.

✔ **Video recording:** If you can make a video or DVD recorder unobtrusive, this can be a great way to capture body language and non-verbal cues as well as what is being said. You don't have to worry about note-taking but some people can feel uncomfortable when being videoed and simply can't relax. Remember, it takes time to set up the equipment, but once you're started people often forget that the camera is there.

✔ **Audio recording:** This is probably the most useful and most used method of recording an interview, although transcribing your recording afterwards can take up a lot of your time. Making a recording can be relaxing for the person being interviewed because you often don't need to use a microphone. But do check that you've switched the recorder on and that the machine is actually recording!

Whichever method you use for recording responses during the interview, make sure that any equipment you're using is in working order and, more importantly, you're capturing what your interviewee is saying and not what you *think* is being said.

Carrying out distance and face-to-face interviews

Sometimes it's just not possible to meet up with the person you want to interview. There are other ways of carrying out an interview though: by phone, video link-up and email, but these methods have obvious disadvantages because you're not actually face to face with your interviewee. If you do have to carry out your interview by phone, video link-up or email, you need to make doubly sure that your questions are as clear as possible because you have less opportunity of explaining exactly what you mean. Receiving email responses to your interview questions can be advantageous, because an email saves you all the extra typing. But you need to think carefully to differentiate your interview from an email questionnaire.

If the person you're planning to interview has personal or other difficulties, it's unlikely that your supervisor is going to allow you to go ahead with an interview. On the other hand, it's possible that your interview may put *you* in a potentially vulnerable situation, and you therefore need to prepare and protect yourself against any undesirable or difficult situations. Remember always to:

✔ Carry out the interview in a public place.

✔ Have somebody else present during the interview.

✔ Make yourself aware of any potential tensions that may arise – try anticipating difficulties and avoiding the difficulties as far as you can.

✔ Don't give your personal details to the person you're interviewing, only pass on the address of your university department.

✔ Plan what you're going to say if you want to end the interview early (have an exit strategy).

✔ Be friendly, but not over familiar.

✔ Make sure that a fellow student or your supervisor knows where you're going, who you're speaking to and when you're due back from the interview.

✔ Be sure to take your mobile phone with you to the interview and leave your mobile switched on throughout the interview.

✔ If you think that it may be useful, carry a personal alarm and keep the alarm switched on in your pocket.

Running a successful interview

Here's a checklist reminding you what you need to do during and in the follow-up to the interview:

1. When you meet the person you're interviewing, smile and try to put the person at ease. Ask her where the interview's going to take place and confirm with her how long you're both expecting the interview to last.

2. Check with the person you're interviewing that you've spelt her name correctly for your own records and ask for her official job title. Go over any agreements you've made about anonymity. Give your interviewee a little background about your research.

3. Make sure that you're both seated comfortably. Think, for example, about whether sitting at a desk is going to make you both more relaxed or may build a negative barrier between you. Offering a cup of coffee or tea or a glass of water is going to help you both feel more relaxed (offering to pay for the cuppa is even better, and a great start to the interview).

4. Remember that the interview is about the person you're interviewing and not you. Keep your questions brief and concentrate on the responses. Try to use non-verbal listening cues, like nodding, looking directly at the person often enough to express interest (but not too much so as to be weird) and making sounds of agreement and understanding such as 'mmhm', 'yep', or 'I see'.

5. You're probably going to need to take notes, but make sure that you look up from your notepad frequently. Where possible get some direct quotations from your interviewee. This is easiest when you're recording but is perfectly possible by just asking: 'Can I quote you?' when appropriate.

6. If you know that you're likely to become tongue-tied during the interview, jot down a few prompts such as: 'Can you please tell me a bit more about that?' or 'Can you just expand on that a little please?'

7. Be prepared to explore interesting trains of thought, but do try to keep largely on track. Keep a close eye on the time to be sure of covering everything that you need to ask.

8. Have a general question prepared for the end of the interview. A general question serves as a kind of summary, which is a good way to end. Something like: 'Is there anything you'd like to add?' is fine.

9. Sometimes it's appropriate to briefly summarise what you've covered in the interview just checking that your understanding matches what the person being interviewed intended to say. (Summarising isn't always necessary – use your judgement.)

10. Keep strictly to your time. If you finish the interview early, it isn't going to be a problem but don't give your interviewee the impression that you're longing to get away. If time is up and you haven't finished your questions, you need to think carefully before asking your interviewee for extra time.

11. To wrap up the interview, say something like: 'Thank you so much for your time, this has been most helpful.' Always give the person you're interviewing the opportunity to add her comments. You can say: 'If a further question pops up, may I get back in touch with you please?' (If the person says no, then don't attempt to get back in touch!)

12. After leaving the interview, try finding somewhere where you can sit quietly and spend a little time sorting your notes and adding in anything that you were unable to fully capture during the interview.

13. Don't forget to jot down the date, time and place of the interview – it's surprising how quickly you can forget details.

14. As soon as possible following the interview, write a thank you note or email your interviewee sending the note or email off straight away.

Don't automatically assume that you understand how your interviewee is feeling about being interviewed. She may be feeling nervous, worried, excited, irritated, defensive or flattered. All you need to do is try to put her at her ease.

Watch your body language – for example, try not to sit with your arms folded because this may give the impression that you're on the defensive, making the other person feel as if she isn't being listened to properly. It's a good idea to try to mirror your interviewee's body language, helping to make the person feel comfortable and at ease. Take a peek at Body Language Expert (www.bodylanguageexpert.co.uk/) for more info.

Transcribing your interview

You're likely to generate a fair amount of data from your interviews or you many have focus group data (see the section above on interviewing people and the section below on 'Running group interviews' for information about focus groups). You'll need to transcribe some or all of your data for your dissertation. Check with your supervisor exactly what needs to be written up. Often, students are invited to transcribe the sections that will be of most use and they're not required to transcribe all their data. Whether you transcribe the whole of the recorded interviews or just small sections, keep hold of the originals until you've received official and final notification that you've passed your dissertation.

Some supervisors require you to put the entire interview in your appendix, others may accept a disc or electronic file – you must check the requirements of your course.

You may find that it's easier for you to work with your data if it's transcribed, but it's a big job, so try to complete a short section first before you commit a lot of time to the task.

You may be asked to submit audio or video tapes of your interviews, or even MP3 files, but the original tapes don't replace the transcription. Don't expect your supervisor to be prepared to scroll through your recordings to find your data.

Once you've recovered from the horror of hearing your own voice on tape, you can get on with the process of converting the recording into written text. Unfortunately there are no shortcuts to making an accurate transcription and because accuracy is key, you just have to settle in for the long haul (unless you can afford to pay someone else to slog it out for you).

You may have your data on a digital recorder, an old-fashioned cassette recorder, a Dictaphone, or an MP3 player with microphone. Whichever method you use to record the interview, basically you need to manually play back, pause and write up over and over again.

Typing and at the same time getting everything down that's being said on the recording is pretty impossible, even if you're a whizz typist – so there's going to be a great deal of stopping and starting as you're transcribing.

If you hired recording equipment from your university, you may be able to get a foot pedal for the pausing and playing, which makes transcribing a little easier. You may need to experiment a bit with the foot pedal until you settle into a comfortable style. Try playing a sentence, stopping and writing up. Compare the foot pedal method with trying to type up as much as you can in one go, to find out which method you prefer.

If you come across a passage that's difficult to understand, try listening to the passage a few times and then note the place, using the counters. As you listen ahead, you may be able to work out what's being said through the context. If you're still none the wiser, describe the section as 'indistinct' and mark the passage using timings or counters. If you have to put in a lot of counters your interview is likely to get too broken up, so try to do as little marking of passages as you can.

Before getting started on your transcription, give each person speaking a code name to protect their anonymity, carefully noting the names you've chosen. You don't want to have to go back into your transcription and spend precious time changing the code names all over again.

When trying to capture patterns of speech and different styles of delivery, you may need to include 'ums' and 'ahs' and make notes about inflexion, pauses, sighs, or laughter. Don't let the 'ums' and 'ahs' interfere with the flow of the conversation – use your judgement.

After finishing your first draft, check for obvious errors. Having made your corrections, listen to the tape again, reading your transcript along as you go. Listening and reading is a good way of picking up any other mistakes you may have missed.

You can use transcription software, but I wouldn't recommend it for the task of transcribing your interview. Some recorders come already equipped with speech recognition software and you can download freeware, such as 'Audacity'. These types of transcription programmes are designed to let you save digital speech files to your computer, which converts spoken words into text. You're still going to have an enormous editing task and the software can sometimes get riddled with glitches. Although, for example, you can buy professional medical and legal software, the software is highly technical and expensive and not really suitable for an undergraduate dissertation.

Wherever possible, try to avoid having to translate your data from your recording into another language. Translating into a different language is time-consuming and errors can creep into your data in the process. You can use standard software to carry out translations, but you're going to need to do a lot of detailed and heavy editing once the software has done its work.

Running group interviews

Holding a group interview or a focus group allows you to interview several people at one time and gets the group interacting with one another as part of the interview process. Your role is more as a facilitator or moderator. You do have to think carefully about the make-up of the group because part of the purpose of a group interview is to get people to bounce ideas off each other and feel at ease together. Beware though of everyone ending up saying exactly the same thing – a bit of disagreement among group members may produce just the data you're looking for!

Always be well prepared and think through your interview before getting started. This helps you to expect the unexpected and be able to handle the situation if things don't quite go to plan.

Taking coherent notes during a group interview is practically impossible. Your best technique is to tape the discussion (audio or video).

Much like questionnaires (see the section 'Constructing a questionnaire' earlier in this chapter), interviews can generate both quantitative and qualitative data, depending on the nature of the questions being asked and the amount of detail the answers draw out.

In group interviews and focus groups, quantitative data is collected in different ways, such as recording the number of people who agree or disagree with specific closed questions. Qualitative data comes from the expression of opinions and ideas and this type of data is often more complicated to capture effectively. Think carefully about the way you go about doing your recording.

Note that the dynamic of a group discussion may inhibit or spark off responses that you don't get in a one-to-one situation. Be careful not to compare group interviews with individual ones for this reason.

Whether you decide on using a questionnaire or carrying out an interview to collect your data for your dissertation, it's a good idea to try out some of your questions or ideas on a friend first. Even if she knows nothing about your area of research, your friend is likely to be able to point out where your questions are ambiguous or problematical in any way.

Making Observations

Carrying out an observation is another well-used method of collecting empirical data – involving watching closely and critically the way a person is behaving in order to gather facts about what's happening in a given situation. As with any research method, there are pros and cons of using observation as a research method and (if you're carrying out your observation carefully) you're going to discover that preparation is key and reflection is essential.

Advantages include:

- ✔ Having a fresh look at a familiar setting
- ✔ Getting candid insights into the way people are behaving
- ✔ Being able to show the gap between what people say they do and what they're actually doing
- ✔ Having the opportunity to take into account the context of a particular action
- ✔ Gleaning rich data
- ✔ Focusing on specific behaviours in detail

Disadvantages include:

- ✔ Observing can be subjective
- ✔ Being watched may influence the way a person is behaving
- ✔ Difficulty of observing more than one situation at a time
- ✔ Mistakenly assigning the way a person is behaving to the situation
- ✔ Not having full control over the observation (such as timing, changes to the observation setting, and so on)
- ✔ Sorting out ethical issues and getting permissions to do an observation can be difficult because of the numbers of people being observed

If you decide that making an observation is a suitable method for collecting data for your dissertation, you need to be clear from the outset exactly what it is you're trying to find out. First, you have to determine if the data you're collecting needs to be quantitative or qualitative. Second, you need to decide the structure of your observation, the part you're going to be playing and how to record what you're observing effectively.

Conducting an observation needs to be done systematically (see the schedule in the section 'Structuring your observation' later in the chapter). The observation needs careful and exact planning – observing involves far more than merely jotting down a few random thoughts about what you see going on.

Rich observations are those that include very detailed data with lots of contextual information. They need to include more than you just see and hear. If appropriate, get yourself thoroughly immersed in the setting. In addition to looking and seeing, bring your other senses into play through smell and touch.

Structuring your observation

The structure of your observation can range from being 'tightly' structured to 'loosely' structured. In Table 8-2 I show you the different approaches you can take to structuring your observation:

Table 8-2	**Looking at Different Styles of Observation**	
Structured	**Semi-Structured**	**Unstructured**
Systematic	Partially planned	No plan
Set criteria	Some prepared criteria	No prepared criteria
Keeps rigidly to checklist	Unexpected events recorded	Everything possible recorded
Interaction minimal	Interaction if needed	Ongoing analysis of emerging patterns

After thinking through and deciding what style of observation best suits the data you need for your dissertation, you should then go on to discuss your option with your supervisor, asking her to approve the choice you're making.

Taking part in the observation

When you become a participant in the observation, you're part of the group you're observing. Generally, you're already known to the group having likely spent time with the group on other occasions. Carrying out an observation if you're already part of a group is less likely to influence the group's behaviour because your being there is natural and expected, making observation a feasible option. However, trying to integrate with a new group can take a lot of your time and isn't generally to be recommended for an undergraduate dissertation.

As a non-participant in an observation you avoid getting caught up in any difficult situations by keeping yourself separate from the group. You must first deal with the ethical concerns and agree the nature and schedule of the observations with the subjects or their gatekeeper (see Chapter 5). Once you've set up things officially (including clarification of the role of the subjects within your study) you can proceed. You still need to be physically in the same location as the group you're observing but you need to make yourself as invisible as possible by keeping in the background and not getting involved in any way. In some cases you may have access to a one-way mirror setting (particularly if you're studying psychology), making being a non-participant in the observation much easier.

Recording your observations

You have a variety of options for recording what you're seeing and hearing during an observation. Here are a few ideas to get you thinking:

- Written notes on a prepared observation plan
- Written notes in a free narrative style (describing or interpreting what's happening)
- Hand-coded schedules and quantitative tallying
- Handwritten movement and interaction maps (recording patterns of behaviour and activities)
- Still photography
- Audio recording
- Video recording

Many factors can influence your decision about which method of recording to use – such as taking into account your own preferences, the limitations imposed by the setting, how your method may affect the group's behaviour and the amount of preparation and follow-up time each method demands.

Freeing yourself up by making a video recording, for example, can give you a big advantage in being able to follow what's going on without the distraction of having to write notes. However, you need to be technically competent when filming and you may find yourself at the mercy of the equipment. A camera of any sort can be intrusive and inhibit group behaviour.

Making a written record of what's going on is generally easier but you need to make sure that you're following what's happening while at the same time getting all the facts down on paper.

Some professional researchers carry out 'undercover' observations to minimise the impact their presence may have on the people being observed. Unless your observation involves working from a distance (for example, counting the numbers of people moving in one or other direction as they come out of the underground station) it's not advisable to undertake a covert study. Ethical, as well as personal issues make this method of observation a non-starter at undergraduate level. Take advice from your supervisor if you're thinking about carrying out a covert observation.

You're only able to record the way people are behaving and what's happening on that particular day, at that particular time. Take care not to make assumptions or generalise until you've got the full picture.

When carrying out an observation, mostly you're looking for hard facts rather than seeking opinions and impressions.

Even if you use mechanical devices to record instances, the observation or record is still subjective. For example, you're looking at whether children are paying attention (or 'on task'). Your interpretation of the facial expressions is part of your observation. You can't tell what a child's *thinking* – and just because the child appears to be daydreaming, doesn't mean the child's not engaged in the task.

Here's an example of a typical record sheet used for an observation being carried out of an adult learning workshop in an art gallery. The record sheet shows the various aspects of the observation that are being noted together with the type of questions that need to be asked and answered.

Workshop Record Sheet

1. **Facts and info:** Date/ participants (group)/ numbers/ timing/ advertising?

2. **Physical environment:** Sketch the space/ethos of the gallery/ think why the gallery has been set up in a particular way/ limitations of space?

3. **Structure of session:** Timetabling/ timings?

4. **Task:** Aims of the workshop/are aims being met/flow of the session and pace/ previous knowledge and experience of participants/ methods/ resources?

5. **Participants:** Emotional and cognitive engagement/ responses/ significant individual responses/ social concerns?

6. **Workshop facilitator:** Communication/ shifts in task/ adapting language used to suit the group?

In Table 8-3 I give you the opportunity of practising filling in your own record sheet for an observation you're carrying out.

Table 8-3	A Practice Record Sheet		
Observation	**What's Happening**	**Impressions/ Interpretations**	**Questions/ Suggestions**
Facts and info			
Physical environment			

(continued)

Table 8-3 *(continued)*

Observation	What's Happening	Impressions/ Interpretations	Questions/ Suggestions
Structure of session			
Task			
Participants			
Facilitator			
Other issues			

You can measure how often something is happening by using a mechanical counter or a tally chart. For example, you're observing how pedestrians are moving around in a town centre, noting the flow of movement. Having an accurate record of the direction the pedestrians are moving in can help you decide where to site a bus stop or a seating area. In Table 8-4 you can see an example of the type of record sheet you can create when using a mechanical counter in observation.

Table 8-4   An Example of an Observation Schedule for Showing Pedestrian Flow in a Town Centre

Observation Schedule for Pedestrian Flow

Date and day
Location
Weather
Level of activity
Sketch of alternative routes (A and B)

	Route A	Route B	Total A	Total B	Comments
12:30–12:35					
12:45–12:50					
14:00–14:05					

	Route A	Route B	Total A	Total B	Comments
14:10–14:15					
17:40–17:45					
17:50–17:55					

Telling a story is another way of recording your observations. A narrative is about describing events and recording your impressions so is naturally subjective. Although a narrative probably has limited use for a social science undergraduate dissertation, the following is an example of a narrative so that you know what one looks like:

> On entering the room the sense of tension was palpable. Most of the participants were avoiding eye contact, keeping their gaze on their work. Materials ranging from charcoal and pastels through to watercolours and richly coloured collage papers were lying on the table but everyone was using pencil. The room was chilly and several people were still wearing their outdoor jackets even though the session had been running for 20 minutes already, giving the impression that the participants were rather uncomfortable and about to leave at the first opportunity. The room had high, small windows, letting in little of the spring sunshine. The strip lights buzzed slightly; one of the lights was flickering on and off, but insistently, adding to the temporary, transient, unsettled atmosphere of the place.

Collecting quantitative and qualitative data

Using an observation schedule is a good way of recording quantitative data, for example noting the numbers of times people behave in a certain way. Or, when recording qualitative data, emphasise the importance, for example, of what's being said and how it's being said, rather than the number of times that somebody speaks.

Wherever possible, try leaving it open for you to return to the place and people you've been interviewing or observing. You may not need to revisit your work but it's possible your analysis leads you to reconsider what you're investigating and the sort of facts you need. I'm not suggesting that new avenues come up and that you need to follow them (so that you get sidetracked), but that you may need to explain what you're doing or have a follow-up question when starting your analysis.

Considering Case Studies

A case study isn't really a research method in its own right, but is more about applying various research methods to one specific case, or subject. A case study is an in-depth look at a particular person or particular situation and often involves using a range of methods for collecting empirical data such as questionnaires, sampling and observation.

For most undergraduate dissertation students, the case study is about one person or one practical issue that has wider implications for a particular section of society. Here are some examples of case studies involving children:

- ✔ A child with autism in a mainstream classroom
- ✔ A teacher dealing with a child with dyslexia
- ✔ Policy on bullying in a specific school
- ✔ A specific cursive handwriting strategy for a child with dyspraxia
- ✔ A clever and able child with learning problems

You can, of course, carry out a case study that makes use of secondary data, rather than generating your own data through questionnaires, sampling, observations or interviews. (See Chapter 9.)

Defining your subject

If you're thinking of doing a case study, your subject doesn't necessarily need to be exotic or unusual. It's actually more useful if the case study is typical of a particular problem or issue. But you do need to make sure that the case study you're doing allows you to link your findings to the wider world.

You need to choose the subject for your case study with great care. For example, think about the implications when choosing someone you know quite well already. If you're already comfortable in that person's company, it can make for more natural behaviour on both your parts but can also lead to a more subjective study where you have difficulty standing back from your subject and making an objective record of what's happening.

Filling in the background

When you're setting out your findings for your case study, you need to provide some background information to put your findings into context so that you're able to draw conclusions. Don't go into too much detail otherwise you're going to end up with a purely descriptive case study that's lacking in analysis. And, importantly, be careful not to reveal the names of any of your subjects; keeping their anonymity is paramount.

However, you do need to give whoever is marking your dissertation enough information to make sense of your case study, making the background detail succinct, clear and useful.

Steering Clear of Bias

While working on your case study, be careful not to become too involved with your subject – this can be a difficult balance when you're focusing all your attention on one particular person or situation. It can be all too easy to slip into a deeply subjective and biased perspective of what's happening. You need to keep some distance from your subject. One way of standing back is to make sure that you talk about your work with different people (keeping the anonymity of your subject at all times). When discussing your work with colleagues, you get to hear other viewpoints, helping you to keep your scrutiny of the situation or subject more balanced than if you're keeping everything to yourself.

No single type of data collecting is better than another. Whichever method you choose you just need to make sure that the method fits the purpose and is relevant to your research question.

Chapter 9

Analysing Data and Drawing Conclusions

· ·

In This Chapter

▶ Exploring analysis and critical thinking

▶ Interpreting your data systematically

▶ Analysing different types of data

▶ Dealing with problems

· ·

*A*fter conscientiously gathering together your data – empirical or non-empirical – the time has come for the grand analysis. You're likely to have a mass of facts, figures, opinions, observations and ideas but your data is only of value if you systematically interpret your findings to support your research question.

In this chapter I talk about the best approaches for analysing your data as well as giving you some ideas on how to present your data visually.

Presenting your data is not the same as analysing your data. It's not enough merely to lay out your findings and expect your reader to draw his own conclusions.

Some courses and fields of study have specific guidelines on data analysis that you're required to follow in order to comply with university regulations. I can only offer you a simplified introduction to data analysis in this book. If, for example, you're studying linguistics, the short section in this chapter talking about discourse analysis is no substitute for the modules provided on a linguistic course, which tackles the subject in much greater depth. If you have any unanswered questions about analysing your data, it's important that you go with your university's guidelines.

Understanding Analysis

Data means very little without interpretation. Whether you generate your own primary data, review secondary data, or shun data altogether and concentrate on argument, you need to analyse the information right there in front of you. You may hear your tutor or supervisor referring to data analysis as 'critical thinking' or 'evaluation', but the gist of the matter is that you need to move beyond description to a systematic and reasoned presentation of the facts.

Whether your data takes the form of numbers and statistics, interview responses and questionnaire replies, or whether you're using existing arguments, you need to show how your facts link with your research question, to the literature on the subject and draw conclusions from what you've discovered.

University courses are designed to encourage students to think and to take an analytical approach to the subject they're studying. One of the most difficult challenges for students moving from school, college or work to university is getting to grips with the idea that effective analysis lies at the centre of the course. If you look up a definition of 'analysis' (noun) in a dictionary or come across synonyms in a thesaurus, you may see the following definitions:

- ✔ Scrutiny
- ✔ Examination
- ✔ Study
- ✔ Investigation
- ✔ Classification
- ✔ Breakdown

These words describe what analysis consists of, but you need to know what you have to actually do in order to analyse. It's useful to think about the act of analysing therefore. The verbs showing what you're doing when you're analysing are:

- ✔ Reviewing
- ✔ Interrogating
- ✔ Assessing
- ✔ Appraising
- ✔ Evaluating

As part of your degree course you've been developing your analytical skills, discovering how to express your views with supporting evidence, how to interpret information and how to compare opinion and ideas.

Your dissertation is your big opportunity for demonstrating your skills when analysing the literature, primary and secondary data (quantitative and/or qualitative) and your own ideas.

Moving from description to analysis

Analysing your data is a completely different activity from just describing what's happening. Analysis is about making an evaluation of the worth of your data. You're saying 'This concept seems to be like this, but can be interpreted like that and the effects of such an interpretation can be this or that'.

Description is important and features in your dissertation, for example, as background information about your case study or source of your data, in parts of your literature review and research methodology and in some parts of the presentation of your data. However, description needs to be controlled and concise. Sometimes you can replace passages of description with a simple table, detailing what you want to say, but if you have to describe an idea fully, the description needs to be woven carefully into the fabric of your work.

Analysis is more complex and detailed than description – it involves evaluation. You're saying if something is good or bad. Analysis is about understanding; showing that you've grasped the general principles of an idea and how your data links to different aspects of your research question.

When you're describing you're just showing that you can paraphrase someone else's ideas. I think that the most frequent comment I make on essays, dissertations and examination scripts is 'Too descriptive', or 'Lacking analysis'. I've even thought about having a rubber stamp made to save me writing 'Lacking analysis' but maybe this is going a bit too far!

Too often students when writing essays and in exams spend valuable time detailing a theory or report that I've presented in a lecture or seminar. The student's task is to analyse the worth of the report and the report's implications (shown in the title), but often what's presented is just a repeat of what the student has noted from the lecture. Sometimes a student even quotes my own handouts back to me. Such an analysis doesn't show analytical or critical thinking and fails to demonstrate the required carefully considered reading of the material. As well as being infuriating, this type of analysis is really boring to mark.

Keep smiling – you can shift from a descriptive approach towards analysis, it just takes thought and care. Here are some suggestions for making the leap from description to analysis:

- ✔ Don't just say where your data comes from and talk about the type of data – evaluate what's good and bad about your data.

- ✔ Don't merely say which research method you're using, decide if the method is the best for the job, saying why you think that the method is or isn't.

- ✔ Don't write a list of information, instead discuss the value of each piece of data. If you must have a list, at least prioritise your data showing you can see degrees of importance.

- ✔ Don't just report what's been happening, explore the consequences of what's happening.

- ✔ Don't just suggest that some ideas are similar to others, show how the ideas link together or how the ideas differ.

- ✔ Don't just repeat a theory, say why the theory matters in the context of what you're investigating.

Considering the general characteristics of analysis

You need to be absolutely clear about what marks out analysis from other dissertation activities. You may have a generally quantitative survey or questionnaire that mainly asks about the facts of someone's role ('how long they've attended Scouts, how old they are, how many badges they've won, how they rank the different activities on offer' and so on) but you may also have a question that elicits their opinions or attitudes to an issue or concern ('If you've answered *yes* to the previous question, please explain here what you think that you've learnt from this year's summer camp in the Peak District.')

In the following list I show you some of the characteristics of analysis – in the list 'data' applies to empirical studies as well as including theories and arguments you come up with in non-empirical work:

✔ Getting some distance from the data, looking at the data from different viewpoints and being objective.

✔ Picking out loaded language designed to persuade and assumptions being made by the writer that you can usefully challenge.

✔ Spotting figures or statistics that lead the reader in a certain direction deliberately; showing how the data can be interpreted differently.

✔ Looking for gaps and flaws in the data – anything missing, anything wrong?

✔ Seeing different possible interpretations – what are the pros and cons of each way of looking at the data? The data with the most pros is going to be stronger than the other data. You need to be able to show how you reach this conclusion.

✔ Searching through the steps of the arguments, and checking that the argument is logical and coherent – do you see any leaps or jumps without back-up evidence?

✔ Looking into the same ideas or data being reviewed by a variety of authors – how do the authors' conclusions differ and why?

✔ After examining your data once, take a break for a few days – go back, looking at your data again with fresh eyes (you're bound to spot something you've missed).

Using Analysis to Explore Ideas

Whether your dissertation is empirical or non-empirical, you're weighing up ideas and theories as your dissertation develops. In a non-empirical dissertation, evaluating ideas and lines of argument is obviously your main concern. Your analysis needs to be concerned with:

✔ Comparing and contrasting

✔ Considering different and/or multiple narratives or perspectives

✔ Evaluating the cause and effect of an action

✔ Speculating about the consequences of different ideas

✔ Understanding that ideas and theories aren't fixed, but are open to being challenged and developed

✔ Distinguishing between opinion and ideas based on evidence

When you're analysing theories and ideas you need to question what you're reading or hearing, by keeping the following in mind and asking:

- ✔ What's the source of this information or idea?
- ✔ How reliable is the source or the basis?
- ✔ How consistent is this theory?
- ✔ What (or who) is missing?
- ✔ What makes the theory or idea persuasive?
- ✔ How can the theory or idea be improved?
- ✔ Is the theory or idea applicable to a particular context?

Try getting to grips with the line or lines of reasoning that are presented to you, seeing if you can spot any errors or gaps in logic or any aspects of reasoning that are short on back-up evidence (both empirical and non-empirical).

Comparing and examining relationships

Your dissertation may be concerned with drawing comparisons between different ideas or issues. If you're examining relationships, you'll be comparing and contrasting. This short section helps you think about the relationships.

Comparing relationships involves breaking down the different aspects of each theory or idea and putting them side by side to find out how far the theory or idea agrees or disagrees with each other. If you find similarities, keep them in mind, and be sure that when you're making your conclusions you highlight the distance between the ideas (if appropriate).

Be careful with comparisons that you're comparing like with like. For example, it's pointless to compare two approaches to working with children in a certain context if one of the approaches was originally designed for working with adults.

Similarly, if you're looking for relationships, don't try to force links where links don't exist. You can't fairly criticise a local council for failing to cater for the needs of Travellers if no Travellers have passed through that area in the last decade. Always try forging relevant links where possible.

Testing out hypotheses

Your dissertation may be concerned with testing out different ideas. For example, you may think that young children who struggle to manage their work can be helped with picture cues, and you want to test it out. It's your hypothesis you're testing. You can also test out a hypothesis you've read about at university.

In cases where you're testing out a hypothesis, you need to kick off with a bit of background, explaining the origins of the idea in question before succinctly delineating the actual idea with clarity. You need to consider the consequences of embracing the idea. When someone has already embraced the idea and shown that it does or doesn't really work, it's easier for you to analyse of course, but do make some limited conjecture if the idea has not yet been put into practice.

You have to include reasons for opposing or supporting the theory and your reasons need to come from theorists or practitioners in your field. This shows that you're expressing your own views. How you set out your views is up to you but, if possible, try not to chop and change between supporters and opposers, because this can put the coherence of your argument at risk.

Analysing to reveal strengths and weaknesses

Showing the strength and weakness of an argument means you're going to need reliable evidence to support your views. Try emphasising the following flaws (or point out the opposite if you're highlighting strengths):

- Making assumptions
- Having breaks in reasoning
- Lacking in theoretical or practical support
- Making false propositions
- Having limits in perspective (such as neglecting the views of a minority group)
- Jumping from idea to idea and lacking a coherent line of argument

Looking at Qualitative Data

Analysing qualitative data can be described as:

- ✔ Noticing or observing patterns
- ✔ Collecting evidence
- ✔ Reflecting on what you've noted

The analysis of qualitative data differs from the analysis of quantitative data mainly by the flowing nature of the analysis, rather than the process of collecting data followed by analysis that you get with quantitative data.

The process of analysing qualitative data is *iterative* – meaning that you're returning to your argument again and again. However, you're not doing the same things over and over, you're building on suppositions about what you can see and the evidence you're collecting. Analysing qualitative data is a progressive process. While you're looking at the details, you're also keeping an eye on the bigger picture because you're aiming at presenting a complete analysis of the topic.

Organising your data

You need to arrange and sort your data so that it's easily manageable and you're showing connections and themes. You can start by *reducing* your data and leaving out the least important aspects and highlighting the aspects that are likely to be most significant, and then coding your data to help you spot patterns.

Reducing your data

Data reduction is about simplifying and transforming your raw data into something that's going to be intelligible to anyone reading your dissertation.

Reducing data is a task requiring skill. You need to make sure of eliminating bias and subjectivity. It's not a case of leaving out what doesn't match what you were expecting to come out of your data, but of focusing on the most significant aspects of your data.

Cutting down your data to a more manageable amount needs to be started sooner rather than later. Get going by summarising your data as you go – for example, creating a Word file noting all the factual details of your interviews such as who you spoke to, length of discussion, location and other basic details. When you next come to summarising all the interviews you carried out, the key facts are ready for you to access easily and quickly.

Finding a single method for organising your data is up to you. You have to come up with a method that suits the data you've been collecting.

Coding your data

You may need to read through this section before getting going on coding your data. Coding isn't the only method of analysing data.

Coding is about looking for patterns and themes in your data to help you illustrate your theories and ideas. As you build up more and more information you're going to need to classify your data, so that you can spot any patterns taking shape.

In Chapter 8 I talk about building codes into your research design; applying coding makes this stage of analysing your data so much easier.

If you look up further information about coding data, you're likely to find taxonomies and typologies mentioned. At present you just need to note that taxonomies are normally for the classification of empirical information (often observable and measurable) and typologies are used for classifying more theoretical information (types of ideas and phenomena).

Begin coding by grouping your data into related areas. Think of coding like doing a jigsaw puzzle. Each piece of data is like a piece of a jigsaw puzzle. At first glance you've a jumble of different ideas that you know fit together but seem impossible to organise. You start by grouping similar pieces of data (like starting with the edge pieces of your jigsaw or pieces of the same colour).

After a short time order seems to be growing out of chaos as you find more pieces that fit together, having neat piles or places to put your data until you're ready for further analysis. As you add more pieces of data to your piles, you're going to see some more complicated issues that need your attention. For example, all the pieces that at first looked the same shade of red can now be separated into smaller groupings or sub-categories. You can now clearly see differences between the scarlet pieces, the purplish red, the pinky red, and so on.

In the same way, as the data from your questionnaire comes rolling in, you find sub-categories popping up unexpectedly. Sub-categories appear like this:

- ✔ From asking one simple question about a student's views on the university library

- ✔ Category from questionnaire – '*Student views on the university library*'

✔ Emerging sub-categories – book stock; photocopying services; opening hours; helpfulness of staff; café facilities.

Coding your data in this way isn't the only way to think about analysing what you've found and some people don't like the jigsaw analogy, but comparing filling in the pieces of a jigsaw with coding a jumbled mass of data makes a reasonable start if you're unfamiliar with the idea of coding. Other social science study skills texts may use different ways of describing coding.

For an undergraduate dissertation, discipline yourself to stick to simple coding as described in the section on coding above. More complex ways of linking data can be used, where you demonstrate complex relationships and show every single connection in a very detailed fashion. But you're well-advised to discuss the codes you're applying to your data with your supervisor.

Seeing themes and patterns in your data

Once you've coded your data, you've a clearer idea about what you've been recording. The process of coding both organises your data and allows you to see how best you can use your coded data for highlighting themes and patterns.

The jigsaw-style method I describe in the section 'Organising your data' earlier in this chapter is suitable for all sorts of data including transcripts of interviews, diaries, some documents, questionnaires and observations.

In the section 'Organising your data' I suggest ideas for dealing with data that's often complex, but you can also have simple codes for basic information, such as gender splits or numbers of people agreeing or disagreeing using 'Yes/No' questions.

Scanning your coded data can immediately highlight clear trends and patterns. Some aspects of your research that you thought were going to feature heavily now seem less important and other aspects stand out much more than you expected.

What's meant by patterns or themes depends on the data you've been collecting. Take a look at the following examples of emerging patterns or themes from dissertations I've supervised, to see how the patterns match or disprove the expectations of the student carrying out the research:

✔ **Questionnaire asking teachers what they understand by the term 'gifted':** *Pattern:* teachers of older children defined 'being gifted' through subjects, whereas those of younger children defined through personal characteristics such as 'curiosity' or 'always asking questions'. Student *wasn't* surprised to see this pattern.

✔ **Project asking nursery children to photograph their least favourite places in their school:** *Pattern:* boys disliking the toilets, saying they were cold and dark. Student felt that the dislike of the toilets wouldn't have surfaced if she'd run the project with less than 20 children.

✔ **Interviews with staff working with children with behavioural difficulties:** *Pattern:* support staff holding the view that 'Boys are generally more difficult to control than girls', contradicting the view of the teachers. Student wasn't sure what the opposing views meant, but mounting evidence suggested that there was a definite split between the views of support and teaching staff.

✔ **Evaluations of museum workshops:** *Pattern:* children misunderstanding one particular display; on looking more closely, the label describing the display was placed too high for the children to read. Student was amazed because labelling wasn't the focus of the exercise, but it explained a great deal about how much or how little the children were involved in the workshop.

Translating the students' findings into patterns was only possible once coding had been applied to the data. Where the student was *surprised* is because the pattern only emerged as a result of the coding. Where the student *expected* the theme to come out, the coding was vital in proving that evidence can be harnessed to support the student's argument.

Interpreting qualitative data isn't an easy option – and you shouldn't be picking it just to avoid maths and statistics. Not only can maths and stats be applied to qualitative data, but you have to be just as systematic, organised and thorough.

Considering alternatives to coding

You may find that your sort of data doesn't particularly benefit from being coded or that only some aspects of your data can be usefully coded. An alternative method to coding is *discourse analysis,* which is a term used to describe a range of methods for analysing written, spoken and signed language.

With discourse analysis you're looking for patterns initially and finding examples, rather than coding the whole narrative and then picking out themes. Discourse analysis is more concerned with studying the structure and features that bind sentences into a sequence and is a significant discipline in its own right. But for the purposes of an undergraduate dissertation there are some useful techniques you can use for making a breakdown of how people use the same sort of language. Techniques include:

✔ **Conversation analysis:** Patterns used in speech and signing.

✔ **Critical discourse analysis (CDA):** Linking a person's language to his social context.

✔ **Feminist critical discourse analysis:** Like CDA, but looking at gender from the post-structuralist standpoint.

✔ **Pragmatics:** How the meaning of words are interpreted differently from person to person.

Most methods of discourse analysis examine the macro and micro aspects of language (being the broader social aspects and specific linguistic elements). Some discourse analysis may also link speech to body language, intonation and emphasis to show what a person is thinking and feeling.

Coding may also be unsuitable if your data is automatically allocated to very clear categories and it's already obvious what themes are appearing in your data. One example of this would be coding data from interviews with five people, say, about their views on visiting art galleries. As part of the discussion, you ask them what they don't like about galleries and they answer high-lighting the costs of the café, the generally quiet atmosphere and the prices in the gift shop. The answers about the café and the gift shop can be coded together as they're about the services for which you need to pay. The other answer is about a less tangible aspect and has a different code. You can use this code to add in any further answers about the general feeling of the gallery.

Although it's unusual not to apply coding in a large-scale study, where an undergraduate dissertation has just a small sample of data coding usually isn't required.

Explaining connections and contradictions

Analysing your findings involves producing evidence for each connection you identify and for each contradiction that occurs. It isn't good enough to explain what's happening because of a hunch or feeling. You always need to use your data to illustrate what you're trying to show.

There are a number of computer packages on the market you can use for analysing qualitative data, such as Ethnograph and NUDIST. But because the sample size in an undergraduate dissertation is small, using such programs can be overkill. See the section 'Meeting more complex statistics' for more discussion of analysis using a computer.

Analysing Quantitative Data

Your job is to interpret and understand the data in relation to your research question. You don't need a degree in maths, but you do need to apply simple maths to your quantitative data – for example, looking at the quantity of people who are thinking something or who are carrying out a certain action. You're attempting to spot patterns showing the frequency of something or picking up on relationships. This activity is called statistics.

Don't panic if maths isn't your strong point. Very simple calculations are often enough for an undergraduate dissertation, such as looking at averages or percentages.

If you need more detailed data analysis, you can apply user-friendly software such as simple spreadsheets (like Microsoft Excel). If you have fewer than 30 subjects, you're likely to find that other more complex software (such as SPSS) isn't going to be that useful, so it's best to stick to more familiar and straightforward methods of obtaining statistical data.

Before getting started on your analysis you need to revisit the original objectives of your research question; checking out what needs analysing. You may find that your data is spot on – exactly the kind of responses you hoped for with the focus matching your research objectives.

More likely, however, you're going to find that something has shifted. The data doesn't really help you with your original ideas, or some other really interesting issues have popped up along the way that are more relevant than your original questions.

If your dissertation appears to be going off course, see the section 'Turning to Troubleshooting' at the end of this chapter.

Looking into simple statistics: Ratios, percentages and means

For the purpose of an undergraduate dissertation just working out an average or a proportion is going to be enough for explaining or illustrating an idea. You can express what you want to get across through a ratio, percentage or mean.

A ratio is a way of expressing a comparison of different qualities, of showing how the qualities relate to one another. Ratios are more commonly used in science and maths than in the social sciences, but ratios have some properties that can be usefully applied to social science data. For example, you can reduce your data (like fractions) making the data easy to interpret. Ratios are also a useful form of shorthand for neatly expressing related amounts:

- ✔ x many girls to y many boys – (girls:boys)

- ✔ x many supporters to y many opposers – (supporters:opposers)

- ✔ x many Chinese to y many Caucasians – (Chinese:Caucasians)

- ✔ When reducing 9:6, you can express the ratio as 3:2

Percentages can be useful for emphasising comparisons as they turn all numerical data into a proportion of 100, allowing the reader to make a simple assessment. Having worked out the percentage, you make it easier for the reader because you've done the maths. For example:

> *13 out of 20 nurses failed to take a daily lunch break compared with 6 out of 32 students.*

An average is usually when you're describing the mean of something, however this may be being a bit simplistic because there are different types of 'average' used:

- ✔ **Mean** – adding up all the values and dividing by the number of values

- ✔ **Median** – taking the middle value once all values are listed in ascending or descending order

- ✔ **Mode** (or *modal value*) – the most frequently occurring value

Meeting more complex statistics

For complex statistical analysis you may need to use a much more sophisticated computer package or spreadsheet program.

The most well-known program used in quantitative analysis is SPSS (Statistical Package for Social Science), launched in the 1960s. SPSS isn't just one single method, but a package that runs loads of different tests. Some tests are for descriptive statistics that quantify the features of the data (such as the frequency of an occurrence or cross-tabulation, which is about the distribution of values, measured with a *chi-square*).

Others tests on SPSS examine the correspondence between variables, known as *bivariate statistics* and the tests being used include the t-test (the most common in undergraduate work as it's good for small samples) and ANOVA (analysis of variance).

Your university library is likely to have the software you need for working out statistics and run courses explaining how to use the different packages. Other statistical packages exist and you can even find these tests on your standard Excel spreadsheet, but be careful because the analysis is rather haphazard and is generally considered to be weak at presenting any subtle differences in your data.

You may find that the SPSS courses and software are reserved for postgraduate students on specific courses such as mathematics or psychology, so do check that you're going to be able to use a particular software before setting your heart on SPSS, for example.

SPSS is a commonly used package but it's very involved and you're going to need training and practice. Think carefully before launching into SPSS. You have to be realistic about the time you can devote to learning the program.

Differentiating between parametric and non-parametric data

A parameter is a constant – setting a boundary or limit to the scope of something. It's a characteristic or attribute that's shared by most people and is spread across a population fairly evenly. Parameters are generally represented visually through a *normal distribution curve*, also known as a *Gaussian curve*. Figure 9-1 shows what a Gaussian curve looks like. Data conforming to a parameter is called *parametric* data.

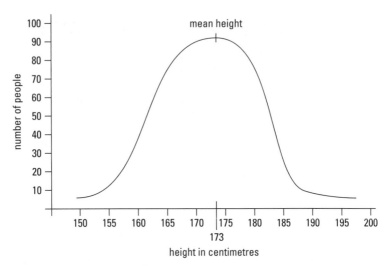

Figure 9-1: An example of a Gaussian curve.

A way of illustrating the use of parametric data is to think of height. Most people are a similar height (that's the average or *mean*), with some very tall and some very short appearing on the extreme of the Gaussian curve (deviating from the mean). The extent of the spread of data is called the *standard deviation* (SD). If the data spread is wide then there's a large SD, conversely a small SD happens when the dispersion is minor and most of the data is close to the mean. When there's no difference and the data is equal, the SD is zero.

SD in action – digit-span tests

Here's a simple example of standard deviation (SD). An often-used psychological test for measuring IQ is simply to remember a string of unrelated numbers. The tester reads out a list of numbers, something like: 3 7 9 2 0 5 4 1 7 8 3 6 9 – a total of 13 numbers.

After a suitable (timed) pause of several seconds, the person being tested is asked to repeat the sequence back to the tester (or write the numbers down). It's a test of short-term memory (amongst other things).

Scores for this test fit the Gaussian curve and the mean is to be able to accurately recall nine numbers correctly. The standard deviation is +/-2, which means that people remembering 7 numbers or 11 numbers fall within the 'acceptable' range. This shows that the spread of data is generally limited to 2 more or less than the mean.

Parametric data is data that can be measured such as heights, depths, amounts of money and areas. For parametric data you're most likely to be using a mean and perhaps also exploring the standard deviations.

Other data (*non-parametric* data) doesn't conform to the Gaussian curve because the data is distributed normally and doesn't rely on parameters. Non-parametric data can be useful when you don't have data on the entire population and you're just looking at a small sample. This is usually qualitative data (see the section 'Looking at Qualitative Data' earlier in the chapter).

Although your data is about ranking and order and looks mathematical – this doesn't make your data parametric. Non-parametric methods are most appropriate for ordinal data (rankings). There are tests for evaluating positions or views, drawing comparisons and analysing more qualitative data, but such tests may be a bit over the top for your purposes. You're likely to be better off leaving out the stats and working on interpreting the data – but check with your supervisor before making any final decisions.

Unless you're a psychology student, or someone who did stats at GCSE or A-level, it's perfectly possible that you've got through your degree so far without needing to do a course on statistics. If you want to methodically analyse your non-parametric data (using say, Spearman's correlation or Mann-Whitney U), you need to take a statistics module or get help from qualified staff.

If you haven't had formal training in statistical analysis, now may not be the best time to take it up. Keep things as simple as you can.

Displaying Your Data

Whether your data is quantitative or qualitative you need to present your data in a way that can be easily understood by the examiner. While you're initially surveying your collection of data, it may not be immediately obvious how best to lay out your data so that your reader can make sense of your ideas.

Always use a method for displaying your data that's appropriate to your sample size. If you have only two subjects for example, don't attempt to use percentages to put across their views. Fifty per cent of two is one. You just need to say 'One of the subjects feels . . . but the other thinks . . .'

Aim for clarity. Your examiner isn't looking to be impressed by your advanced computer skills or superb colour illustrations.

Trying tables, charts and lists

In general, when you write essays you avoid using bullet points and lists, but in a dissertation the chapter where you present your data is an exception to this rule. Clearly introduced bullet points are fine in these cases. Here are some other ways of presenting your data:

- ✔ **Pie charts** show percentages and are presented in a circle. Try to limit the pie chart to less than eight segments for clarity. Merge very small values into a segment labelled 'other'.

- ✔ **Bar charts** show how different data compare with one another. Try not to have too many entries and keep the distinguishing features clear. Make the scale match the data equally and don't skew the data too far just to fit in a value deviating from the norm. (Note: histograms appear to be like bar charts, but histograms are different.)

- ✔ **Line graphs** show how things have changed over time – trends and developments (always moving from left to right). For clarity you may want to label your lines on the diagram rather than in a key.

- ✔ **Histograms** show data that's presented in a continuous scale. The bars touch one another to show these links (it may be data like ages, say 10–15 years, 16–19 years, 20–24 years, and so on).

There are other ways of displaying data, but pie and bar charts, line graphs and histograms are likely to be the best ways of displaying data in an undergraduate dissertation.

Tables of all sorts can be easily put together using basic word processing and spreadsheet software. Tables and spreadsheets need to be concise. Give your table a heading and each cell of a spreadsheet may possibly need a brief description only. Keep tables and spreadsheets compact and tidy. If your data starts to spread or becomes unwieldy, you've got too much detail, or you need to make more than one table. The other possibility is that the data isn't suitable to present as a table, and you may need to think of another way of presenting your data.

Always make tables and charts readable by making sure that they're contained on one page. (Use a foldout sheet if necessary.)

What looks clear and simple on your computer screen can come out muddled and confusing once it's printed out, particularly when you're printing out a colour chart in black and white. You want your reader to be enlightened, not perplexed. Limit your colours so that your chart is easy to read and avoid using too many complicated black and white patterns and textures that can be difficult to follow.

Considering case studies and other narratives

If you're writing a non-empirical dissertation involving a case study it's likely you're going to be using a narrative format for analysing your data. Some form of discourse analysis is likely to form part of the study of your narrative, but this is probably going to be a micro-examination of the structure and use of language. However, if you only focus on the micro-aspect of your data, you may miss the broader picture.

Your narrative needs a plot line or chronology and clear statements about what's happening. Usually you highlight key features like any significant changes occurring or any shifts in the subject's ideas and views. It's best to explain such happenings with a timeline (a linear outline of the development of the 'story' and explanation of the key 'events').

There may be particular characters or actors featuring in the narrative (real or fictional) and you can place them in your narrative using a thumbnail sketch. You may also need to outline your characters' setting and show the results of actions that are central to the story.

A flow chart can be a useful device in a narrative because flow charts show horizontal and backwards connections as well as links that are vertical and forwards.

Try keeping in mind the value of researching an idea through narrative, biography, diary and storytelling:

- ✔ Storytelling conveys meaning.

- ✔ Narratives are good for resolving dilemmas, reducing tension, bringing problems out into the open.

- ✔ Diaries and memoirs are useful for helping to explain actions and for following changes in behaviour.

- ✔ Narratives allow you to stand back and give opportunities for seeing patterns and logic in apparently disconnected and chaotic events.

Interpreting people's diaries and memoirs can be a very time-consuming and complicated activity. You're going to need a coding method: coloured tabs, highlighters and other materials do the job. Because a diary is a personal document you may be better off making a photocopy or even have an electronic version so that you can start getting on with the analysis as soon as possible.

Including data in an appendix

Go to Chapter 15 for finding out how to manage your appendixes. Broadly speaking, you need to include information that's necessary, but that doesn't interrupt the flow of your work. For example, you may want to include the permission letter if it's significant, or a blank version of your questionnaire, or an interview schedule. You can also include details of your coding system if your coding threw up interesting categories, or you may have samples of handwriting or extracts from transcripts you want to put into your appendix.

Keeping hold of all your raw data until you get your official confirmation that you've passed your dissertation is a must. If a query arises and you've shredded your data and put it on your organic compost heap, you're going to be in serious trouble.

Turning to Troubleshooting

If you find things starting to go wrong with your data analysis, you know that you're in trouble. Disaster can strike if your research methodologies trip you up by doing the opposite of what you intended.

Take, for example, a questionnaire where your respondents have consistently misunderstood a particular question. The likelihood is that you've designed that particular question poorly. You may be able to get round this mini-disaster by having another question elsewhere in your questionnaire that throws light on what you're asking – allowing you to get hold of the data you need. In your analysis you can discuss the difficulties you've been having with interpretation because your respondents haven't fully understood the questions you've been asking.

Help! My data completely changes my research question

Panic! Students have been known to start panicking at the analysis stage after discovering that the data they've collected completely changes their research question. The answer is to keep calm and start rereading and reviewing what your subject is actually saying rather than throwing out your research question altogether. You're likely to find that you're (unintentionally) reading the response you expect from your subject, rather than the actual response your subject is making.

Help! My data is rubbish

Analysis of quantitative and qualitative data is obviously different, but one aspect that many undergraduates are unprepared for is how data collection affects the general direction and experience of a dissertation. You may well find that your data doesn't match your idea of what you thought you were going to discover. With quantitative data, the common disappointment is that what seems to you to be a significant issue turns out to be rather mundane and has no useful statistical significance.

For qualitative data, you're most likely to find that your research shifts and changes shape as you go along. For example, an interview where your subject answers one question in a way that changes the direction of your discussion and you start to question what you're investigating.

Help! No one's answering my questionnaire

Having disappointing data, or data you're not expecting, is one problem – but having no data at all is really bad news. If you find yourself in this situation, it looks very much as if you simply haven't been following the guidelines for your dissertation. Early on in your planning you needed to have sussed out what sort of return you were likely to get from your questionnaire. For example, if there was a possibility that you weren't going to get any responses you should have made contingency plans earlier in the process.

Sadly, this kind of error happens too often when students leave things to chance. In many cases it's best to accept that you simply need more time and speak to your supervisor about deferring your dissertation until such time when you're properly organised and have the time and inclination to complete your work satisfactorily.

To get going again on your dissertation you need a strategy for collecting new data relating to your research question. How you go about restarting your dissertation depends on your subjects and access to people and resources that can help. In Table 9-1 I offer you a strategy for moving forward on your dissertation once again.

Table 9-1   Strategy for Restarting Your Dissertation

Original plan	Problem	Strategy
Questionnaire	No response	Interview
Interviews	No access	Library research
Observation	No ethical clearance	Use published case studies
Email survey	Technical	Paper-based questionnaire

Whatever problem you're having with your dissertation, you MUST contact your supervisor. Having no data and trying to pull a dissertation out of thin air is a recipe for disaster.

Chapter 10

Staying on Track

Writing a dissertation is a long process and you need to stand back and take stock from time to time to be sure that you're moving in the right direction towards your goal.

In this chapter I give you tips for reviewing your progress and checking that you're keeping on track – and that you're able to submit your dissertation finished and on time. I'm also going to show you ways of getting to grips with problems that are stopping you working effectively. When you're feeling as if you've tried just about everything – I point you in the right direction for that extra bit of help.

 When you plan your dissertation, build in some review time so that you can be certain that you're not neglecting any aspect of your dissertation.

Seeing How You're Getting On

Writing a dissertation is a major undertaking. You need to review your progress regularly as it's easy to veer off-track as you have so much to manage. This section helps you review where you are and be sure that you're heading in the right direction. It also helps you rethink a little if you seem to be a bit lost.

Reviewing your progress

You need to consider honestly how you're getting on with your work. It's not just a question of how many words you've written or how many books you've read. What you need to review is how far on the journey have you come and whether you have sufficient remaining time to ensure that you can do a great job in completing your dissertation.

Having a Gantt chart up on your wall or notice board is an excellent way of monitoring your progess. A Gantt chart is a table with overlapping lines showing the different tasks you've set yourself and how the tasks run alongside one another. (If you want to see an illustration of a Gantt chart, go to Chapter 4.) Or, design your own plan – whatever you decide, make sure that you can easily see your Gantt chart or plan from your desk. Use colour to mark your progress through your work, showing where you've got to and what you've achieved. More specific to-do lists (with all those smaller tasks listed) are best kept in your notebook or diary. You need to keep generating new daily and weekly lists crossing off the tasks as you get them done. Carry your list of smaller tasks around with you as a reminder and enjoy the satisfaction of ticking off items as you go.

Some people find having a plan of campaign staring them in the face a bit threatening and overpowering. If you feel this way, rely on your to-do lists for a while, and mark each item off boldly when completed. Only display your Gantt chart or plan when you're about halfway through your dissertation or at a point where the Gantt chart doesn't fill you with horror when you see what still needs to be done.

Readjusting your goals

Writing a dissertation is like going on a journey. As you're going along you can find yourself changing direction or thinking about a slightly different emphasis or route. After spending some time working on your dissertation, it's worth reviewing how long the journey's taking, where you've got to, what you've accomplished and where you're wanting to go next.

Your goal is to finish your dissertation. However, you may find that some aspects of your dissertation change along the way. For example, imagine your plan was to carry out interviews with four people, but one subject was unwell and another cancelled. (You've no need to think that *you've* failed in any way.) If you and your supervisor think that two interviews are going to give you all the data you need, you can scrap your original plan of carrying out four interviews rather than spending time looking for substitute subjects.

Now that you've two less interviews to do you can adjust your timetable. Where you set aside a day for each interview amend your schedule, saving the two unused days for another activity.

Moving in the right direction

If you find that the direction you're moving in isn't matching up with your plans you need to stop and take stock. Do any of the following situations strike a chord?

- ✔ You're confused about what you're supposed to be researching and not sure how to go about things.

- ✔ Your research is changing emphasis because you've found a new area of interest or your data/reading is leading you to new ways of thinking about your topic.

- ✔ Your dissertation topic isn't manageable in the way you originally expected and is morphing into a more practical project.

- ✔ You're no longer interested in what you started off doing and have got sidetracked by following what really interests you rather than sticking to your original plan.

How you respond to a change in direction depends on your reasons for moving away from your original plan for your dissertation. Here's what I suggest to students coming to see me with the above concerns:

- ✔ **Confusion about methods:** You probably need to go back to your original objectives, defining exactly what you're trying to find out. Once you're quite clear about what you want to achieve, your methods are likely to fall into place. If not, go with the most practical approach for meeting your objectives.

- ✔ **Shift in interests:** If your new interest relates to your original objectives that's fine because your ideas are likely to be covered by the work you've already done in your literature review (although your review may need tweaking). In your rationale or introduction explain how your research has shifted, or while you're doing your data analysis, whichever suits best.

- ✔ **More practical approach:** Taking a more practical approach is usually fine and normally means cutting down your original rather over-ambitious plans. You just need to check that you can generate enough data in the time available for completing your dissertation.

- ✔ **Loss of interest:** Clearly it's hard keeping motivated when you aren't really interested in what you're doing. Having enough time to pursue your new idea depends on how far away the topic is from what you've already covered in your research and how long you've got until the submission date.

At all costs avoid submitting a half-hearted and poorly thought through dissertation. Instead, face up to your change of direction and set about thinking through how you can overcome the difficulties involved in taking a new approach.

A supervisor sees making a change of direction as only a minor hitch if the student is prepared to commit to sorting out what needs to be done. When a student comes to me lost, panicky and with no suggestions, it's much harder to give the student any help. If the student has some tactics worked out for getting moving again on her dissertation, we're both onto a winning formula.

Be sure always to talk to your supervisor if you're thinking about changing direction. Most tutors are pleased to support a student who's facing up to a shift in plans, especially when the student is coming up with ideas for a new approach to her work.

Backing up your work

Regularly backing up your work is as necessary as breathing. You need to be aware of two important activities: one is keeping track of different versions of your work (keeping the drafts clearly labelled), and the other is keeping copies of your work in case the original version on disk, memory stick or hard copy is lost or damaged.

As you churn out more and more text without having a system in place for keeping your work in order, safe and secure, you can easily become overwhelmed. Having too many piles of paper on your desk or too many files to keep track of on your desktop or your memory sticks means trouble.

The best place to save your work is on your university Intranet. Automatic back-ups are made all the time and if you have a disaster you can call on the IT service staff to help you recover your work.

Don't name all your files 'Dissertation' – because you're going to end up lost and confused. A simple system is to save things chapter by chapter and each time you make substantial revisions to your work add a number. When you're happy with your final version, call the version 'Final'. If you have to cut out material or you have some bits and pieces that don't quite seem to slot in, save them and call them 'Extras' or something similar. If you have lots of notes that you need to include in your dissertation, it can be handy to put the notes in separate files so that you can delete as you go (or better still move the notes to named folders). For example, creating a folder for your literature review and putting all the versions of your review into the folder together with any notes or items you want to keep for a bit longer is going to stand you in good stead. Your folder may end up looking something like the following:

Folder – *Literature Review*

File – Lit rev notes: Web

File – Lit rev notes: Library

File – Lit rev notes: Other

Folder – *Literature Review Notes*: (finished)

File – Lit rev: 1

File – Lit rev: 2

File – Lit rev: 3

File – Lit rev: Bibliography

File – Lit rev: Extras

File – Lit rev: Final

 To keep a firm grip on your work, copy your files to more than one memory stick, keeping each memory stick updated with the latest version of your work. This may seem a bit over the top but just think how you're going to feel if your one and only memory stick gets corrupted.

No matter how reliable you think your computer is, print out a hard copy version of your work from time to time. Your tutor or supervisor is going to be far more sympathetic about your computer crashing if you're still able to wave a draft copy under her nose, showing how hard you've been working for all those months.

 Most people find proofreading on paper much easier than trying to proofread on-screen. Give yourself a break by using hard copy for proofreading purposes.

 If you're feeling really paranoid, copy your work to a disk and ask a friend to store the disk on your behalf. You can also email your work to a friend or colleague but make sure that you arrange this with your friend beforehand in case the attachment is big, as you don't want it clogging up your friend's inbox.

Sorting Yourself Out

Go to Chapters 16 and 17 to pick up tips and tactics for staying focused on your dissertation and keeping yourself healthy and happy. In this section I focus on the most common difficulty students experience with a long project – temporary loss of enthusiasm and coming to a halt in writing – and suggest ways of staying calm in a crisis.

Dealing with procrastination and writer's block

Nothing seems worse than having that cursor flashing at you in the top left-hand corner of a blank screen – it almost seems as if the cursor's mocking you! Anyone who's ever written anything substantial (like an essay, for example) knows only too well the difficulty of getting that first paragraph down on the page and then being completely stuck. While I'm writing this chapter I'm sitting in a local café because I simply can't get going at home today. A deadline is looming over me and I need to find a way of motivating myself.

Writer's block is more serious than just having an off-day. When the lack of motivation or inability to get going with your writing lasts for an extended period, you know that it's time to find a solution, fast.

Procrastination takes many different forms. Pretty much everyone puts off doing things from time to time. But you need to face the problem if it's becoming a barrier to getting on with your dissertation.

Looking at some general procrastination behaviours

Here are some of the behaviours that you may find yourself exhibiting when you get writer's block. Looking at this list can help you decide on the seriousness of your situation and take action if needed:

- ✔ **Ignoring the task** – carrying on doing other things (pretending that you aren't procrastinating). You've a nagging feeling that you ought to be getting on with your dissertation, but you've managed somehow to convince yourself that nothing needs doing.

- ✔ **Avoidance behaviour** – finding other things that are suddenly 'urgent' and simply must get done, such as putting on some laundry, cleaning the kitchen floor, polishing your door handles (almost anything to avoid getting on with your writing).

- ✔ **Repeated false starts** – getting started and then stopping; you can't keep up your writing for more than a very short period.

- ✔ **Being openly lazy** – watching TV, listening to music or just reading something for pleasure when you know very well you ought to be working on your dissertation.

> ✔ **Paralysis** – literally doing nothing/staring into space/sitting in one place without moving (not even watching TV or listening to the radio).

Whichever way writer's block manifests itself, you're likely to feel guilty, hopeless and maybe also angry with yourself for being so idle and useless. Don't give in to these feelings as they're only going to make things worse.

Procrastination is a common problem amongst writers, and students don't escape either. Academics especially experience writer's block and your tutor or supervisor is likely to appreciate and understand your frustration.

Understanding your reasons for procrastinating

Your first step in overcoming procrastination is facing up to the reasons why you're avoiding getting on with writing your dissertation. See whether any of the following reasons ring true and if my suggestions for getting going again can help you:

> ✔ **Your dissertation topic wasn't really your choice – you're doing what your supervisor/friend/mum recommended and you're not that interested:**
>
> *If you're at an early stage of your dissertation, think about changing your topic – if you don't, the situation is only going to get worse. If you're at a late stage, you need to stop and review the situation carefully, setting yourself new and practical goals that you know you can achieve.*
>
> ✔ **You're used to doing everything to a high standard and because your dissertation is such a big project and you haven't enough time, you may as well not bother.**
>
> *You're aiming for perfection and this isn't feasible. Face up to what you can actually manage and make plans to help you achieve the best you can within your limits.*
>
> ✔ **You aren't clear what you need to do and so you simply don't know the way forward.**
>
> *You need to review your overall plans for your dissertation with your supervisor, checking that you're on the right lines.*
>
> ✔ **You're afraid that you're not up to the task of writing a dissertation.**
>
> *If you've successfully managed two years of your degree course, completing a dissertation should be well within your capabilities. If you've done less well, you need to talk with your tutor or supervisor to make sure that you're getting all the help you need. With the right support, a hard-working student can overcome the difficulties and successfully complete a dissertation.*

> ✔ **You're scared you're going to be in trouble with your supervisor**.
>
> *Remember that your supervisor is there to help you. A supervisor usually enjoys and is interested in working with students on an in-depth project. What annoys a supervisor varies of course, but generally, giving in your work when you're asked and finishing tasks as arranged isn't going to cause annoyance or anger. It's important that you keep in touch with your supervisor; if your supervisor doesn't know what's going on (or not) she can't help.*

(Only) fooling yourself

Sometimes you tell yourself you've got writer's block when in reality you've quite a different problem. For example, not being able to get down to writing your dissertation may be caused by poor time-management skills and you just need to rethink your plans. Failing to face up to emotional worries causes other (related) problems (see Chapter 17).

Take a look at the different ways people can fool themselves into believing that writing a dissertation is no big deal. Do you recognise any of the following reasoning?

> ❏ I don't think that my dissertation is particularly important so I don't need to work very hard and I'm not bothered about doing that well. I've had reasonable grades after doing all-nighters and I'm sure I can manage to do the same again for my dissertation.
>
> ❏ I know I often underestimate the amount of work I need to do. I think of myself as capable and efficient, but I know that this can't really be true because I'm always rushing to meet deadlines.
>
> ❏ I planned on taking just a 15-minute break, but it's turned into a mammoth TV session and is stopping me from getting on with my work. Fooling myself that I have the time to watch 15 minutes of TV is being unrealistic.
>
> ❏ I've been away for the weekend and I took loads of work with me – books, photocopied articles and other papers. I fully intended to do some reading, but I never got around to it in the end. I suppose that I convinced myself I'd get on with some work when I knew there was no chance.
>
> ❏ There's no point working on my dissertation because I've ages before I need to get going and anyway I can only work when I've got a deadline hanging over me. A deadline is my way of motivating myself.

❑ I know that I have other things to get on with in my dissertation but I just seem to be doing and re-doing the same bit of dissertation. I've persuaded myself that getting a passage right is important when the truth is that I've far too much new work to do than I thought but I'm staying in my comfort zone by fiddling with something familiar. New work seems too daunting.

❑ I've got a lot of reading to get through and until I get at least four more references there's no point in starting writing. I suppose that I'm tricking myself into believing this is the best tactic rather than seeing what I'm doing is using reading as a safety blanket and an excuse for not facing up to what needs to be done.

You can see that most of the reasons being given for not getting down to work are emotional rather than practical. Go to Chapter 17 for some tactics for dealing with the emotional issues and to Chapter 4 for managing your time and to help you in avoiding such difficulties right from the start.

The emotions linked to procrastination vary from person to person, but you're likely to be feeling anxious, guilty and overwhelmed. Everyone can feel disappointed in themselves from time to time and you may be genuinely mystified as to why you just can't get down to the business of writing your dissertation.

 Some people experience a more extreme reaction to procrastination and descend into depression and having feelings of self-loathing. If you're having these feelings, don't ignore them, but arrange to see a counsellor or your GP, who are there to give you any help you need.

Stamping out procrastination

Once you've recognised why you're indulging in work avoidance behaviours, you're well set up to righting the situation.

 Think of a time when you finally managed to get that job done that had been hanging over you like a black cloud. The joy of crossing the job off your to-do list and recalling the feelings of relief, the way you felt lighter and happier (even if only for a short time). That's what you're after recreating; the 'phew!' factor.

Be honest with yourself. If the truth is that you really aren't that bothered about the amount of work required for your dissertation, you just need to decide how much time you're prepared to put in to get your dissertation completed. However, distinguishing between the barriers that are affecting your work and your imagined barriers is important for getting moving on your dissertation once more.

Be realistic about what you need to do to get your dissertation completed and how long you're going to need to get the job done. Avoid spending too long on the parts of your dissertation that you really enjoy and neglecting those aspects that are a bit of a bugbear. Thinking of the 'easy parts' as a kind of reward for getting some of the dreary tasks out of the way can keep you moving forward.

Try keeping your goal in mind at all times while you're working on your dissertation and fix your eye firmly on the finishing post.

Here are some suggestions for dealing with writer's block. (Over the years I've tried them all with varying degrees of success – persistence pays off!):

- ✔ **Read something – anything.** First try reading a text linked to your study and see if it gives you a flash of inspiration. If that's no good, try reading something totally different but well written. It can be the excellence of the writing that lights a spark inside you.

- ✔ **Look at your dissertation or chapter as a whole.** Rather than focusing on the bit that's left you stuck, you can benefit from looking at the bigger picture.

- ✔ **Get up and go somewhere else.** I don't mean upping sticks to a different location. In this instance, I mean just taking a momentary breather. Go and wash your face, or brush your teeth or make a cuppa, or put away the dried dishes or tidy up your shoes from the hallway. Doing something minor or trivial for a short time can help you to get moving again on the real task in hand.

- ✔ **Have a complete break – go to bed early and set your alarm for an early start.** Just switch off and try thinking about anything except your dissertation for a few hours (obviously this isn't going to work if you've only a few days until submission, but can be reviving if you still have a bit more time in the bank).

- ✔ **Just write any old thing that comes into your head – but get writing.** If you're working on your dissertation, try using a different colour or font so that what you're writing stands out. If you simply can't bear to look at your dissertation, try writing something else altogether such as a thank you card or answer some emails – things you've been putting off. After a while, go back to writing your dissertation – you may find that it's the actual writing that's a pain rather than trying to work up your ideas.

Some people, believe it or not, find their creative juices flowing when they're feeling worn out rather than when they're feeling fresh. I'm not going to recommend this as a general tactic for getting down to your writing (partly due to the number of typos that creep into your dissertation and the nonsense you're going to have to correct later). However, working under pressure can sometimes be stimulating, releasing you from the distress of writer's block.

✔ **Go chat with someone.** Someone in your support group is your best choice, but failing that, anyone who's willing to listen! When I'm experiencing writer's block I find myself calling my Mum and chatting about all manner of things totally unconnected with my work – escaping from my own problems – and yes, there's another world out there.

✔ **Have a change of scenery.** This time I mean pack up your work and go somewhere else, a café, the library, a shopping mall with nice seating, a park (if it's fine weather), a museum café – anywhere but where you are now.

✔ **Do some more research on the area of your dissertation where you're stuck.** Even if you don't find anything new, it can be reassuring to discover that you actually do know quite a lot. If facing what's difficult in your dissertation is scary, you may need to go right back to the drawing board and start afresh on the part that's troubling you, before getting back on track with your writing.

✔ **Although this has never worked for me, some people swear by it – pouring out on paper the anguish you're feeling because writer's block can be your cure!** Telling the world what's making you angry and annoyed can be cathartic. And having got all that out of your system you're ready to start anew.

Handling information overload

Dealing successfully with the sheer amount of information coming at you from every direction means having the right tactics up your sleeve to help you cope. Being subjected to an information overload (such as too many emails) and the demands of daily life can overpower you, stopping you from focusing on what's important – writing your dissertation. Added to this, when researching your dissertation topic you're coming up with a massive amount of data that needs sorting and organising. In this section I give you some tips on handling large amounts of information and at the same time keeping sane.

Living in a digital age

So, you've got a huge amount of information that needs organising. (It used to be quite easy to cut yourself off from unwanted information – now, even libraries have moving message boards, video screens and cafés for receiving and sending emails, making it difficult to find a space for quiet study). It's your job to filter out the information that's totally useless and unnecessary.

Disable your wireless connection on your laptop and switch off your mobile phone when you're in the university library. You can always turn your phone and laptop on again after an hour or so, check for urgent messages and then switch off once more.

To stop yourself being overwhelmed by incoming info, try the following:

- ✔ **Limiting your email availability** – by logging off from your computer and leaving your computer switched off for long stretches, only logging on when you need to. When you do go into your email, limit the amount of time you spend reading and answering your messages, and prioritise ruthlessly.

- ✔ **Filtering your ideas** – just letting ideas sink in for a while. Your subconscious is going to be busy mulling over your ideas even while you're sleeping. Those ideas still demanding your attention next day are likely to be the ones most useful to you in your dissertation. Letting ideas simmer is also a good technique for getting your ideas into perspective.

- ✔ **Unplugging your phone** – switching your landline phone off (unless you've dependants who may need to contact you urgently). You can always plug your phone back in when convenient to you and check for messages, so your phone needn't be off all day.

- ✔ **Avoiding the stimulus from the radio, TV or Internet** – watching TV or surfing the Internet means you're going to be bombarded with facts and figures that you can well do without. Try a hot bath or a brisk walk instead.

Too much stuff

In Chapter 6 you can find some useful tips on note-taking and Chapter 7 is great for discovering how to collect and manage data, but even the most conscientious among you is still sometimes going to feel swamped by the amount of information you need to structure and organise.

You need to match what you've collected with what you actually need. Prioritise your tasks by deciding what to do first and what may take you the most time to complete (see Chapters 16 and 17 for help with this). Then you need to be ruthless. Imagine you're going to be shipped to a desert island to complete your work and you're only allowed to take papers (no electronic resources) in a small basket. What are the essentials for getting your work under way? Choose these and put everything else away for the moment. You can always come back to it if you need to amplify your ideas. Do what you can by focusing on the minimum.

Another key thing to remember is to stop collecting new material. Simply stop and work with what you have. The library is still there if you urgently need something additional. You don't need it all before you start writing.

The key tip is to keep focused. Set yourself reasonable, manageable short-term goals, prioritise them above everything else and then you're more likely to actually achieve something daily.

Despite giving you lots of ideas for handling and managing the information overload, I'm now going to urge you to keep an open mind – always being ready to receive and consider new ideas. Pasteur is recorded as saying that 'Fortune or chance favours the prepared mind'. If you close your mind to new ideas, enlightenment may well pass you by – so try keeping focused, and open not closed.

Keeping calm

Try breathing in and out – slowly. Practising breathing is definitely a good way of calming yourself down and helping you stay on track. While you're writing your dissertation it can feel as if you've been holding your breath for months; longing for the moment when you can let out some deep breaths and relax at last.

Feeling fraught is understandable. While you're writing your dissertation you're going to experience moments of tiredness, irritation and even pure panic. But try keeping everything in perspective. Remember, many other people have been through what you're going through and although that doesn't get your work written, it does prove that you're going to come out the other side in one piece and a much better person!

As far as I know, although students have had colds, headaches, repetitive strain injury and sore eyes, no one has given up the ghost as a result of writing a dissertation. Even if your dissertation takes longer than planned, if you follow the advice in this book all is going to come right in the end.

Flick ahead to Chapter 17 for hints and suggestions on keeping yourself emotionally and physically well balanced while you're busy with your dissertation.

Getting Support in a Crisis

Owning up to the fact that life is getting on top of you is an important step towards dealing with pressure. If you're being asked 'Are you sure you're okay?' and you're replying 'I'm fine thanks' to every genuine request about how you are, chances are that no one is going to be aware that you're having difficulties.

Seeking help from your supervisor and university support services

As you're probably in your third year of undergraduate study, you're likely to be familiar with the support services your university has to offer. Of course, you must tell your supervisor that you're having problems, but remember that your supervisor isn't likely to be a trained counsellor. (If it so happens that your supervisor is a trained counsellor, generally it's not such a good idea for her to get involved in your emotional difficulties as well as supervising your work.) Your supervisor is more likely to refer you to the student counselling services that can give you practical help and support.

Most universities have support services dealing with the following:

- ✔ Counselling
- ✔ Medical issues
- ✔ Advice on contraception and sexual concerns
- ✔ Financial concerns
- ✔ Technology courses and support
- ✔ Library help
- ✔ Study skills courses
- ✔ Support for people struggling with their sexual identity
- ✔ Disability services
- ✔ Careers advice
- ✔ Religious guidance

These are professional services and you can easily find the details of each service on the university Intranet.

 If your tutor or supervisor isn't up to date on what support services are available at your university, try asking the administrative staff for details, or even better hot foot it to the Students' Union, which is sure to have all the information you need.

Networking with friends and colleagues

You don't necessarily have to rely on the professionals for support and help. Anyone who is ready and willing to sit and have a chat over a cup of tea or coffee and listen to your hopes and fears is going to be a great help.

If possible, find someone to talk to who understands the sort of problems you're experiencing and who themselves has been through the trauma of writing a dissertation. Try not to bore the person to death though. Your friend or colleague may never have heard of the theorists you're writing about, but she's likely to know what it feels like having too much to do in too little time and how miserable you are because your supervisor is a hard woman!

Try focusing on some positive aspects of your work and while you're getting things off your chest, keeping things in perspective is a must. No matter how awful your questionnaire has turned out, it's not the end of the world. You want your friend to sympathise and have a giggle with you about your little calamity; not get up and shake you.

Having the mutual support of fellow students who are likewise doing dissertations is the ideal support group. If you don't have a support group on your course – set a group up yourself. Ask the administrative staff if you can put up a notice on the office board or even on the Intranet.

Staff aren't allowed to give out personal details of students or staff, so don't ask your tutor or supervisor for other students' phone numbers or email addresses. You can, though, ask your supervisor if she can kindly pass a message on to a student if you know the student's name but have no idea where she's living.

You can run a support group in any number of ways:

- ✔ Formal meetings held in a study room (pre-booked), such as at the university library.

- ✔ Email or phone support where you just contact each other for a friendly chat.

- ✔ Social groups where you meet at someone's house or digs and get on with some work together.

- ✔ Arranging gatherings at a coffee bar or pub (choosing a quiet time of day so you're not disturbing other people and vice versa).

✔ Accidentally bumping into a friend or colleague and having a really useful chat. Don't be afraid of then inviting that person to meet up again and joining another more formal group.

Having a plan for your meetings, especially if you don't know everyone that well can be a good idea. To avoid one person in the group dominating the meeting, give everyone present five minutes to say what they're stuck on in their dissertation at that moment. You can follow this up by asking further questions, with the group working out a strategy to help the person solve their problem.

You may feel that a structured meeting is a bit too formal when you're in a group of people you know quite well – but make sure that you're not wasting valuable group time just chatting about unrelated matters. Even if you don't want a structure, it can be worthwhile agreeing on the length of the meeting and deciding on a theme for your session.

Holding a meeting of your support group in the bar is highly likely to turn into more of a social gathering. This isn't a serious problem in itself – getting together in the pub can even help, but it's not the best way of trying to keep focused on your work.

Part IV
Writing and Polishing Your Work

'So this is your dissertation, Mr. Mafielli – and
you've brought your support team with you.'

In this part...

It's show time. This is the part you want when it comes to getting your material down on paper or on disk. I show you how to grasp the differences between the different sorts of dissertations and the way you need to approach and structure each. These chapters take you through the nitty-gritty of writing up your work and presenting it to maximum effect. I give you the inside track on putting together a comprehensive bibliography and reference list, and there's plenty here too on tone, style, and the intricacies of revising and editing your work.

Chapter 11

Managing Your Argument: Writing Up Your Non-Empirical Dissertation

· ·

In This Chapter

▶ Understanding the key elements of your dissertation

▶ Setting out your ideas

▶ Constructing opposing arguments

▶ Drawing conclusions

· ·

*A*re you a person who enjoys a good argument? Then writing up a non-empirical dissertation is likely to be a rewarding experience. A non-empirical, or theoretical, dissertation doesn't have any data you've generated at all. You won't have interviews, questionnaires or observations to present but you do need to manage the structure and flow of argument effectively so that the conclusion is logical and the finished piece is coherent and clear. In this chapter I run through the key elements you need to write up your work, help you to present a strong argument, and show you how to reach some logical conclusions.

Following the Prescribed Format

In Chapter 3 I explain the structure of the typical dissertation, based on some common musical terms – prelude, main movements, and finale. In this chapter I guide you through the compilation of these key elements. If you feel vague about these aspects of your work, take a look at some theses in the library and read some journal papers to refresh your memory about things such as referencing.

In this section I take you through the key elements of your dissertation. For full details on these parts, I suggest you read this section in tandem with Chapter 3.

Check your university or college regulations. They may have a specific word limit for your prelude items, or particular requirements that you need to fulfil.

Prelude: Title page, acknowledgements and contents

One of the weird things about writing a dissertation is that you write most of the beginning bits after you complete most of the work. You'll see that nearly all these items can only be tackled when you've completed the bulk of your writing. Start a fresh page for each of the items in your prelude.

Title page

The items you need to include on the title page are the ones that identify you as the author (by name or code as demanded), show which course you've been doing and the date you completed your work. You also need to write the title of your dissertation. Some institutions require other information such as your supervisor's name or your student code number and some are very specific about the kind of font style and size that are permitted.

Acknowledgements

Acknowledge the people who helped you complete your work such as family, friends, partners and children. It is courteous to thank your supervisor and can be a nice touch to mention any particular library or support staff who lent a hand on the way. Be sure to show appreciation for any organisation that has been kind enough to offer you financial support.

Although it is undoubtedly a great personal achievement, your dissertation has not passed until it's been marked, so refrain from using grand statements along the lines of 'After this arduous learning journey I can hardly believe that I will be graduating in a week and starting my dream career in the world of shoe production'; this is tempting fate (it's also corny, hackneyed, banal and trite).

Contents page

Although you may know your way around your dissertation, no one else has much of a clue how it all comes together into your perfect whole. You need a detailed and accurate contents page to guide the examiner through your dissertation. Incorporate headings, subheadings and any further sub-subheadings using the same numerical coding as in your text and provide the page numbers for each entry (even when you have more than one entry for the same page). Include the bibliography in your contents list. If you have any additional material such as appendixes, be sure to include them in the table of contents. (See Chapter 15 for more on structuring your dissertation.)

Prelude: Abstract and introduction

Again, start a new page for each of these items and check the required order of presentation and exact word limit as this may differ from course to course. (Also see Chapter 15 for more information on these sections.)

Abstract

Your abstract must be made up of flowing paragraphs and you must adhere to the word limit set out in your course details. Start by restating the overall aims of your project. This is likely to be an extended version of your title. You can then present a little about the context of your work, maybe explaining the background to the study or saying why you think the area is important. You may feel that you don't need to mention anything about research methodologies as you're unlikely to have much to say here, but if very specialist resources were pivotal to your work, you may want to mention these here.

You should lay out your key argument very briefly and state the opposing view, mentioning the names of the main theorists where only one or two are used and they're very significant. If you're arguing for/against a school of thought (such as feminism or post-structuralism), you should mention this, rather than the names of thinkers.

If you have a particular stance that affects the tone of your dissertation, you may want to raise this in the abstract, but if it's very much in the background, don't mislead your reader by emphasising it in the abstract alone.

You need to reveal your conclusion in your abstract. This isn't a novel where the grand denouement is left to the end; you must divulge your final deductions in the abstract.

Your abstract must reflect the content of your dissertation; it isn't an opportunity to mention a few things that you realised you should have covered!

Introduction

The introduction contains similar content to that of your abstract, but it's longer, probably around 300–500 words, but check with your supervisor. Unlike the abstract, the idea is not to summarise everything, but more to stimulate the examiner to want to read further and discover what you think about the research question you've constructed. This is a chance for you to help readers acquaint themselves with your dissertation.

Start by noting the overall aims of your work and say something about the context and background. You can present a few sentences of a rationale, explaining how you came to this topic. Next, sketch out the core ideas that you address and any key counter arguments. If needed, you can talk about the particular approach you've taken. If your dissertation structure warrants a remark, this should be in the introduction, but often non-empirical work is a little shorter and the structure is basically the flow of the argument.

Try and make your dissertation sound exciting and interesting (without exaggerating) and tempt the reader to turn the page.

Main movements: Literature reviews and research methodologies

Because your dissertation is non-empirical, the boundaries between your main argument and a 'literature review' are somewhat blurred. The main purposes of a literature review include:

✔ Demonstrating your understanding of the general field

✔ Explaining your theoretical stance

✔ Contextualising your work

✔ Showing the significance of the area you've chosen to study

As you can see, these issues are different from the main argument you're making in your dissertation and they need to be addressed. You may not, however, need a full chapter that can be described as a literature review, in the way that such a chapter exists in an empirical dissertation. A reasonable solution is to have a short chapter entitled Background or Context.

A similar issue exists concerning research methodologies. For an empirical dissertation, you would be describing the methods you used to collect your data, reviewing the pros and cons and writing a little about your experiences. If your work is all library based, you won't have the same amount to write about in terms of methods, obviously.

You do need to explain your general stance and approach to your reading. If you don't have a separate literature review, explain the types of literature you've been using. Say if you researched in a particular archive example, or if you've relied on specific research tools (such as those described in Chapter 7).

Main movements: Key and counter arguments

Whatever style your dissertation, you must apply logic in building your argument toward a conclusion. In the section 'Presenting Your Arguments' later in this chapter, you can find more detail about inductive and deductive reasoning, but the broader issue is to avoid careless thinking where you surmise inappropriately, paying insufficient heed to logical statements. You're trying to avoid mistakes, which are known as *fallacies* when talking about logic.

An error in reasoning is known as a fallacy. A fallacy differs from a factual error, which is an error about a particular fact.

Finale: conclusions and further research

In this section you need to make your conclusions clear (see the section on 'Coming to a Conclusion' for more details). You should also highlight opportunities for additional research. By doing this, you're aiming to show that as well as providing some conclusions, you're very aware of the additional questions raised by your research. Imagine you're writing a sequel to your dissertation – here are a few questions to ask yourself about carrying out further research:

- ✔ What additional topics could form the basis of an interesting further study?

- ✔ Which issues have you identified that would benefit from more in-depth research?

- ✔ Which aspects of literature do you wish you'd been able to spend more time interrogating?

You don't actually have to write this sequel dissertation, only identify areas of further research.

Some dissertations end with recommendations for a specific audience. You are encouraged to consider this with care – try not to come across as arrogant or as a know-all, but do express any useful ideas that have arisen as a result of your research.

Finale: references and bibliographies

You're likely to have a large number of references throughout the text and you need to take care that these are all very clear. The key to success is careful record-keeping throughout your research. See Chapter 14 for more details.

Laying Out Your Ideas

In this section I offer lots of ideas about constructing your arguments and presenting a logical dissertation. I show you different ways of using quotations and help you see how to decide when to use a quotation and how to check it illustrates the point you're making.

Saying what you think

Degree programmes, fields of study, courses, modules and tutors vary with their attitudes to the use of the personal pronoun (I) in academic work. In some types of research, identifying yourself as a researcher and using 'I' is often absolutely essential, as your personal perspective is central to your argument. In other cases, however, mentioning your own view using 'I' is considered completely wrong.

Regardless of your supervisor's view about the relevance of personal experience and the use of the personal pronoun, your dissertation must present your argument, your research and your views in relation to the research question you've chosen.

You can express your view without using the personal pronoun in a number of ways and to a lesser or greater degree, depending upon the emphasis you want to give to the point you're making. You can, for example, present a positive view of a particular argument through threading quotations together and using language that shows your favourable view.

Ensure that you use the conventions required by your course concerning the personal pronoun and how far you should or should not infuse your personal opinion across your dissertation.

Backing up your opinions with references

References can be used in a variety of different ways for assorted purposes and you should be careful how you refer to different quotations. It would be an error to present somebody's opinion as if it were a fact, for example. To avoid making these mistakes, you need to be absolutely clear about the nature of the quotation or idea before deciding to use it in your work.

Here are some useful questions you can ask yourself about your reading that help you clarify the nature of the evidence and ideas:

- ✔ What is the viewpoint of this writer? Does it detract from his judgement?

- ✔ Is it okay to accept this fact? Would other people agree with this point?

- ✔ What evidence is this writer citing? How can the validity be assessed?

- ✔ Why should I give this author any credence?

- ✔ Is this writer using commonly accepted definitions?

Your use of this writer should be affected by your answers to these key questions. Here are some examples of how this works:

- ✔ **'I was the political Beatle,' says McCartney.** The viewpoint here is likely to be biased in favour of the supporting statement. It is unlikely to be objective since the person making the statement is talking about himself. In this case, McCartney is 'identifying', 'describing', 'postulating' or 'classifying' and any quotation is his perception or assumption (rather than a proven, universally agreed fact). This quotation comes from an article by Gray, S. in *The Independent*, 14 December 2008.

- ✔ **'Even "Harry Potter, the most profitable film franchise in film history" isn't totally secure.'** This statement about the credit squeeze and the success of fantasy films is not a 'fact', but a prediction. You would need to decide if it's okay to accept it and one way is to look at the source – it comes from *The Independent*, 28 December 2008. Consider whether other people would agree with this point and what evidence can support the collective view.

- ✔ **'Michael Jackson's 1982 album "Thriller" is the highest-selling album in the world to date.'** In order to accept this information, you'd need to check the evidence that's being cited. You'd also need to consider the validity of the claim and specify further detail about which measures are being used in this instance. It comes from the Michael Jackson fan site and so it would really need to be verified.

✔ **'Madonna's intentions and impact on Western culture have been even bigger [than the Beatles].'** In this instance, you need to decide whether this author has credence. Do they know what they're talking about? What experience and background do they have in the field? What measures would they be using for making such an assertion? It is from *The Times*, 22 April 2008.

✔ **'*Ulysses*, by James Joyce, is the 20th-century's best novel in English.'** This statement makes use of a commonly used word ('best') that requires clarification. It's undoubtedly true that *Ulysses* is a brilliant novel, but ascribing it the label 'best' requires some very clear criteria. Many avid readers would dispute this choice, which comes from the *New York Times* 100 Best Books in English list (www.nytimes.com/library/books/072098best-novels-list.html), accessed March 2009. Many people, including some literary critics, would want to question the use of the adjective 'best' in this context.

Using quotations effectively

A common error is to sprinkle quotations liberally throughout the text without showing how they link to the points that are being raised. Often this is due to lack of understanding for what is being quoted. Examiners can sometimes read between the lines to discern why a student has quoted as he has, but this is no good; it should be clear how the quotation connects to the student's ideas.

It shows immediately in your writing if you've not understood the quotations you're using. If you don't understand what you're reading, leave it out.

Before you use a quotation, ask yourself these questions:

✔ What is the significance of this quotation to the point I am making?

✔ How does this quotation link to what I've just said?

✔ Why is it relevant to this aspect of my dissertation?

✔ How can I avoid just repeating the quotation when I'm explaining how it connects to my argument?

✔ In what way is this quotation going to enhance the point I'm making?

Presenting Your Arguments

Many different ways exist to argue in a dissertation and what you choose to do depends on your research question, your field, and the available literature, amongst other things. However, some elements are to be expected in all fields regardless of the research question or the literature, and these include logic, coherence, careful use of evidence and clarity.

In a non-empirical dissertation you use desk research and argument to answer your research question. You can approach this task in a variety of ways, for example:

- Reject someone's idea using reason and logic
- Corroborate a particular viewpoint providing new or additional evidence
- Compare two contradictory views and decide which is the most compelling
- Re-evaluate an existing idea, improving it somehow
- Present a new way of understanding something

Differentiating deductive and inductive reasoning

One issue to take into account concerns different types of reasoning. Commonly, you may find guides and support for dissertation writing that discuss *deductive* and *inductive* reasoning and so it's worth getting to grips with what these words mean.

Deductive arguments tend to verify theories and hypotheses. They're more associated with quantitative research and a kind of positivist framework. Often, but not always, deductive thinking moves from the general to the particular, and results in clear statements. A good deductive argument is described as 'valid'.

Deductive arguments can play out in numerous ways and some of those most useful for undergraduate dissertations involve *syllogism*, which is a form of logic. Here's an example of an argument that is trying to show a cause-effect relationship:

> Start with a main idea, or premiss, for your work, in this case
> improved funding for youth work. This leads to a connected idea –
> more facilities can be provided for young people. The effect of
> better facilities is that fewer young people hang around the street
> in the evenings, getting into trouble. With these premisses and

through examining the cause and effect, the next logical move is to the conclusion that increased funding will result in less trouble caused by young people.

Inductive reasoning usually (not always) involves deriving theory from specific examples and because of this, results in statements that are more or less likely to be true, rather than a fixed absolute response. A good inductive argument is strong or 'cogent'. As with deductive reasoning, different ways of arguing are possible. Here are examples of the ones most likely to be used by undergraduates:

- ✓ **Deriving evidence from an expert:** In this case you need to be completely certain that the source of your evidence is authoritative, accurate and valid. 'Professor Brown construes that children in care are less likely than children in families to achieve a university place in the UK. This conclusion is based on several major longitudinal research projects . . .'. (Here's where you cite dates and other details and really get down to the nitty gritty.)

- ✓ **Using relevant examples:** Rather than the single key source noted in the previous example, this form of inductive reasoning relies on building a conclusion from a selection of relevant, valid examples from reliable literature. 'Various studies have clearly demonstrated that university places are more commonly won by students whose parents have degrees.' (Green and Black, 2003; Lilac, 1999; Gray, 2000.)

- ✓ **Cause and effect:** You need to be very careful with cause and effect and be absolutely sure how the connections are made. Has x caused y or has y caused x? Are the connections any more than coincidence?

Some people argue that deductive and inductive reasoning work in a kind of cycle and can't be separated as plainly as others suggest. You can adopt a more nuanced and careful approach to different aspects of logic, but need to be sure that you understand how you're constructing your argument. This requires some research into types of reasoning.

Facing your protagonists head on

There's no point pretending that no disagreements exist. It won't be a strong case if you assert that you agree with someone but provide no evidence that you've thought through potential criticisms and discovered ways they can be rebuffed. The most convincing arguments take into account all aspects of an issue and concede points when necessary.

Each argument should get the same treatment – interrogate the premiss, evidence and problems of all the arguments, as this allows the strongest arguments to emerge.

Some arguments will be more central than others, but all need to be treated reasonably. By this, I mean don't over-criticise the arguments that you dislike and give an easy ride to those you feel you'd like to support. You need to dispense even-handed analysis, but don't shy away from pointing out fallacies.

Criticise, don't denigrate, otherwise you'll weaken your own argument. Garner support genuinely, don't twist people's words to suit your purposes.

Following threads of logic

In building a strong argument, there's no one single absolute correct structure. Whichever route you choose, you must ensure logical links through your argument. In the subsections that follow, I offer some alternative structures for building argument in non-empirical dissertations. These structures include all aspects of the thesis (such as literature review, methodologies and conclusion), so for clarity, the parts that constitute the central argument of your dissertation appear in italics.

Visiting the virtues of alternative arguments

Present the context of your argument; discuss the academic literature; discuss any relevant professional literature; *explain the underpinning assumptions of the main argument; corroborate with relevant academic and professional evidence; present alternative arguments, highlight their deficits and fallacies with reference to relevant academic and professional evidence;* show how the conclusion is inevitable as the main thesis has superior supporting evidence.

Evaluating an existing study

Present context; give rationale for why the study is being evaluated, including the impact of this study on policy and/or practice; present an overview of the literature; explain the evaluative methods to be used, taking into account issues such as validity, reliability, quality of evidence; *evaluate the study, providing support for any criticisms of the study's research design, conclusions and implications; make an overall judgement on the quality of the study including implications and recommendations for improving policy and practice;* conclude by summarising the key themes (without repeating everything).

Critiquing a particular theory

Contextualise this theory within the current field; provide a rationale for evaluating the theory; explain (briefly) any methodologies you may utilise; show the importance of the theory through a review of the literature; *describe the origins, nature and impact of the theory; critique the theory by referencing evidence, examining its validity, consistency and suppositions; compare the inferences made from the theory with those you can now make having identified fallacies in the theory; suggest improvements*; conclude by summarising the key themes (without repeating everything).

Coming to a Conclusion

Your supervisor isn't likely to have a preconceived view about the conclusions he's expecting you to draw. In actual fact, the conclusion itself is less important than showing that you've used the requisite logic, reasoning and evidence in constructing your argument.

In your conclusion, make every effort to ensure that you:

- ✔ Show that your findings are drawn from critical analysis.
- ✔ Demonstrate links to your research question and original aim.

To help you balance different views and present a strong conclusion, try using the following guidelines:

1. Start by restating your research question as this helps you keep your conclusion relevant.

2. Draw together the significant findings of your argument.

3. Place your findings within the context of the literature in your field (without repeating your literature review).

4. Present answers to your research question, without falsely trying to twist your ideas.

5. Be frank about the limitations of your study (both methodological and conceptual).

6. Relate your conclusions to your original aims and objectives.

When you summarise what you've laid out, resist the temptation to merely repeat what you've already said. You can avoid doing this if you focus on the themes of your argument rather than the details.

Chapter 12

Writing Up Your Empirical Dissertation

In This Chapter

▶ Following the prescribed format for the prelude

▶ Getting to grips with the main movements

▶ Making an impressive finale

---

*I*f your dissertation includes data that you've generated yourself – such as questionnaires, interviews or observations – your work is *empirical*. This chapter shows you how to structure the overall piece, from the prelude through to the finale. You should find an empirical dissertation is generally easy to structure – it is logical and tells the story of your project in a straightforward fashion. When writing up your dissertation, you're going to be following a step-by-step approach so that your examiner knows what's coming next and you meet expectations.

Perfecting Your Prelude

In Chapter 3 I introduce you to the structure and main elements of the standard dissertation based on some common musical terms – prelude, main movements, and finale. In this section I give you lots of detail about actually writing these elements. If you haven't already done so, it's a good idea at this point to pay a visit to the library and peruse some dissertations and papers, so you have a clear idea of what you're aiming to achieve. Even though your reader starts at the beginning of your work, you'll probably write the prelude items at the end of your dissertation process. Most of the elements of the prelude can only be attempted once you've completed the greater part of your writing.

You are responsible for finding out about the exact requirements of your university or college when it comes to the specific word count and order. What I present here is, of necessity, general.

Prelude: Title page, acknowledgements and contents

The opening sections of your dissertation set the scene for the weightier arguments and data to come. You'll have to follow a reasonably simple structure and ensure that you include the appropriate bits and pieces the examiner expects to find such as the abstract and introduction. You can find further details of the exact way to present these elements in Chapter 15, but here you can read about the content of each section. You may also find it useful to look at Chapter 11 where I explain these same elements for a dissertation that doesn't have empirical data (that is, a non-empirical dissertation).

Start each of the prelude items on a fresh page.

Title page

On the title page, you usually present your name and course and put the title of your work and the submission date. See Chapter 15 for further information about the layout of the title page, but also check what else is needed for submission at your university. You may be asked to note who has been supervising you, or to give some kind of numerical student code that may be required in place of or in addition to your name. Adhere to any rules you may be given about font style and size.

Acknowledgements

Acknowledge the people who helped you in writing your dissertation: family, friends, partners and children. It's polite also to thank your supervisor and can be a nice touch to mention any particular library or support staff who lent a hand on the way. Be sure of thanking any organisation or body that gave you a grant or a bursary, or any other financial support.

If you want to thank any research subjects, take care not to compromise their anonymity. If you've just spent 10,000 words calling your subjects 'Donald Duck' and 'Minnie Mouse' from the 'Cartoon Academy', don't blow their cover by thanking John Little and Marion Maid from Sherwood Primary School in Robin Drive, Nottingham.

Be grateful, relieved and pleased you've completed, but don't go overboard and portray yourself as a martyr, saint, hero, conqueror or Nobel Prize winner (yet). Be modest without being too humble or obsequious. And never write anything like: 'I have worked so hard and if I get more than 65 per cent I'll have achieved the degree result that my sick grandfather always longed for in our family'.

Contents page

Although the order of many of the elements of a dissertation is pretty fixed, you need a detailed and accurate contents page to guide the examiner through your work. List all the headings, subheadings and any further sub subheadings and be sure that you match any numerical labels for these to your text. Provide the page numbers for each entry (even when you have more than one entry for the same page). You must also have the bibliography and any appendixes catalogued in your contents pages. For more information on what this should look like, see Chapter 15 for further information about the layout.

Prelude: Abstract

Your abstract should be one (or maximum two) paragraphs that don't exceed the word limit you've been prescribed. If none is mentioned, stick to a top limit of 250 words. Begin by reiterating the overall aims of your dissertation, using many of the same words as you have in your title. Next, provide a bit of background as this helps the examiner understand the context of your work. You must now outline your research methodologies. You can also mention here any very significant aspects of these, such as sample size, or the timescale of your work, but only where these aspects are of particular significance; remember that this is a *summary* of the dissertation.

Outline your main findings where these are clear. If you have rather more messy findings (a common issue), just report something like this: 'The investigation of role was not conclusive, as only 20 per cent of the subjects responded to the questionnaire. However, the data presented demonstrate that men are more able to multitask in the kitchen on Wednesdays than on Saturdays and I explore
reasons for this in the data analysis section.'

Note the names of one or two key theorists whose ideas have been helpful in supporting your study. Also declare any dominant standpoint that has deeply affected your work, such as Marxism or pragmatism, as readers need to understand your perspective.

Your abstract should end with a sentence or two about the conclusion. You shouldn't expect your readers to flick to the conclusion pages to find out what your deductions are in relation to your title. This, of course, is why you need to write this part when the dissertation is actually complete. See Chapter 15 for information about the layout of your abstract.

Use the words of your title in summarising the conclusion in your abstract. That way you ensure that the closing statement really links to what you set out to explore. Say for example, your title is something like: 'An exploration of the effectiveness of background music to aid school children's study'. Your conclusion to the abstract could read: 'In this study, I show that the use of specific types of background music can aid the concentration of school children undertaking independent study.'

Prelude: Introduction

Your introduction is similar to your abstract, but with the following two main differences:

- ✔ You don't need to reveal your findings and conclusions in the introduction.
- ✔ The introduction should be longer than the abstract, at around 300–500 words.

Generally what you're doing in your introduction is providing the outline of your dissertation, highlighting the focus of your work (such as the key argument you're making). You should also summarise the methods you've used, but you can save discussion of the pros and cons to the research methods chapter.

I have said (in the bullet point a few lines above this sentence) that you don't need to reveal your findings. This decision is rather up to you and your supervisor. Some feel that the findings are more exciting to read if not previously discussed in your introduction, whilst others think that it's a grave omission to leave them out of the introduction. Check what's expected of you on your course.

Obviously, a direct instruction from your supervisor about length trumps what I say here, but generally, the introduction is a preamble to the core of your dissertation. You need to orient and prepare your reader by raising the aims of your work, saying something about the context and outlining the key issues you address and the approaches you've taken.

See Chapter 15 for further information about the layout of the introduction.

You should also explain a little about the structure and this should be more detailed if you've departed from the traditional layout. You're providing more detail than in your abstract, putting your work into a clear context through showing the overall, big picture of what you've done. Your objective here is to hook the reader into your work, encouraging her to read on.

Getting the Prelude in Order

The order of the prelude items is usually as follows:

1 Title page

2 Acknowledgements

3 Abstract

4 Contents pages

5 Introduction

Managing the Main Movements

Unless you've been given other specific instructions, you should stick to the standard layout of an undergraduate dissertation, which is explained here. You'll start with the literature review and then move onto something about your methods, both of which are explained in this section. Working out whether to split your data presentation and analysis is also quite important and discussed in this section. All these elements constitute the Main Movements of your dissertation. Have a look at Chapter 3 first if you want an overview of these different parts of the dissertation.

Reviewing the literature

The literature review should provide a conceptual framework for your dissertation. Of all the aspects of the dissertation, the literature review is probably closest in style to previous essays you've written on your undergraduate course. In an empirical study, your literature review is an essential explanation of the trends and developments in your field as they relate to your research question. You're aiming to demonstrate your awareness of the diversity of literature that relates to your research question through an understanding of the central relevant theories, studies and methodologies.

One way of thinking about the literature review is to consider it as a clear, detailed, substantial essay. Ensure that your literature review is more than just a list or summary of work that you think may be relevant. Try to do the following:

- ✔ Show the links between different theorists
- ✔ Emphasise how the literature informs your research

✓ Demonstrate where theorists concur

✓ Illustrate instances of effective criticism of theorists

✓ Conclude by showing how your research fits into your field

Structure your literature review carefully. The most effective composition usually starts with a broad overview and narrows your focus until you reach your research question. Chapter 13 helps you with the tone and style of your literature review as well as providing tips about different stages of drafting your work.

Some students find it very useful to use sub-headings as they write their literature review but then delete these headings for the final version. If you like this idea, perhaps have a go with these four headings:

✓ **Background to the topic:** Discerning the trends; setting the scene; explaining some of the wider issues; starting with the past and moving up to date; explaining accepted conventions.

✓ **Key issues in the field:** Raising the key issues saying who discusses them in your field; picking out the main points as presented by the leaders of your field; showing the central ideas that generally arise in your field; citing evidence from literature to support these main contentions.

✓ **Other (less central) issues:** Presenting particular viewpoints that support or illustrate the central ideas; mentioning other key thinkers or ideas that relate to the key ideas; mentioning evidence from literature to support these peripheral or related contentions.

✓ **Conclusion:** Don't just reiterate everything you said in your literature review, but try, instead, to summarise the main themes, showing how they connect to your research question.

In order to help you write your literature review, follow some of the suggestions:

✓ Look at good models in other dissertations and journal articles.

✓ Structure your literature review with a clear purpose, perhaps thematically, chronologically or by argument.

✓ Think of your literature review as an ongoing project, adding in, revising, moving or deleting things as you go along.

✓ Ask for your supervisor's help – submit a draft and be prepared to redraft your work.

Here's a sample of writing showing a bad approach to a literature review on using museums and galleries for children's learning:

> Hein is the main theorist and I've looked at his work. It shows that museums and galleries are important, in terms of learning for children. Different theorists might have different ideas about this and in psychology of education writing they have put across different views of what learning is. Some of these theorists are Piaget, Vygotsky and Gardner for example. Constructivist educationists who have written about learning will be important for this research. Various approaches to two museum and gallery education will be used. Concerns about learning in museums and galleries will be significant and relevant.

Now here's a sample of writing showing a much better approach to the same thing:

> This study draws on diverse approaches to museum and gallery education, taking Hein's work as central. Within the field of cognitive psychology, constructivist notions have shown that engaging children in learning is easier within a positive social context. Clear definitions of learning in gallery and museum contexts will be explored and these will be informed by wider literature including the work of Hooper-Greenhill and Dierk and Falking.

> The recent history of education in museums and galleries will be considered in order to explain current policies and understandings. The contemporary context will help to highlight the barriers and challenges to effective provision. Museum policy is an important part of this study, but the focus will be on issues surrounding learning, rather than financial restraint, in order to explore this issue in some depth.

 A literature review must be more than a summary of different reading. You need to show the examiner that you've been reading critically and that you've properly grasped what you've read.

Regarding research methods and methodologies

Hang on, aren't research methods and methodologies the same thing? Not quite – your collection of data constitutes the 'methods' of your dissertation, and the 'methodologies' are the broader issues surrounding your research in general. You need to consider both aspects in your chapter. It's as much about the reasons and rationale as it is about the specific methods you've selected.

Although I distinguish here between methods and methodologies, call your chapter whatever your supervisor recommends.

In many ways, the chapter 'writes itself' since you're basically describing:

- ✔ What you did
- ✔ Why you did it that way
- ✔ Who you did it with
- ✔ Where and when you did it
- ✔ Why you chose to do it the way you did

In most cases, it's a good idea to start with the general and move to the particular. This means opening with some explanation of the perspective you're taking and your point of view about your question.

In Chapter 2, I explain something of the different stances you can adopt. These different stances are important as they link to the methods you then adopt to address your question.

Skinning a cat

Over two consecutive years I had two students doing very similar research questions, but due to their distinct stances, the work came out very differently and incorporated diverse methods. Both students were interested in the experience of twins when they started schooling. One student felt that in order to support children starting school it would be useful to collate as many experiences as possible, and the other student was keener on looking at only one case, but doing this very fully.

The first student used a questionnaire to survey all the local schools, asking about the number of twins and their policies about keeping them together or separating them (where possible) as they joined school. The other student spent time with one pair of children (non-participant observations) and conducted interviews with their teachers and parents. The data was different; the first was largely quantitative with some anecdotal illustrative exemplar, whilst the case study generated detailed qualitative information.

These diverse studies stemmed from different stances on the same question.

As part of the research methodologies chapter, you need to evaluate the different methods showing the positive and negative aspects of those that you've chosen, and explaining your reasons for those you've rejected. Each field in social science has its own key text evaluating the range of research methods commonly used in that area. Your dissertation support materials from your course should have the key texts listed in your bibliography. Make use of these, as they've been recommended by your course tutors.

In the research methodology, consider general pluses and minuses of different styles of collecting data. In your data collection chapter, you can go into details of your actual experience.

 When exploring the pros and cons of different research methods, take care not to overlap with your discussion of your own experiences of the data collection (which comes in the data section of course).

Dealing with data collection and analysis

In Chapters 8 and 9 I cover collecting and analysing your data. In this section I deal with writing up your data and your various options for approaching this task: should you keep the collection and analysis clear and separate or try and integrate them into one flowing chapter? My advice to students has always been based on two main factors:

- ✔ **The nature of the data**: Whether they're expansive or narrow and whether they fit clearly into themes or are more disparate. Some data are so dense, or diverse, that they need lots of explanations all the way through, whereas other data can stand alone rather better.

- ✔ **The quality of the student's writing:** That is, whether you can craft your writing very skilfully or if you have difficulties. If your writing is predominantly clear and succinct, you'll find it easier to manage complex explanations than if your writing is more laboured and harder to understand.

Often, the nature of the data dictates whether there should be separate chapters for presentation of results and analysis or if the collected data should be displayed in the same chapter as the analysis, in a more integrated fashion.

It's generally a little easier to write two separate chapters, although the presentation of data can be wearisome to read if it's merely descriptive. A way to avoid irritating your examiner is to keep this chapter short, clear and self-explanatory. You can then get stuck into your analysis in the following chapter which can be a little longer. In this instance I would suggest titles something like these:

- ✔ 'Data Collection', or 'Presentation of Data', or merely 'Data'.
- ✔ 'Data Analysis', or 'Analysis of Results', and so on.

In this instance, the first chapter should include any tables, pie charts, graphs, diagrams and models, as well as sample responses from questionnaires and summaries from observations.

If you're an adept writer and able to weave your analysis into your discussion of what you found, an integrated chapter is a more effective way of writing as it negates the necessity of flicking back and forth and it avoids excessively descriptive passages.

If you find writing problematic, I highly recommend that you write one chapter for the presentation of data and a second chapter for data analysis. This is a perfectly acceptable way to structure your work and requires less 'crafting'.

Inserting images, tables and other extras

Images, models and diagrams can be extremely useful at portraying your data in a brief, neat and impactful manner. You can make use of pie charts, graphs or tables to summarise ideas and findings. In Chapter 9, on Data Analysis, a section is devoted to displaying your data using visual methods.

Usually students aren't expected to create visual representations of their data unless it really enhances what has been found. Social science makes use of a great many different methods of presenting ideas and data so you wouldn't be able to cram them all in to a dissertation anyway.

Only bother with models, charts, tables and images when they actually have something to say. They shouldn't be used in a dissertation to provide decoration, they need to add something to the value of the text.

For example, if you have some stark data showing differences in opinion or behaviour, this can look great in a bar chart. What you'd have is a presentation of contrasting findings next to one another so the reader can see at a glance that you discovered something showing different ideas or actions. In this case you should use the chart.

If your data are more subtle, however, your graph would look pretty wishy-washy and you'd be better with some interesting analysis of language for example, which can't be as well presented visually.

A word about models: social science uses a great many models to show the relationship between different ideas and processes. By all means use the published ones you find in your literature searches, but don't spend ages creating your own (unless your supervisor has advised you to do so). Models look easy to make, but are actually very complex to create; as soon as you think that you've covered everything, something new pops up that you didn't think of, so take care if you're trying to make a model.

When using any kind of images, take great care that you have ethical and copyright clearance for what you're presenting.

Formatting the Finale

In this last section of your dissertation the most important aspect is probably the conclusion, but this finale contains many other parts so be sure to leave yourself sufficient time to complete this section effectively.

Considering your conclusions and further research

Your conclusion will probably fall into two parts: the conclusions that link strictly to your data; and those that are more general, relating to your aims and objectives. Both aspects of your conclusion need to be combined in order to fully answer your research question. (For more detail about how to draw a clear conclusion, see Chapter 11 and for ideas on building your conclusion from analysing your data, take a look at Chapter 9.)

As well as drawing conclusions from your data, you should make such suggestions for recommendations or implications for practice that have arisen from your work. You have a choice about how best to present your suggestions. You can divide them up into recommendations for your own development and further research, and those ideas that would most affect your subjects. You can look at the additional questions that your dissertation has raised, perhaps providing directions for others to take up in the future.

Your project may be small scale but, assuming you've done a good job, your conclusions are valid and should be of interest to the people with whom you've been involved.

Referencing and building a bibliography

Chapter 14 deals with this in detail. Remember, however, that throughout your dissertation you should be referring to theory and evidence; it's not confined to your literature review. For example, in your research methodologies chapter, you need to reference the recommended texts for your field to help support your choices for different methods and use the main theorists to back up your theoretical view.

Presenting your data is less reliant on other theory since you're describing what you did – the links come when you're analysing your results.

Be very clear about how to reference in the text and how to present your bibliography as required by your course guidelines.

Adding appendixes

In Chapter 15 I give you lots of info about managing your appendixes and also mention what to put in your appendixes in Chapter 9. At this point, however, it's worth thinking about which aspects of your data, analysis and theory can interrupt the flow of your work and would be better placed as a reference at the end of your dissertation.

These are the kinds of materials that examiners would generally expect to see in an appendix:

- Any ethical clearance or letters requesting permission for you to undertake your research
- A copy of any questionnaire or interview schedule
- Examples of responses to questionnaires
- Additional material from observations or questionnaires that serves to amplify samples from your main text
- Background information about any institution you may be examining
- Theoretical models that you've mentioned on more than one occasion, but which don't really fit in the main flow of your discussion
- Pictures that explain something about your dissertation
- Portions of transcriptions that serve to illustrate some of your key points

Chapter 13

Writing Effectively

- -

In This Chapter

▶ Reviewing your own writing style

▶ Ensuring your writing meets the required standards

▶ Revising and editing

- -

*N*o matter how fantastic your questions and your research, if your writing is lumpy and unclear and your ideas come over as thin and wishy-washy you can forget about getting a great grade. Throughout your dissertation you need to show off your best writing and this is particularly important when you get to the end. Often students make the mistake of merely repeating everything in their conclusion – do your best to avoid this common error!

Pretty much everyone can improve their writing. Authors and academics use handbooks and style guides and ask colleagues to read through their work. You may not have a specific problem, but you can still benefit from this chapter.

This chapter doesn't go through the nitty-gritty of each grammatical aspect of writing, nor does it show you spelling and punctuation tips. If you need these, get yourself a guide to writing in the English language.

Improving Your Writing

The information in this chapter should help you tackle issues concerning the quality of your writing but you first need to be clear about what you're aiming to produce.

Your academic discipline may have some conventions that differ from other fields. Some disciplines even vary within themselves, so you must be sure that you meet the expectations for your area.

The two best practical ways to improve your writing are [1] reading good authors and [2] doing a lot of writing yourself.

Looking at dissertation writing styles

Your dissertation writing style is just the same as most of your essays. However, essays and dissertations need to conform to some academic conventions that are worth reiterating and keeping in mind:

- ✔ The audience for academic writing is academics (!). Therefore, the best model of such scholarly writing is that of other scholars.

- ✔ You're expected to provide informed argument (this includes what is known about a topic, presented in a balanced way and also your view on the subject, supported by logical argument).

- ✔ Unless you've been asked for a specifically personal paper (not typical for a dissertation), your paper is almost certainly required to be much more than an individual response – it must incorporate evidence.

- ✔ You're supposed to be providing illumination or bringing something useful to an argument or discussion.

- ✔ You're expected to conform to the conventions of an academic style (correct grammar, non-colloquial language, references and citations).

What's different about a dissertation is that you need to sustain these things throughout the whole project. You'll also find slight shifts in style depending on different parts of your thesis. For example, when working on your conclusion, you need to be much more succinct than when you're writing the literature review. Similarly, you'll adopt a rather descriptive style when presenting results but it'll be more critical for the analysis. Throughout, however, you need to keep up the points raised in the above list.

Visit some websites to help you get a feel for university-level writing, if you'd like some examples and exercises. A couple of good ones are Dr Jay's 'Write' Home Page (www.csun. edu/~vcecn006/) and the Learning and Teaching Institute at Sheffield Hallam University (http://universitywriting.shu. ac.uk/good/intro.htm).

Your examiner wants to mark your research, not your grammar. Most university tutors expect that you've already mastered grammar and that you've come to university as a reasonable writer, so only submit work after you've checked it carefully.

Tutors expect your writing to be correct. Some tutors mark the grammatical errors in your work, but others won't, so don't assume that no markings means you've turned in a perfect paper.

Knowing your writing strengths and weaknesses

It's feasible to improve your writing but you first need to identify what should be changed and what is perfectly acceptable. The amount of coursework that remains uncollected by students at my university is quite shocking. Many students forget, some can't work out where to collect it from (despite the many signs and information we provide) but lots just can't be bothered. Unfortunately these tend to be the students who could most do with the comments tutors have provided.

So, the first step to improving your writing is to read the comments on previous coursework. If you can't decipher what's written, get back to that tutor and make an appointment to go over what he said about your work. Even busy lecturers are willing to help out students genuinely trying to advance their work.

Take note of the comments, especially when the same points have been made by different tutors. Find out how to rectify your errors using some of the methods in this chapter.

Using the wrong words

It's a very bad idea to use language you don't fully understand. Make use of a dictionary and specialist glossaries or encyclopaedia. Most reasonable textbooks have a lexicon included or a section devoted to explaining key terms.

It's very clear when a student doesn't understand a word they're using. Often the word is used in the wrong place or is just inappropriate, like these actual phrases from student essays (the mistake is underlined and I have included what I think the student meant to say):

- ✔ This shows how the teacher can <u>ameliorate</u> children more clearly. *This shows more clearly how the teacher can help children improve.*

- ✔ It's a good example of <u>ensuing</u> the curriculum. *It's a good example of following the curriculum.*

- ✔ The museum visitors were <u>subordinating</u> at the exhibit. *The museum visitors were examining the exhibit.*

- ✔ I think that White makes a good point that I concord with my alignment of ideas. (Not sure what to emphasise as it doesn't make any sense at all!) *I find that I agree with the point that White makes.*

- ✔ No teacher would <u>obscure with</u> a group who has disabilities. *No teacher would ignore a group who has disabilities.*

I've no doubt that the students had heard and used these words before, but it's glaringly obvious that they haven't understood their meanings. Just like my colleagues, although I'd really like students to extend their vocabulary, when it comes to assessments, I feel people should stick to what they really understand.

Attempting to suddenly incorporate a whole new vocabulary generally makes people sound at best bewildered, and at worst pompous and rather silly.

If in doubt, leave it out.

Avoiding typical mistakes

As well as the incorrect use of words, common weaknesses in student writing include the following (with correct forms also shown):

- ✔ Incorrect preposition:
  - I'm bored of reading that galleries are different to museums. *I'm bored with reading that galleries are different to museums.*

- ✔ Shift in tenses:
  - I was observing the group and I hear the argument start. *I was observing the group and I heard the argument start.*
  - When he saw the outline of the course, he want to register. *When he saw the outline of the course, he wanted to register.*

- ✔ Missing capital letters:
  - The english legal system is well developed. *The English legal system is well developed.*
  - Philosophy would be poorer without kant. *Philosophy would be poorer without Kant.*

- ✔ Indistinct reference to pronoun:
  - The boys spoke to one another and he recognised the solution. *The boys spoke to one another and they recognised the solution. Or, The boys spoke to one another and one of them recognised the solution.*

✔ Missing commas (or 'and's):

- The research project shows children teachers and parents were upset. *The research project shows children, teachers and parents were upset.*

- Socrates was a Greek philosopher his ideas are influential today. *Socrates was a Greek philosopher and his ideas are influential today.*

✔ Wrong form of verb (usually from a dialect):

- I was sat at my desk / I lay on my bed. *I was sitting / I was lying.*

✔ Pronoun disagreement:

- A visitor to the workshop is encouraged to show what they make. *Visitors to the workshop are encouraged to show what they make. Or, A visitor to the workshop is encouraged to show what s/he makes.*

- Everybody can choose their favourite tune. *Everybody can choose his or her favourite tune.*

✔ Subject–verb disagreement:

- She spent a while looking and were obviously interested. *She spent a while looking and was obviously interested.*

- The data is useful. The media was to blame. *The data were useful. The media were to blame.*

✔ Incomplete sentence/sentence fragment:

- Which the manager did not provide. *Something missing at the start of the sentence – whatever it was that the manager didn't provide: Which the manager did not provide.*

- Government sources have stated . . . *Government sources have stated. Have stated what? Something missing at the end of the sentence.*

✔ Misuse of apostrophes:

- She watered it's roots thoroughly. *No apostrophe required for possessive words.' It's' is only used for the contraction of 'it is'. It should read: its roots . . .*

- In the 60's fashion became more accessible. *No possessive required here but does need the apostrophe to indicate the missing '19'. It should read: In the '60s . . .*

✔ Run-on sentences:

- In my essay I will explain how the theories of child development from the behaviourist schools of the 1950s still resonate today when you look at the context of day care and schooling where such ideas as attachment are still valid although they have changed over the years to reflect the development of society shown through the shifting role of men in caring for example.

In my essay I will explain how the theories of child development from the behaviourist schools of the 1950s still resonate today. When you look at the context of day care and schooling, ideas such as attachment are still valid. They have changed over the years to reflect the development of society, shown through the shifting role of men in caring, for example.

This list is not exhaustive – not by any means. I've included it so you can take a look and assess your own writing. If you can't see the errors, you need to seek some help with your writing.

See the University of Wales, Cardiff site on Writing Good English for a useful grammar guide (www.uwic.ac.uk/ltsu/u_area/ studyskills/unit08.html).

Auditing your writing

Using the lists in the sections above can help you review your own writing and decide what sort of changes you need to make. If you (and your tutor) can only find one or two of the errors from above and they're clearly the result of being hurried or a bit sloppy, it's not a serious concern. What you need to guarantee is that you leave yourself generous time for proofreading.

If, however, you're making many of the errors and/or your mistakes are liberally scattered across your writing, you need to address this more urgently and thoroughly. You need to understand the rules of grammar that you're breaking.

Often, people use grammar correctly by intuition, but where errors are found, they need to be put right through understanding and explanation. You can't rely on instinct in this instance as you'll wind up repeating your mistakes.

It may feel like a steep mountain to climb if you've a number of issues to address; so start by prioritising your mistakes. (Get help with your prioritisation if you find this hard to do by yourself.) The errors that change the meaning of your writing are the most serious. If you're using words you don't fully understand, stop using them or find out what they mean and use them correctly.

A good way to evaluate your writing is to run a readability test, which is a simple procedure that's normally found in your software. The most commonly found are the Flesch Reading Ease test and the Flesch–Kincaid Grade Level test. Either would be useful as they both examine word length and sentence length that are common areas of concern. In terms of student writing, having a poor score generally indicates that the writer has used phrases that he doesn't fully understand or that he has constructed sentences weakly.

What constitutes a good score on a readability test depends on which one you're running, but the Flesch-Kincaid has a score from 1–100 and you should generally aim for a high result if you want more readable work.

Readability tests aren't a perfect way to establish the quality of your writing, but they highlight some factors, such as where your work is laden with jargon, or where your sentences are far too long.

Having someone to help audit your work is going to be really helpful, but it's worth having a go at spotting your own errors before handing it over to someone else. That way you gain more out of their support and won't waste time going over what you already know but just forgot to correct.

Seeking support for your writing

Every university has different systems for supporting students, but many have a central support service that's available to all undergraduate and postgraduate students. These services normally run courses on improving your writing and may have workshops or seminars during which you may have your writing style diagnosed by a professional.

If you're lucky, your own degree course team includes support staff dedicated to helping students on your course alone. In these cases, the support is specialised and the people helping you should have particular knowledge of the field and area in which you're working. As early as possible, find out what kind of support is available for you and what kind of timescale support staff require in order to help you.

If you need particular support due to a learning difficulty or because English is not your dominant language, such provision should be clearly advertised wherever student services are based.

Writing circles are a great idea. You get together with other students and share sections of your writing, giving each other feedback. You're all in it together and you've several heads working on the same problem (five is probably the optimum number). It works best if you know a little about each other's topic, but not too much.

Your supervisor's advice usually trumps 'help' books (including this one) and your friends' pearls of wisdom. Your university probably publishes writing support materials that you can access for free. They're probably available both online and on paper.

The student guide market is buoyant with loads of different books to choose from, all of which seem to be offering useful advice and ideas. Don't just buy anything over the Internet with a title you fancy. Try and check what the book covers and flick through it to see if the writing style and layout appear helpful or annoying.

Consulting friends about writing issues is a strategy that can meet with mixed results. The quality of advice depends on the nature of your relationship and the level of knowledge and expertise of those you consult. Don't accept what your friends say about grammar as always accurate. Just because your friend is absolutely certain that every word that ends in the letter 's' needs an apostrophe, doesn't mean that your friend is right.

Using your computer effectively

Some students, by saving up, or through luck, decide that a new computer will be a great help for them when writing a dissertation. If you can afford a state-of-the-art machine, so much the better. It's a bad idea though to buy a brand new computer just as you're getting started with your writing. Managing your dissertation as well as learning how to use new keyboards, word processing software, printers, and so on, is going to overload you when you're already pretty stressed.

The most important thing is to understand how your computer works and to make the best use of it possible. It's worth getting a 'health check' for your computer and checking that you have the requisite storage facilities (such as compatible memory sticks, floppy disks, CDs) so that you can hit the ground running.

Despite the prices of computers crashing down over recent years, many students don't have access to a computer at home. This can be inconvenient, but it's not a disaster. Most universities have 24-hour access computer suites and on-site technical support services. Just make sure that you have access to the facilities.

Avail yourself of courses that can help you find out how to use software. These courses are usually free at university since they're heavily subsidised but can be very costly in the 'outside world'.

Dealing with dyslexia

Having dyslexia (or a similar problem such as dyspraxia or a general difficulty with processing information or writing) should not prevent you from writing a great dissertation. It's likely to make it more important that you focus on the mechanics of writing your work clearly and that you have enough time to review and rewrite as necessary. Be realistic and build strategies for coping with your particular learning difficulties.

By their third year of study, most students are quite clear about their strengths and weaknesses in terms of writing, reading and studying in general. Some may have managed to get through their entire schooling without anyone picking up on their dyslexic-type problems, however. It's not uncommon to be diagnosed with a reading or writing problem as late as the second year of your degree course. If you happen to be such a student, you're likely to understand the problems that having dyslexia brings and know about building up strategies for managing your dyslexia, as well as coping with the emotional side of the condition.

In Chapter 17 I help you think about strategies for practical tips on identifying your difficulties and seeking appropriate support. Importantly, see your supervisor and student support services sooner rather than later.

A really useful study skills website with loads of writing tips is available on the Middlesex University web pages. The website is very well designed for people who learn best with colours and different types of layout, rather than just linear expression of ideas. You can find it at www.mdx.ac.uk/WWW/STUDY/Glossary.htm.

Saying What You Want to Say – Succinctly

Clear writing is to make your sentences a reasonable length and to construct your paragraphs effectively (as well as using the correct words, of course).

Although sentence length isn't an exact science and varies according to topic and context, a useful rule of thumb in academic writing is to try for no less than 12 words and never more than 40.

Students who submit weaker papers tend to overlook paragraphs. They frequently make the common error of putting too many points in each paragraph. Sometimes, students ignore them completely by treating each sentence as a separate paragraph, or (more daunting to read) by writing continuous prose with no delineation of paragraphs on a page.

The characteristics of a good paragraph are:

✔ Making one clear point, supported by evidence

✔ Relevant to the argument

✔ Being made up of linked sentences of reasonable length

✔ Usefully developing the argument

✔ Grammatical perfection

✔ Concise and to the point;

✔ Being in the right place (to contribute to a coherent, logical argument)

✔ Connecting to both previous and following paragraphs

✔ A reasonable length

The appropriate length is determined by the subject and discussion. When you introduce a new idea or change the focal point, you need a new paragraph. Normally, a paragraph is more than two sentences long. Avoid very long paragraphs or more than 15 sentences (although you need to use your judgement, as the length of the sentence is also relevant).

Each paragraph should be a clear exposition of the main point. Start the paragraph with this exposition and then develop your idea. Once you've done this (in a couple of sentences) go on to provide quotations or exemplar to support the idea.

When you're providing a kind of 'compare and contrast' paragraph, use linking words such as:

✔ Although

✔ However

✔ Alternatively

✔ But

✔ Yet

When you're trying to use examples to support an idea, you should use words like:

- ✔ For example
- ✔ In addition
- ✔ Similarly
- ✔ To illustrate
- ✔ Moreover

The opening and closing paragraphs may depart from some of these suggestions, for the obvious reasons that you're introducing or concluding rather than developing your argument.

Concentrating on your conclusion

Your conclusion needs particular attention and is often one of the weakest aspects of student writing. A reasonable argument can be undermined by a poorly concluded paper. It should be a coherent follow-on from your earlier writing and should summarise neatly whilst avoiding repetition. Summarising differs from repetition. A decent précis or summary draws out key points from the passage without going over all the same ground.

So, whilst you may have an element of summary, this must be brief and only a minor aspect of your conclusion. Anything that you've noted earlier in your dissertation should now be modified or affected by your research in which you've shed new light on a previously stated concern. An example of this is to reconsider any of your earlier definitions of key concepts, highlighting developments you've made.

One useful way to start your conclusion is to use the title or research question. If, for example, your title concerns an investigation into the relationship between the form and function of public architecture, start your conclusion: 'As a result of investigating form and function in public architecture, it is apparent that . . .'. Even if you don't keep this introductory sentence in the final draft, it helps you ensure that your conclusion is relevant and does actually conclude your work.

Another tactic is to use a fitting and apposite quotation or example, but don't let this veer off the topic or be too lengthy.

Words like 'therefore', 'thus', 'finally', 'in conclusion' are likely to surface in your conclusion. They signal the ending to your reader.

Make your conclusion pithy and memorable. You need to be punchy and succinct, leaving an impact on the examiner without going over the top.

Tackling Tone and Style

Expressing ideas can be done in many different ways and you need to ensure that you use the right tone for an academic project. Aim for an authoritative voice that demonstrates your conviction that what you're saying is valid and relevant. This should be tempered with some acceptance that you're open to discussion and persuasive argument, rather than writing as if no one can ever change your mind. It's appropriate to be swayed by well-evidenced facts and information and if you present your ideas as incontrovertible, you could give out an impression of stubborn arrogance.

Getting straight to the point

Academics marking your work can recognise waffle when they read it and they know when you're using elaborate words and phrases for the sake of it, rather than to enhance meaning. Eliminate extraneous words such as:

> In ~~his book~~ 'Das Kapital' ~~Karl~~ Marx states . . .
>
> In my opinion, ~~it seems to me that~~ the best . . .
>
> It is ~~a~~ valuable ~~background~~ to have ~~a little~~ experience of . . .

Avoid waffle and irrelevancies. Say what you need to say and then stop.

Cutting out colloquialisms

When you speak up in a seminar or supervision, your tutor expects you to use casual, everyday language, but in an essay, more formal language is mandatory. In Table 13-1 I show some corrections I've made in a recent batch of student essays.

Table 13-1	Colloquial and Formal Language
Student's Colloquial Wording	*Replaced with Formal Wording*
kids	children
a fab workshop	an enjoyable workshop
the kids went ballisitic	the children lost control

Student's Colloquial Wording	Replaced with Formal Wording
way over the top	extreme reaction
a rubbish argument	a flawed argument
not sure what it's on about	it was unclear

You can leave informal language in place if you're quoting from something like your focus group. Don't alter someone else's words.

For clarity, don't be vague or too general, try and provide specific data. These sentences are annoyingly imprecise:

- ✔ The National Curriculum was introduced a while back now . . .
- ✔ In recent years it's changed a great deal . . .
- ✔ It's generally thought that . . .
- ✔ Most nurses think that . . .
- ✔ It was the government of the day who thought up the idea of . . .

Your aim is to meet the word requirement without lots of 'padding'. Students often have the impression that producing more words is better than fewer and that academic writing should be wordy and fussy. Whilst academic language is specific to the field and meanings can be different from common usage, overuse of jargon and technical terms interrupts the flow of a dissertation and should be avoided.

Using quotations to excellent effect

Just because you've painstakingly typed out some quotations that you really like the sound of doesn't mean you must put them all into your work. Only use quotations when they illustrate a point or elucidate an idea, not just to bump up your word count. Some suggestions for effective usage include the following:

- ✔ Limit the number of quotations you use – don't sacrifice your own voice to produce a list of other people's views.
- ✔ Be certain the quotations link to the point you're making.
- ✔ Don't ever use a quotation you don't understand.
- ✔ Before and after the quotation, don't preempt or repeat the quotation, just let it speak for itself.
- ✔ Always reference fully and correctly (see Chapter 14).

Aiming for assertiveness, not arrogance

Whilst your tutor is interested in your viewpoint, he's also aware of other people's views on the topic you're discussing. Many of the other ideas they've studied come from rigorously undertaken research, evaluated by the academic community. Your ideas may be just as remarkable, but for now they lack the support of established research and as such have less currency.

This doesn't make them less valid, merely less tested. You need to recognise this and without false humility you should show awareness of the limitations of your work. To meet this requirement you need to express your ideas clearly and assertively without being overconfident.

A long-dead theorist doesn't agree with your views; you agree with his. Don't therefore say 'Plato backs me up when I think . . .' as you're wrong. In actual fact, what you mean is: 'My understanding of this concept is based on Plato's work . . .'.

Examiners hope to read concise and persuasive writing. They can spot occasions when you've used language you don't really understand in order to try and impress.

One way that scholarly writing differs from other writing styles such as journalism is that academics are typically wary of making too many bold statements without qualifying what's been said with evidence and support. That's not to say that scholars are nervous about expressing their views, on the contrary this is what they tend to enjoy. The difference is that they recognise that there may be caveats or qualifications to make to ensure that people fully understand what they're expressing.

In journalistic writing you find sentences that state 'All people think *x*' or 'It's a fact that *y*', whereas academic writing is characterised by phrases more like these:

- ✔ Evidence shows that
- ✔ Research suggests
- ✔ Generally, it is thought that
- ✔ Many advocates of *x* consider
- ✔ Not all findings support this, but
- ✔ Some data verify
- ✔ In some instances

You can express your thoughts about an idea together with any reservations. This comes across as thoughtful and shows awareness of contradictory ideas or cases with limited support.

Being tentative because of a balanced, thoughtful appraisal of evidence isn't the same as being weak or vague.

For more in-depth help on tone and style, see Explore Writing at www.explorewriting.co.uk/UseOfAppropriateTone.html, and also 'Get Ready for University Study' from Edinburgh Napier University: www2.napier.ac.uk/getready/writing_presenting/style.html.

Revising and Editing Your Work

Revising your work is a central part of the process of writing. Your dissertation will emerge in blocks of writing and passages of drafted and redrafted text as you go along, probably not in the order you intend them to be read. Different levels of redrafting and editing exist and you're better off if you know the difference between them and then apply them appropriately:

- ✔ **Major Revisions:** Rethinking argument and checking for coherence in ideas. You need to be prepared for major rewrites of key sections if required.

- ✔ **Minor Revisions:** Focusing on a part of the dissertation that seems unsatisfactory (within a broadly reasonable section).

- ✔ **Editing:** Cutting out any extra words, aiming for a concise, clear paper.

- ✔ **Proofreading:** Using your computer spell check and then going through everything with a fine-toothed comb to pick up on small errors and inconsistencies, especially spellings, grammar and typos.

- ✔ **Final check:** Double-checking and making sure that it's all perfect.

It takes a certain amount of courage to genuinely revise your work. You need to accept that parts of your work may be on completely the wrong lines and need to be abandoned altogether.

You need to be in the right mood to manage drastic changes. Don't embark on revisions if you're feeling insecure and precious about your work on a particular day.

I find it useful to have a print out of my work for editing and sometimes I read through, marking sections in colour by theme. This helps me spot where I've repeated myself so I can see what to eliminate.

If it's so hard, is there much point in spending time on revisions? In short – yes! One of the best ways to improve the quality of your writing is through the process of writing and rewriting. By doing so, you continually review and analyse your work and reconsider your own ideas. You can then discard irrelevant points and seek more persuasive ideas that result in a stronger argument.

Through continual rewriting, you pick up the common errors you make as they're the things that you need to keep changing. You can then cut them out at earlier stages of your writing – eventually you'll have eliminated them and that's how your writing evolves (and hopefully improves).

You need to manage the different versions of your dissertation carefully as they build up alarmingly fast once you start writing. See Chapter 10 for help with this process.

Looking at a first draft

Here's the introduction to this section written in a first draft style:

A first draft is a set of notes with which to start you off, written in loose sentences, sort of to yourself (and with informal bits in to remind you to check things out ***). I've included this bit, hopefully it'll help you get started – the good news is . . . there's no single way a draft should appear, it should suit your style and content.

A first draft can be one of several things, depending on the writer:

- ✔ A concept map (visually conceived and prepared).
- ✔ A list of headings and sub subheadings (eventually to be eliminated).
- ✔ A few notes in some sections and loads in others.
- ✔ The odd note or start of a sentence and a marker *** so you know what to go back to.
- ✔ A work in progress with amendments. For example, you may use CAPITALS, or ??? or ***** to mark bits that need revising.

The look of the first draft depends on how you'll write your dissertation. If you're asked to produce a first draft by a certain date, be sure to clarify exactly what's expected of you. Some of the methods in the bullet points you've just read a few lines above may be unacceptable for tutors checking over your work, whilst others may not mind.

Tackling tracked changes

Some supervisors get back to you having looked at your electronic documents and made changes to them using the track changes tool. Using track changes allows your supervisor to edit directly onto your text using a colour. The process allows you to respond in return. After only one or two back and forth sessions with your supervisor, your document can become impossible to read with all the crossings through, comments and so on.

If you have any kind of visual difficulty or dyslexia that causes you to be unable to read red writing on a white background, ensure that you make this clear to your supervisor, or be certain that you're able to change the text into a format that you can read easily.

Picking up proofreading techniques

Spelling and grammar checkers are undoubtedly fantastic, but they don't pick up a lot of errors, and they don't notice when words are used wrongly. They're unable to decide whether you've used the correct word as they're unable to comprehend what you've written. If you rely on a grammar and spell check for your dissertation, you're relying on a machine when you should be using your own intelligence. It's very easy, however, to read through your own work at some pace and miss minor errors, as you know what you want to say and you're reading what you want to read.

Your supervisor isn't paid to proofread or edit your work. It's your responsibility to master the art of effective written language.

Simple proofreading techniques can help you with this onerous task. One idea for word-by-word checking is to read your work backwards. Starting at the end of your work means you're simply checking each word rather than reading for meaning. It's laborious and pretty dull but is a pretty good way of getting through your text and checking for mistakes.

Another technique that's really helpful is to listen to your work being read aloud by someone else. Choose your reader with care. It can be a long drawn-out process if you try to tackle the whole dissertation in one go, but can be eased with tea, wine, chocolate or whatever helps you along. Even though this may take ages, it may be better as you have the benefit of reading the dissertation as a coherent whole. If your reader reads out something that's nonsensical, you should stop and check what it is he's just read. For this task to succeed, you need someone who is a reasonable reader and a good critical friend.

Watch out for punctuation in your dissertation. Ask your reader only to take deep breaths when he comes to punctuation, especially full stops. If the person is trying to hold his breath as he's reading, it's likely that you haven't used enough punctuation in your dissertation.

Find further tips from the Plain English Campaign – try their website www.plainenglish.co.uk/proofreading.pdf.

If you know that you have a serious spelling problem, or if you tend to write in incomplete sentences, or you have difficulties such as dyslexia or dyspraxia, you must seek professional help. Your university has support services: Contact them early.

If you find that the support services are overloaded and unable to help, you can engage a proofreader. Often you can find masters and doctoral students earning extra cash through proofreading undergraduate dissertations. They normally charge a very reasonable amount and if you can afford it and feel you need it, it's worth it for peace of mind (they won't rewrite or edit for you however).

Chapter 14

References, Bibliographies and Appendixes

In This Chapter

▶ Fathoming the fundamentals of a good bibliography

▶ Meeting the different referencing systems

▶ Understanding the purpose of appendixes, footnotes and endnotes

Examiners want to be able to follow up any reference in your work by simply flipping to the bibliography and seeing all the information you've used in a clear and recognisable format. In this chapter I define the different parts of references and bibliographies, explain how to follow your university's required referencing format, and help you decide what to put in your appendixes.

Defining the Terms

In writing a dissertation, you come across a number of technical terms for the different parts of the work. Some brief definitions should help:

✔ **Bibliography:** A list of all the sources you've used to research and write your essay or dissertation. A bibliography is usually ordered by authors' names and placed at the end of your work. Usually the bibliography includes only the references that you've used directly in your writing, but sometimes tutors ask for all your broader reading as well – you need to find out what's required of you.

✔ **References:** The word 'references' has two main meanings. A reference list is essentially a catalogue of all the sources to which you refer in your dissertation. Your reference list should include only sources that you mention directly in your dissertation. Your reference list usually comes at the end of your document.

✔ A different use of the word 'references' means sources that you mention in your text, within a sentence. Generally you just mention the author and date (and page number if you use a direct quotation) – your readers can then look up the author in your reference list.

✔ **Further reading:** This is a list, separate from your reference list (which includes only what you mention specifically in the text) that indicates your suggested additional reading.

✔ **Citation:** This is similar to a reference. With a citation you acknowledge the source of an idea. With a reference you provide the exact details of the source.

✔ **Works cited:** This is the same as a bibliography or reference list.

✔ **Appendixes:** These are pages at the end of your work for any information that you feel is vital to your work but would interrupt the flow of your argument if you included it in the text itself.

✔ **Footnotes and endnotes:** These are additions to the main text at the bottom of the page or end of the chapter or dissertation, respectively. You can use them to elaborate on the main ideas without digressing from the main themes and arguments.

Myriad different approaches to referencing and listing sources exist in the world of academia. Some fields do things one way, whereas others follow a completely different system. Even within the same field you may find variations. As you read different journals, note the range of assorted approaches that you see.

If you follow your university guidelines with care, you'll be fine. The key is giving yourself sufficient time to proofread your references. References and bibliographies aren't difficult, but they're fiddly and time-consuming.

Students often get into a spin about bibliographies and referencing. But creating a good bibliography is a pretty easy way to gain points. A well-crafted list of sources is an expectation and prerequisite for getting a decent grade. Not attending to the bibliography and references is a really pointless way to work and you'd be foolish not to spend time on this task.

I can't emphasise enough how fundamental it is that you ensure that you meet the requirements of your course concerning the bibliography and references.

Building a Brilliant Bibliography

Turn to the back of any academic book or journal article and you'll probably see some kind of bibliography. The bibliography is a vital component of the work and provides validation for everything written in the book or article as it allows the reader to go back to the original sources and decide whether they agree with the author's interpretations. In this section I show you how to perfect your bibliography.

Looking at the basics of a good bibliography

Some general rules for your bibliography are as follows:

- ✔ Place it at the end of the dissertation.

- ✔ Put everything in alphabetical order, by author (unless you're using the Vancouver style, normally only used in the medical sciences).

- ✔ Don't split books, articles and websites into separate lists unless specifically requested to do so.

- ✔ Format your bibliography so it's easy to read and meets your university's style requirements.

- ✔ Use spacing that makes your work clear; leave a line between each entry. See the examples in the section in this chapter on Harvard bibliographies for examples of correct spacing.

 In general, don't list dictionaries and encyclopaedias in your bibliography. If, however, your dissertation focuses on comparing different definitions, or a dictionary from a particularly special source (such as a seventeenth-century dictionary), and you draw attention to a comparison or change in meaning, then you need to include these sources too.

Creating your bibliography as you go along

Your dissertation bibliography is going to be pretty long and will almost certainly extend over several pages. Managing your bibliography is a hassle, but you can reduce your difficulties significantly by undertaking the process bit by bit, working as you go.

Develop a habit of recording all sources as you use them. Your bibliography then becomes a working document rather than some mountainous task left to the last minute. If you have all the substance of your bibliography (names, dates and other details), the job at the end is reduced merely to formatting and laying out the list correctly and neatly.

The devil's in the detail. Always note seemingly minor concerns, such as which edition you use.

For further information about compiling a bibliography as you go, check out Chapter 6.

Sussing out the different referencing systems

So many different ways of referencing exist, so check with your supervisor which system you need to follow. In this section I describe the most commonly used referencing systems in social science in the UK.

Your own university or course details always trounce anything I say in this section, as this book is a general guide rather than specific to your course.

Even among the recognised styles of bibliographies and referencing, you find variations that match specific requirements of a field or the tastes of the team of tutors who teach you and examine your work. Discrepancies you may encounter may relate to the following:

- ✔ Use of capital letters (especially following a colon)
- ✔ Size of font and acceptable fonts to use
- ✔ Punctuation in general (some use commas, others like full stops or spaces)
- ✔ Use of italics, bold and underlining
- ✔ The specific location of information, such as the date, within the reference

If you use any translated texts, include this information in your bibliography. Usually you list the original author first, unless the reason you discuss the text is because you compare different versions of the text. Use your head and think it through.

You should have all the information you need. When in doubt, strive at least for consistency to show that you've considered your methods with care.

The Harvard system

This is the system used in science and many social science disciplines. The full details of the source are included in the list of references or bibliography at the end of the work. Only minimal information (the author's name and the date) is included in the text. See below in the section 'Referencing in the Text' for further details about
referencing in the body of your writing.

If you're missing data due to your sloppy recording, fill in the blanks correctly – even if that means yet another trip to the library. If data are missing from the original source, note where any gaps exist and show that the information isn't available. For example, where there's no date, you should put 'no date' and where there's no author, state 'no author listed'.

Books

Include the following general information:

Author/editor's surname and initials. (Year of publication). Edition (if not first). *Title of book: including subtitles*. Place of publication: Name of publisher.

Here are some real examples:

- **Single-authored book:**

  Sutherland, M. (2005) *Gifted and Talented in the Early Years: A Practical Guide for 3–5-year-olds*. London: SAGE Publications.

- **Edited book:**

  Marples, R. (ed.) (1999) *The Aims of Education*. London: Routledge.

- **Book by two authors:**

  Robson, S. and Smedley, S. (1996) *Education in Early Childhood: First Things First*. London: David Fulton.

- **Book by multiple authors:**

  Orchard, J., Clinton, C., Lynch, S., Weston, D. and Wright, A. (1999) (2nd edition) *Islam In Today's World, Teacher's Resource Book*. London: Hodder Education.

- **Chapter in book:**

  Terzi, L. (2006) 'Beyond the dilemma of difference: the capability approach to disability and special educational needs' in Cigman, R. (ed.) *Included or Excluded? The Challenge of the Mainstream for some SEN Children*. London: Routledge.

Journal articles

Include the following general info:

Author's surname, initials, (year of publication) 'Title of article', *Journal Title* **volume number** (part number), page numbers.

Here's an example:

> Hand, M. (2007) 'Should we teach homosexuality as a controversial issue?', *Theory and Research in Education* **5** (1), 69–86.

Newspaper articles are referenced in the same way as journals. If there's no author, list by the name of the paper and say 'no author listed'. With the names of newspapers, drop 'the' from the name of the paper, except for *The Times* that states that the 'The' should always be included, with a capital T and the whole names should be italicised.

Conference papers

Include the following general info:

Author's surname, initials. (Date of publication) 'Title of paper', Paper presented at (title of conference), place of conference, exact date.

Here are some examples:

- ✔ **Single presenter:**

  > Gereluk, D. (2007) 'Bong HiTS 4 Jesus: Defining the Limits of Free Speech and Expression in American Schools', paper presented at the Education and Extremism Conference, London, UK, 5 July 2007.

- ✔ **Two presenters:**

  - ✔ Winstanley, C. and Peat, J. (2006) Keeping Hold of First Year Students: Dealing with Retention, paper presented at HEA, Nottingham, UK, 4 July 2006.

Websites

Include the following general info:

Author/editor's surname, initials (or, if no author, name of organisation, for example, BBC) (year of publication). Title. URL. Date accessed.

> Brighouse, H. (no date) How Should Children Be Heard? http://www.law.arizona.edu/Journals/ALR/ALR2003/vol453/Brighouse.pdf. Accessed 17 November 2008.

Considering other common bibliographic systems

You may have come across the American Psychological Association system, known as APA. This is similar to the Harvard method as it cites the author and date in the text. Some of the differences are minor, but experts marking your work will notice:

✔ Within the text:

- **APA:** (Baum, 1900, p. 17) [no other options]

- **Harvard:** (Baum, 1900:17) or (Baum 1900, 17) and so on [slightly less prescriptive]

✔ In the reference list or bibliography:

- **APA:** Baum, L.F. (1900) *The Wizard of Oz*, Chicago: George M. Hill.

- **Harvard:** Baum, L.F. (1900) *The Wizard of Oz*. Chicago: George M. Hill.

✔ Listing journal articles:

- **APA:** Ritter, G. (1997) 'Silver slippers and a golden cap: L. Frank Baum's The Wonderful Wizard of Oz and historical memory in American politics', *Journal of American Studies*, Vol. 31, No. 2, 171–203.

- **Harvard:** Ritter, G. (1997) 'Silver slippers and a golden cap: L. Frank Baum's The Wonderful Wizard of Oz and historical memory in American politics', *Journal of American Studies*, 31, (2), 171–203.

Some other systems are very different, however, such as the numerical Modern Humanities Research Association (MRHA) system and the Oxford Standard for the Citation of Legal Authorities system.

In numerical systems, you assign each reference a number in your text, either in brackets or as a superscript. The numerals in the text relate to the sources in the order they're used. You then provide a list of all references as they correspond to the numbers. These lists can be presented in different ways, such as:

✔ In footnotes on each page

✔ In endnotes at the end of each chapter

✔ In endnotes at the end of the whole dissertation

Depending on the type of numerical system you're using, the list of references or bibliography can be presented in a number of ways. You use the same information as in Harvard, but it looks a little different. Here are some examples:

✔ **Book:** [1] Suissa, J. *Anarchism and Education; A Philosophical Perspective*, London: Routledge, 2006.

✔ **Journal:** [2] Richardson, M. 'Identifying gifted students around the world', *Educating Able Children*, 8(1), 15–24 2006.

Whichever method you use, if you have more than one publication by the same author in the same year, differentiate between them by adding a, b, c, and so on.

If you have a learning difficulty, such as dyslexia or dyspraxia, you may find referencing more difficult than other students and you may be less good at spotting mistakes. Give your support worker plenty of time to help you with the proofreading process.

Referencing in the Text

As well as listing all your sources at the end of your dissertation, you must reference clearly in the text. The information in the text must match what's in the bibliography or reference list exactly, but in a more succinct manner.

Your text citations need to show what you've researched and acknowledge the source of your ideas. Your reader may want to follow up something you've said and go over your interpretation of a primary source. They can only do this if you clearly identify the original you used.

The main point of careful referencing in your university work is to avoid accusations of plagiarism. If you put down someone else's ideas or words without acknowledging them, it's as if you're claiming that the work is yours – that you thought it up, that you wrote it, that you chose those words to express your idea. It's considered a serious academic offence to pass off someone else's work as your own.

When a student just starting out at university fails to reference effectively she certainly fails the work in question, but hopefully she then has a session with her tutor who refers her to the support systems for help with study skills and referencing in particular. If you fail to reference beyond the first term, you're likely to be in a great deal of trouble. Universities expel students for such offences and by your final year there's no earthly way you can claim not to know anything about referencing.

Don't use others' ideas without providing accurate, full references.

Citing using the Harvard system

With the Harvard system (which I describe in the earlier section 'The Harvard system'), you give only basic minimal information in the text – usually just the author's surname and the date of publication. You also put a page reference if you quote directly. You add the full details of the source in the bibliography at the end of your writing (see the earlier section 'Building a Brilliant Bibliography' for more info about referencing).

To cite the author in the text, give the surname of the author, followed by the year, as part of the sentence or at the end of a sentence. Here are some examples:

> Challoner (2003) notes that the media have failed to report science objectively . . .

> . . . reports of these concepts were simplistic and emotive (Challoner, 2003:46)

If you quote directly or make a very specific point, provide the page reference as well. I've done this above using a colon, but other options exist too:

> 1979:36–8
>
> 1979, p.36–8
>
> 1979, p36–38
>
> 1979, pp36–38

As long as you're clear and consistent, and your supervisor doesn't have a preference, the way you show the page number isn't desperately important.

Where you have multiple authors, in place of writing out all their names, put the first author, followed by *et al.* (In Harvard use this for three or more, but in APA, use it for six or more.) For example:

> Aylin *et al* (2007) note that students reported difficulties with . . .

Noting the numerical system

You usually only need to put in the author and number (superscript or brackets) for a numeric in-text reference:

> According to Wright [7], post-nuclear apocalyptic scenarios are . . .

Wright[7] notes that the future of political systems . . .

For other types of reference, use the same style as Harvard (see the earlier section 'Citing using the Harvard system'), adapting them to the brackets and superscript style.

A couple of handy shortcuts to writing out the full in-text reference if you use the same reference in a short period of writing are the Latin terms *ibid* and *op cit*:

Ibid means 'from the same source'.

Op cit means 'already cited' and refers to the most recently cited work.

If you reference the same text, but different pages, *ibid* is really handy. After the first reference, say to page 17, when you want to cite the next part you used on page 25, you can just put (*ibid:25*).

If you've written about one source in paragraph [a] and then use it again in paragraph [b], you can simply put (*op cit*) in place of referencing it all again.

Adding Info in Appendixes and Notes

An appendix is an add-on. An appendix contains additional information that amplifies or illustrates, but needs to be separated from the main development or stream of your argument.

For further information about how to present your appendixes, have a look at Chapter 15.

Deciding what to put in the appendix

You may have models, diagrams and lists in your appendixes. If you conduct an interview or questionnaire, the schedule and questions or sample answers can be included. You may have longer paragraphs of transcriptions whereas in the text you have a properly referenced fragment or phrase. The appendix provides the context in this instance.

Appendixes are normally only allowed to contain about ten per cent on top of the wordage. For example, if you have a 10,000 word limit, your appendices should not normally exceed 1,000 words.

When you need to refer to an appendix, put this clearly in your text. Include the page number and label each appendix clearly. Often this is done with roman numerals to distinguish from normal page numbers.

> Before agreeing, she had explained the background to the offence (see Appendix iv, page 46) and shown me the . . .

Using footnotes and endnotes

Unless they're being used for references (see above), footnotes and endnotes serve to allow you to amplify ideas from the main text. They can be preferable to stopping in the middle of an argument to explain something basic or enter a digression.

Some university regulations require a footnote to be on the exact same page as the reference to it, whereas others are less fussy. Endnotes can go at the end of a chapter or at the very end of a document, in which case they're normally divided into chapter sections.

The main guideline for using footnotes is usually this: if you haven't been specifically required to write footnotes, then don't do it! It is perfectly possible that they're disallowed in your regulations. Some examiners absolutely hate flicking back and forth (with just eyes, or with eyes and hands) and those of us who don't mind them don't really miss them if there aren't any at all.

For further information about how to lay out your footnotes and end notes, see Chapter 15.

Chapter 15

Presenting Your Dissertation

● ●

In This Chapter

▶ Looking at layout and formatting

▶ Printing and binding your work

● ●

*I*f you look at other students' dissertations in your university library, you see a variety of presentations. You may notice that some forms of presentations work better than others, that some are clearer than others and some are easier to read. Many restrictions govern the size, shape and layout of your dissertation and these are articulated in your course regulations – it's your responsibility to familiarise yourself with the requirements.

In this chapter I help you work out how to format your dissertation to your university's requirements, where to put all those extra bits and pieces, and how to present the finished product in a way that makes your examiners smile rather than cry.

Working on the Main Text

Most of your dissertation will be paragraphs of writing that must be readable. This section explains the fonts, titles, headings, margins, page numbers and so forth. If you'd like more information on writing styles, take a look at Chapter 13.

Focusing on font types and sizes

You need to aim for lucidity and clarity rather than trying to be groovy or distinctive. I suggest you choose a plain font such as Times, Arial or Courier. Steer well clear of italic fonts for your main passages, and avoid fonts with elaborate *pothooks* (loops extending high above and below the line), which can be really hard on the eye.

The smallest font you should consider would be 11 (10 is just too much of an eye strain). I would also suggest that 12 is ideal and is pretty much the largest you should use for the main body of the text.

Keep the same size font for subheadings, but for chapter headings, cover pages and your titles, use something a little larger. Don't go over the top, however.

For headers and footers, use a smaller font, .8, .9 or .10, so as not to interfere with the main text.

Your examiner probably has to read around five dissertations, which adds up to a staggering 50,000 words along with other essays, portfolios and examination papers. Make it easy for him to like your work.

Managing margins, spacing and layout

Your university probably has certain regulations about the size of your dissertation and the margins for printing the pages. If you use a standard word-processing programme and don't mess around with the settings, you generally find that it adheres to the recommendations of your programme. The standard setting is 2.54 centimetres at the top, bottom right and left. For a soft-bound document (as most undergraduate dissertations are) this is fine. If in doubt, check with your supervisor.

Print out a page or two as a test before you print the whole document. Imagine what it will look like when it's bound. Check there's sufficient space for the binding and that it's possible to read all the words on the page once there's a spine.

You can affect the way your work looks on the page through *justifying* it differently. I'd stick to one clear style but here's some information to help you decide:

This text is justified, which is standard. Here I have also justified the whole paragraph (which is standard in printed books, but not usually in student work), so that you can see the effect. It often leads to awkward breaks in the text and isn't recommended for your dissertation.

Here is an example of text ranged to the left (that is, lined up on the left-hand side). In this example I have left the paragraph unjustified. It's generally accepted to help improve the flow in essays and less formally bound documents.

Here's an example of text that has been centred so you can see what it looks like. It's most useful for titles and sometimes headings.

> Here is an example of text ranged to the right (that is, lined up on the right-hand side). You aren't likely to need this, although occasionally it's useful when you're placing a heading of a table or chart and it just seems to look better laid out in this way!

When you look at the pages of your work, you should be able to spot easily anywhere you have too much long flowing text that's not broken into clear paragraphs. Conversely, you'll notice any pages that contain predominantly short sentences and phrases, where there's no flowing text. Either of these extremes would be inappropriate. See Chapter 13 for information about length of paragraphs and so on.

Handling headings and page numbers

The key with headings and page numbers is to be sure that things are in order. I mean this in both senses of 'in order'; (a) consecutive, numbered, logical, and (b) well organised and clear. So, to recap:

✔ Main headings should have the following characteristics

- Font about 14pt
- Short and conventional titles (such as 'Research Methods')
- Centred or ranged left

✔ Subheadings

- Normal-sized font
- Bold if appropriate
- Number if required
- Ranged left

Page numbering is easily done automatically on word processing software. Check with your supervisor and your course materials any specific rules about where on the page numbers should appear. Usually they appear in your footer (the text at the very bottom of the page), but you may be asked to put them in the text at the very top of each page, known as the header. If it is left up to you, I'd recommend one of these three alternatives:

(i)	37	Chapter 4
(ii)		37 of 70
(iii)	Chapter 4	37

You may be required to supply your student number, or name on each page (in case any pages are lost). Ask your tutor if it's not made clear in your course documentation.

Using bold, italics, underlining and colour

You should **absolutely** avoid **bold type,** underlining and _italics_ wherever possible. If you use them to **emphasise** certain words, it comes across as _patronising_, almost as if you don't trust your reader to _manage_ to read **your** work without _your_ voice intonating for **emphasis** in the _background_. See how annoying that is? Generally, follow this advice:

✔ If you use a quotation with italics or bold already incorporated, then you should put these in the text exactly as they're written in the original.

✔ On very rare occasions you may need to highlight a word or phrase, but it's probably best to use 'quotation marks'.

✔ The only part of your dissertation that should have lots of italics is the bibliography.

✔ Bold can be used for subheadings.

Using capitals for emphasis is a no-no. Reading work in capital letters is like BEING SHOUTED AT BY THE AUTHOR.

Formatting figures and tables

All tables and figures should be labelled clearly with a title and a number. Roman numerals or letters are a good idea as they avoid confusion with the page numbers of your dissertation.

Check that the numerals or letters flow accurately from the start to the end of your dissertation.

If you include any tables, make sure that wherever possible, they don't run over more than one page. If you need a bit more space you should consider a fold-out A3 page rather than splitting over a number of pages as you lose the coherence if you have to keep flicking back and forth.

If it's utterly impossible to avoid splitting the table, you should repeat the titles of each column on the new page to make it easier to understand.

 Aim for clarity!

Formatting the End Pages

I devote all of Chapter 14 to the minutiae of your bibliography, but in this section I offer some tips on laying out your bibliography and other end pages, such as the appendixes. As with other aspects of this chapter, clarity is the important word to remember.

Laying out your references

Here's a checklist for your bibliography. You should be able to tick all these off:

- ❑ Spacing is correct between each entry.

- ❑ It's in alphabetical order.

- ❑ You've used underlining and italics correctly.

- ❑ 'Other sources' (websites, videos and so on) are integrated into the list, or separated, as required.

- ❑ Everything is lined up and ranged to the left.

- ❑ You've used capital letters in the correct places.

If your dissertation has endnotes and footnotes (which I explain in Chapter 14), check that you've done the following:

- ❑ Used endnotes or footnotes as recommended.

- ❑ Started a new page for endnotes.

- ❑ Located any endnotes at the end of each chapter, or at the end of your dissertation as required.

- ❑ Used numerals or numbers as per the regulations.

- ❑ Used superscript or parentheses as recommended.

- ❑ Avoided footnotes that take up too much space on any page.

- ❑ Kept all footnotes and endnotes to a minimum, only using them when absolutely necessary.

Dealing with appendixes

Appendixes are difficult to generalise about as they're all different and sometimes contain awkward bits of information. Of course that's the reason you've probably decided they should be in your appendix, since if they were in the main text, they'd break up the flow of your writing and ideas.

Appendix matter is often personal to your specific dissertation, but a general rule is the old chestnut of being as lucid as possible, combined with an additional concern about purpose. You need to blatantly lay out what the purpose and aim of the appendix actually is, and it should be plain how this fits into the dissertation overall. How best to achieve this is to use the following checklist:

❑ Clear title for each page of the appendix.

❑ Easy to find the appropriate appendix from the text through clear numbering of appendixes and pages.

❑ Any models or tables confined to one page only (prefer a foldout A3 page to spreading over two A4 pages).

❑ Obvious purpose for each appendix.

❑ You have references for any appendix, stating the exact source.

Although appendixes are often individual, some common appendixes can be identified and it would be perfectly normal to find these elements in an appendix:

❑ Permission letters from organisations for data collection.

❑ Sample questions/answers from structured interviews or questionnaires.

❑ Theoretical models or diagrams referred to in the text more than once, but not necessarily central to the thesis.

❑ Subjects' responses (samples only) including transcribed conversations, anonymised handwritten responses, drawings and so on.

Your appendixes should not be more than 10 per cent of your total word limit. Many undergraduate dissertations are around 10,000 words long and so that gives you an additional 1,000 words, which fill about three pages of fully typed A4 paper. You may possibly have more pages, as appendixes tend to have fewer words on each page as they're composed of models, diagrams and letters and so on.

For your titles and contents page, try to remember that 'appendix' is the singular form of the word 'appendices' (or 'appendixes') – the plural form.

Don't fall into the trap of spending too little or too much time on the presentation of your dissertation. I'll say it again – clarity!

Considering the Cover and Front Matter

Generally, course requirements don't allow for much inventiveness or flexibility on your front cover. In your dissertation guidelines you're likely to have a prescribed layout with specific regulations stipulating what you must include.

Tackling the titles, abstract and acknowledgements

At several points through the process of writing your dissertation, I encourage you to check that your title is really what you think it should be and that your dissertation actually addresses what your title proclaims. Just before printing is your final opportunity to make any alterations to your title. Try and be succinct and clear. You can aim for interesting and attention-grabbing, but not at the expense of coherence.

A silly title doesn't work, even if it's snappy, and usually just bemuses or irritates your examiner.

The layout must follow any given guidelines and this includes the order of items such as the abstract and acknowledgements. See Chapters 11 and 12 for more detailed information on writing these elements.

Start a new page for your abstract and even if it's fairly short, don't be tempted to bump up the font to .14 to make it look more substantial. Take a look at some dissertations in the library to see how smart and neat it is to have a clear abstract, with delineated paragraphs as required. Keep it plain.

As mentioned in Chapters 11 and 12, your acknowledgements should be short and sweet. Just because you have a full page for presenting them doesn't mean you should try and fill it up trying to name everyone you've ever met. Make it clear and succinct.

A title often looks best centred on the page.

Compiling your contents page

Your contents page includes a list of all your chapter headings with the relevant page numbers listed alongside. If you have subheadings that come immediately after the main headings, you should include these as well and perhaps subheadings for further subsections.

You should find that you have no more than three levels of headings: chapter heading; next level heading; further level heading. If you have many more than these, you end up with far too much detail in your contents page.

You should also include any appendixes and the bibliography as these are essential items. Non-essential items include any other items such as pictures, graphs and models. If you only have one figure or table in your whole dissertation, you can incorporate it into your contents list, but if in doubt check with your tutor. As you'll have seen in books, a simpler (and often more effective) method for listing diagrams and charts is to create a list of figures and tables on a separate sheet. This is standard practice in publishing, but you may only have a single figure and can therefore leave it in the contents list.

From your own reviews of other people's dissertations, you'll have seen a spectrum of different contents pages from fantastic to dismal. Aim for clarity. Some people use their word processing software to produce their contents page, but you may find the automatic formatting can be a little annoying and you have less flexibility around changing the order or adding in extra items (such as tables and appendixes).

Think carefully about how best to format your contents page. Here are a few alternatives:

Chapter 2

Literature Review 15

Chapter 2 Literature Review   15

2: Literature Review _____ 15

2. Literature Review

    2.1 Introduction   15

    2.2 Main theories   15

    2.3 Other theories   17

Any of these, or similar ideas are perfectly acceptable, as long as they're clear and as long as you stick to one system throughout.

Once you've completed your contents page, 'challenge' a friend to find a few key things in your dissertation, such as the research methods section, or the third appendix, or the bibliography. See how easy they find it to navigate around your work and make any necessary improvements.

Introduction and rationale

For your introduction (and rationale if you have one), be sure to find out whether your university prefers this to be part of the front matter or part of the main text. Your course requirements may specify that you need to provide a certain length of introduction/rationale that starts on a fresh page and comes before the dissertation starts fully (with the literature review). If this is so, your introduction/rationale are part of the front matter and need a page each.

If your introduction/rationale (where you're asked to provide one) are just part of the Main Body of your dissertation, you may not decide to start them on new pages but to integrate them into your work more generally.

Whatever you need to do to satisfy your course regulations, you should make sure that it clearly links to the introduction so a reader can find his way around your dissertation without becoming lost and frustrated.

Planning the Printing and Binding

Your aim is to present a manageable document where all the pages are intact, clear and readable. Most undergraduate dissertations are A4 in format and consist of only one volume. However, if you have a large number of images (for example, your dissertation is about children's drawings) you may consider an A3 format, or A4 with foldout extended pages.

Un-numbered and loose pages that fall out in a jumble as soon as the examiner opens the folder are a disaster. Don't go too far the other way, attending more to appearance than context. More important than aesthetic appeal, your top priority is a dissertation that can actually be easily read.

You have various options for binding your dissertation and you need to weigh up factors such as cost, ease and time when making your final decision, taking into account the specific needs of your dissertation, such as the number of pages, or any unusual layout issues.

Don't assume that you'll be able to bind your printed pages in a quick couple of hours the afternoon before the thesis is due to be submitted. Give yourself time and do some preparatory homework to ensure that you make the right decisions.

Printing out your work

Your dissertation is a long document and just printing it out can be a complicated affair. During the process of writing your dissertation it would be quite proper to save paper through printing on both sides, using scrap, single spacing, printing two pages to one sheet and so on. Now, however, you need to print on one side of the paper only, with the correct margins, and it needs to be double spaced (or 1.5) as required.

Using the professionals

If you prefer to have your work printed out at a print shop or at the media shop in your university library, make sure that you find out their exact requirements in terms of what you need to provide. Ask if they'd prefer a disc or memory stick, for example, or if they can access your work from the university network itself. Also make sure of the length of time it's going to take and the actual costs before you make a decision.

Doing it yourself

If you're doing this yourself, print out your dissertation in stages. Send it to the printer from your computer one chapter at a time and as the pages come out, check through them for any problems. It's easier to rectify if you only have bits at a time, rather than the whole thing in one go.

Considering comb binding

Most university libraries or media centres provide comb binding facilities for students to use themselves and also offer a reasonably priced professional comb binding service. The main advantages of comb binding are that it's economical, flexible and you can do it yourself, meaning you're completely in control. Another great aspect of comb binding is that if you adjust the thickness of the 'comb', you can manage any number of pages and when the examiner opens your dissertation, the pages lie flat.

Using a comb binding machine takes a bit of getting used to but is essentially straightforward: put the pages into the machine and punch specific holes in your pages; insert the 'comb' into the machine, and then place the pages in order. Voilà – the machine closes up the comb, transforming your loose pages into a bound document.

Even though comb binding is a cheap process, your document can look pretty snazzy if you use some decent coloured card for the front and back covers (although you may need to get the media centre to print on this card for you). You should use a clear plastic sheet on the front (and maybe back) to protect your work and give it a really good look.

If you're planning to do your own comb binding, you should first practise on a less important document before risking making an error with your precious dissertation!

Using a professional binder

You can have your work professionally bound in a number of ways and generally the most suitable for undergraduate dissertations is comb binding, as described above. If you want to be sure of a professional job, it's probably better to have your work comb bound by the people who've done it before. It's up to you to be sure that:

- ✔ You have all the pages.
- ✔ They're in the correct order.
- ✔ You allow sufficient time.
- ✔ You're able to print a spare copy in case something should go wrong.
- ✔ You've included any appendixes, or extras.

Other options for professional binding exist, such as coil binding (where a metal coil is used, much like a comb), tape binding (where cloth tape is used and heat sealed), 'screws' (aluminium screws are used a bit like staples) and so on. You're more likely to come across these alternatives at professional print shops than at your university library.

An even more expensive choice would be hard cover binding, but this is usually only required for a master's degree or other higher level work and it generally takes a few days to do. You need to book in and visit the printers to discuss your requirements in detail.

Don't get carried away – the content of your dissertation is far more important than the presentation. The top tip for binding is to make sure that the pages lie flat.

Including appendixes and other additional material

Appendixes should be incorporated at the back of your dissertation (see Chapter 9 for details of what should and shouldn't go into your appendixes). Some people use different coloured paper to help the examiner distinguish essential material from supporting work. If you do this, make sure that the different colour is not too strong and that your work can be easily read. Choose a pastel shade to ensure that the text is legible.

You don't get extra marks for putting into your dissertation excessive notes, interview schedules, data, images, quotations and so on. Think very carefully about any additional material and ask yourself: 'Is this really adding value to my dissertation?' If it isn't adding value, leave it out.

If you need to include a DVD, video cassette tape, memory stick or some kind of audio file, you should speak to your supervisor about acceptable formats for this submission. Generally, it's sufficient to submit the material in a suitably protective case, clearly labelled with your name, student identification number, the date and maybe also the title of your dissertation. If you can find a way of attaching this to your dissertation, so much the better. Incorporating an additional plastic folder into a comb bound dissertation is perfect – you can just slip your DVD into the plastic folder.

Keeping extra copies

Throughout this book, I stress the importance of backing up your work and keeping electronic and paper copies (preferably in separate places) to help you avert potential disaster. This is true even once your dissertation is printed, bound and submitted. If there's any query about your data, or any of your research, you may need to reprint a section or send something to your supervisor.

Another possibility – too dreadful to contemplate – is that your dissertation is somehow lost between you submitting it and the examiner receiving it, or even after it's actually been marked. In this instance you need to print out a copy (although you'll find your department is only too willing to pay, if you can prove you gave it in and it's their fault it's been mislaid).

Many courses require you to submit two copies of your dissertation so that they can be marked by two different examiners who then meet to compare their notes on your work. Some courses ask you to provide two copies but you only need to submit one – the other is for your reference.

If your course involves an oral examination, you should definitely have a copy of your dissertation for reference during the examination. Your own copy doesn't have to be fully bound, in fact it may be easier if you have it in an ordinary ring binder with the different sections separated using Post-it notes and file dividers. This way you can easily move around your dissertation to answer questions as required.

Part V
Managing the Overall Experience

'I must say I like the preliminary notes in your dissertation, Mr. Rothsberger.'

In this part...

The experience of writing a dissertation can be a gruelling one. You need to gather a load of data, make sense of it and get everything you need to say down on paper (or screen) while maintaining you focus over a long period of time. It's demanding stuff.

In this part I walk you through what you need to do to work as efficiently as possible, from sorting out your working environment to maintaining your enthusiasm for your subject. I also cover the important business of looking after yourself physically, from knowing when to take a break through to coping with the aftermath of submitting your finished work.

Chapter 16

Organising Your Work Habits

*I*n this chapter I help you understand your own work habits and encourage you to think about building on your good habits and breaking the bad ones. By discovering what distracts you, you can create strategies that help you get down to work quicker. I suggest you read this chapter in conjunction with Chapter 17, where I offer lots of info on looking after your well-being during the process of writing your dissertation.

Working Out Where You Can Work

The optimum scenario, if at all possible, is for you to set up a workspace where you can leave some of your papers and equipment laid out all the time. It needn't be a huge space, but having a place for working helps you keep focused and organised, both key aspects of a successful dissertation.

 If it's impossible for you to have a desk or table where you can leave your work undisturbed, make use of a shelf or a large plastic box with a lid. The main point is to have everything together in one place so that nothing gets lost.

Arranging your workspace and knowing about your work habits are both useful preparation for your dissertation, so sort them out before you actually start work.

Making your workspace your own

People work in different ways, but some basic aspects of setting up need to be considered, no matter how you choose to resolve them to meet your needs. Here's a list of the main things to bear in mind and the common recommended solutions. If you differ from the suggested responses, that's fine, as long as you know why and you aren't impeding your ability to work effectively. (I offer lots more information about health issues in Chapter 17.)

✔ **Desk height and depth:** These aren't easy to adjust, especially if you're having to work at the dining table or similar. You may find that you need different heights for reading and longhand writing than for using a computer. A deeper desk allows space for a wrist support and for more of your books and papers.

✔ **Healthy computer use:** Guidelines abound for safe computer use, but just think about being sensible rather than worrying if you're complying with regulations: don't sit too close to the screen; rest your forearms on the desk; use a relaxed grip on the mouse; position your monitor so you're looking slightly downwards; use a screen filter if it eases the strain on your eyes; use a foot rest if your feet aren't flat to the floor; choose glasses over contact lenses (due to the drying effects of a computer suite or individual monitor – eye drops can help); take regular breaks, and so on.

✔ **Lighting:** Illuminate your work to reduce eye strain. Place your desk lamp so you don't cast irritating shadows on your screen, keyboard or books. Invest in a daylight bulb if you find normal lighting inadequate.

✔ **Pinboard:** Having to-do lists and information pinned up near where you work can be useful or oppressive, depending on how you like to work. If you start out one way and change your mind, that's okay, just try and make it as easy as possible for you to get your work done efficiently.

✔ **Seating**: If possible, a stable computer chair is the best option as these are adjustable and designed to support your back. For most people, having a range of places to sit for different tasks is also desirable. If you want to do your reading curled up on the sofa, still remember to have appropriate lighting.

✔ **Ventilation:** Don't let your work space become stuffy and airless, but avoid sitting in a draught as your muscles can become achy and stiff. Some people get headaches seemingly associated with all the electrical equipment in their homes. A plant here and there can help reduce this if you're a sufferer.

✔ **View**: If you have any choice about the placement of your workspace, think carefully about your view. Some people find a blank wall the best for reducing distractibility, whilst others prefer to have a view to contemplate. This is not just about lyrical daydreaming; a view (urban or rural) allows you to refocus your eyes to long distance for a short break – episodes of staring are healthy!

Sorting out sound and vision

The important thing to note about sound and vision is the amount of background noise that suits you best and the point at which it becomes distracting. We have our own preferences and if you know your tolerance level well you can adapt your environment to meet your needs, taking into account the effect of your behaviour on the people around you of course.

It's probably a bad idea for most people to have the television blaring out while trying to work, just as commercial radio stations can be really irritating as background noise. However, if it's too quiet, some people report feeling very self-conscious and too detached from reality to get on with their work.

Playing some background music that you enjoy is a controllable way to block out other, more disturbing sounds, especially if the outside noises are erratic and unpredictable. Using headphones on your computer or MP3 player is a great way of listening without disturbing the people around you and also for drowning out other people's conversations in cafés and the noisier parts of libraries and computer suites.

Do try and ensure that your music doesn't leak out too much, bothering other people, however.

Your own selection of music is better than radio that breaks off into adverts and weather reports as most people find speech more distracting than music. Following the same logic, music with no words is generally easier to work along with than music with words.

The genre of music doesn't matter except for how well it suits you. Some studies report that classical, jazz and rock (ambient rock in particular) make no real difference to a listener's performance. It's predominantly personal taste rather than the music style. Some claims have been made that Mozart and Bach are especially good for studying to and it's definitely the case that the music is clearly structured and 'clean', but if you hate the music, you won't be soothed or focused, you'll be annoyed. If hip-hop allows you to be more productive, go with it (but not so it disturbs your house-mates).

 If you live in a shared flat or house, talk to your housemates openly about the levels of noise that you expect and keep to your side of the bargain. Agree what times (morning and night) are acceptable for having music playing and the television on and discuss the volume that's appropriate.

Getting everything you need within reach

Consider what you need to work effectively on a daily basis and ensure that you have all the supplies to hand. It seems like a small aspect of your work but makes all the difference between getting on with it and becoming really distracted and using a vain search for a pencil sharpener as a reason to give up work for the day. You probably need the following essentials close to hand:

- ✔ Dictionary and thesaurus

- ✔ Light and music (as above)

- ✔ Pad of A4 paper (smaller isn't really any good for decent notes)

- ✔ Small notebook (this is what you carry with you all the time so make it one where you really like its look, feel and paper)

- ✔ Plastic folders that zip or clip shut (for ultimate portability)

- ✔ A way of separating notes into some kind of order (different-coloured folders, file dividers or a ring-binder)

- ✔ Pens that you enjoy writing with, in a range of colours

- ✔ Highlighters and a thick felt pen for labelling things clearly

- ✔ Different-sized sticky notes (big ones you can write on and small ones to use as page markers for your notes and your own books – don't use on library books as they can cause damage)

- ✔ CDs and memory sticks for backing up your work (get a pen that writes on discs and label everything clearly)

Optional extras may include correction fluid, glue and sticky tape.

Try to have a clear-out every now and then, although don't be too fastidious. When you're in a hurry, you need to feel okay about leaving your things a little untidy and not beating yourself up about the mess. After all, you won't be examined on the neatness of your workspace.

Using common scents

Whether you know that you're sensitive to smells or not, you can benefit from using some essential oils to lift your mood and help you concentrate. Some research has been conducted on this and it has been shown that for most people, at the least, the oils positively affect their moods. I'm not making any grand claims for aromatherapy here, just pointing out another way to make your studying a bit more pleasant.

You may therefore find that a drop of an essential oil on a tissue or cotton hanky is helpful for keeping you alert – you just sniff it from time to time. Cold air diffusers are the best (technically speaking) as they don't affect the oils through heating, but you still get an effect from an oil burner, light bulb ring or a few drops in a bowl of hot water. Do follow any safety tips on using the oil diffusers or burners.

Try and use good-quality oils (get them from health food stores or pharmacies) and be aware that you only need tiny bottles as you're just using a drop or two for each study session. They don't really have an effect if you use them constantly, so use them for the first ten or fifteen minutes of each session. If you have allergies, don't try this without medical advice.

Be sure that you choose an oil for alertness. Those that supposedly help include: lemon; cypress; peppermint; black pepper; eucalyptus; basil and bergamot. You can also get blends of oils that have been combined for optimum effect. Only choose those that you like the whiff of and steer clear of sandalwood (unless you want to feel sensual) and don't use lavender or chamomile, as you'll drop off to sleep at your desk!

An organised workspace saves you precious time and reduces your stress levels.

Finding Out What Kind of Worker You Are

It's useful to examine what tendencies you have in your approach to tasks and to match your dissertation strategies to your strengths. Think about these honestly:

- ✔ When you're eating, do you eat your favourite bits from the plate first and save the best 'til last, or the other way around?

- ✔ When you were at school, did you do the easy bits of your homework first to ease yourself in, or did you tackle the hard bits and then leave the easy stuff as a kind of treat (if there can be such a concept in homework)?

> ✔ Do you leave your housework to pile up and then blitz it, or do you like to keep on top of it regularly?
>
> ✔ Do you enjoy tasks such as ironing, where you create order out of chaos, or do you find it frustrating?

What you're trying to discern is how you like to work in general and where you've fallen down in the past. Say you used to do the easy homework first, did you honestly always get the hard stuff done effectively? If you did, this is a great tactic for you, but if you didn't, you should think about approaching your dissertation in the opposite way rather than putting off difficult tasks.

Consider which ways of working and approaching tasks are the most satisfying and least stressful for you.

Be honest with yourself when you think about how you work best. Fooling yourself is only going to impact negatively on your own work.

Taking an all-or-nothing or bit-by-bit approach

It's great if you can dive headlong into tasks with amazing fervour. However, it's only great in the long term if you can sustain high levels of energy and gusto. For people who like the 'get straight in' approach, they tend to enjoy a kind of top-down overview of a project. If you're like this, you need to clarify the big picture of your research before knuckling down to details. That's fine as long as you can guarantee that you'll get the minutiae under your belt in plenty of time.

Try and maintain some of your enthusiasm for the meetings with your supervisor. A supervisor is more likely to help a student who shows that she cares about her work and really wants to do well.

The other way of working is more of a bottom-up, stepwise strategy. If you like this way of studying, you'll be happy with managing bits of your dissertation at a time, building up the full picture as you go. This is a very steady and useful way to work, but you need to bear in mind that the bits have to come together to form a coherent whole.

Most people have some tendency for both views, depending on the task in hand – and perhaps also affected by the hour of the day, the day of the week, and even the weather. You may prefer one style for a particular aspect of your work, but approach another part quite differently.

It's easy to lose sight of the overall project if you focus too much on the components. Remember to stand back from time to time.

Aiming for perfection – or not

Being a perfectionist can be helpful in your work, but taken to extremes (like most things) it can cause you damage. Having high standards is admirable, but aiming so high that everything must be absolutely perfect may result in you feeling like you can't ever give anything in at all. This level of perfectionism is known as *maladaptive perfectionism*.

If you're only able to submit work that's absolutely perfect, you can end up procrastinating, which cuts down the amount of feedback you get. You may also suffer from anxiety, worrying about details and losing sight of the whole picture. Many people with perfectionist tendencies have rather low self-esteem, although the plus side of these high standards is that it can help you press on and keep up the required high energy level.

Being flexible and realistic

Once you've thought about the working style that suits you best, you shouldn't make that a fixed and unbending approach. At times you'll need to break your schedule for very good reasons and at other times you may just be unable to meet specific deadlines because you miscalculated some aspect of what needed doing. (In Chapter 17 you can find some information about tackling these situations and facing up to difficulties.)

Changing Your Scenery

Sometimes you just need to get away. A change of view can reinvigorate your work for the day, although moving around all the time for the sake of it can be disruptive. The chance to escape the same four walls or tired view is worth making a short trip for and it can be far harder to procrastinate if there's no pressing stuff to do at home such as doing the dishes or cleaning the kitchen floor.

Changing your scenery can also make you happier to get back to your home workstation and appreciate your own space.

Keep an eye on your productivity. If café or library-hopping isn't helping you to get your work under control, don't do it! Changing your scenery is only valuable if it improves your work.

Sometimes you notice your productivity dropping due to a sense of habit and sameness pervading your daily routine. You've been lulled into a rather safe but stultifying comfort zone and it's worth breaking out to rediscover your enthusiasm.

Your comfort zone is a mental construct, not a physical place, but it may be that changing your physical space helps you jolt back into a more effective type of action. It can be a little disconcerting if you've settled into a comforting schedule, but it'll refresh you if you allow yourself to experiment with modifying your work habits.

Slipping into Good Habits and Breaking Bad Ones

If you can establish positive work habits from the outset of your project, so much the better. In this context, I mean not putting off tasks such as keeping your bibliography updated (more on your bibliography in Chapter 14) and backing up your work (see Chapter 10). Since people are habitual beings, it's a great idea to try and just make good habits part of your work. If, for example, you always back up your work to disk and memory stick before you tidy up at the end of a session, you find you do it without thinking after a time – sort of on autopilot.

Most of us tend to slip into bad habits from time to time, which is not generally a huge problem. It's as well to keep aware of how you're working so that you don't suddenly realise you have heaps to do because you haven't taken notice of your bad routines, such as not bothering to back up your writing, add references to your bibliography or tidy notes away.

Other types of bad habit can be more problematic, especially when they get a little out of hand and become more like addictions, compulsions or dependencies. Here, I'm referring to things like habitually staying up all night watching TV and consequently not getting enough rest, or always deleting writing that you think isn't perfect rather than keeping it for redrafting later. Phobias (such as fear of showing your work to your supervisor) can also be habit-forming and it takes lots of emotional effort to confront these concerns.

It takes at least four weeks of sustained, consistent focus to break a mild habit and longer if it's really ingrained. Generally you first need to make yourself aware of your habit through honestly and regularly reviewing how you're getting on (see Chapter 10 for help with this task). You then need to isolate the behaviours that are blocking your progress and impeding your work. As soon as you've identified what's difficult, you need to work out an alternative behaviour that is more productive. You need to adopt this behaviour consistently for at least a month. Take heart, it can be done, but most people need support to accomplish these changes (depending on the severity of the situation). You can get support from your GP, student health centre, student help groups and from friends and family, if appropriate. See Chapter 17 for more information on your emotional health.

Try to tackle your poor habits using the ideas in the Tip directly before this paragraph, before you see your supervisor for the first time. Let your supervisor know that you're aware of your strengths and weaknesses in terms of managing a long-term project as this helps her support you more effectively.

Maintaining Your Enthusiasm and Keeping Momentum

No one expects you to work on your dissertation at fever pitch for a whole year, but you do need to sustain interest in your work if you want to enjoy the process. Probably the best way of ensuring that you maintain interest is to break up what you need to do into manageable tasks.

Monitoring your moods

It's easy to let a day slip away from you because you aren't noticing your own mood. You should expect that some days you just get up feeling irritated, miserable or annoyed for no apparent reason. On such days there may not be much you can do to snap out of your bad mood, but at least by being aware of your moods you can adjust your tasks for the day to make the most of how you feel.

For most people it's not necessarily a big deal, but if you know that your mood really affects your productivity significantly you need to think about trying to even out your frame of mind so you're disposed to work more often. One way to do this is to keep a mood diary.

Take a few minutes each day to consider your mood and jot down some notes about how you've felt and behaved. After a couple of weeks you should be able to notice patterns in your moods and then you can try and alter the triggers, issues or environments that are causing your lack of balance. Here are some mood diary tips:

✔ Keep your diary with you during the day and jot down the honest answers to these questions concerning a moment when your mood changed:

   • How did I feel before the mood change?

   • What is happening around me?

   • How do I feel right now?

   • How can I shift out of this negative state?

✔ Consider the following three issues separately (as well as examining the links between them):

   • Behaviour

   • Thoughts

   • Feelings

✔ Make summaries or reflective notes on the day just before you get ready for bed.

✔ Write these notes somewhere quiet so that you can really focus.

Overall you're trying to decide what it is that affects your mood and how surmountable the difficulties are, so you can decide how to tackle your moods. The kinds of actions that many people find helpful are to take some time out or have a brisk walk in some fresh air. If appropriate, communicate with the person who may be affecting your mood, perhaps talking out a particular problem. Some people find that meditation, yoga or breathing exercises can help.

If you're new to any yoga, meditation or breathing exercises, you can pick up a book or DVD to help you get started, or perhaps download an audio file to play on your MP3 player.

I would recommend that you contact your GP or local health club to find a list of registered practitioners running classes that conform to high standards. You can injure yourself trying advanced yoga without help, although some gentle stretching may be beneficial. The same recommendations apply for meditation and be sure not to part with any money until you're sure of the quality of the organisation or individual. If they're good, they'll offer you access to references. For help with breathing exercises, the same people can help, or an experienced singing teacher. For all these services, you can also contact your university.

If you know that you're really moody and have an on-going medical concern, such as a mental health issue, consult your GP for support and report any problems to your supervisor or counsellor.

Just getting on with it

If you've read the previous section, on first reading this section you may think that it seems rather contradictory. I exhort you to build a better understanding of your moods and your work habits and to spend some time thinking about the best way that you can work. This is the right tactic for your dissertation overall. You should learn about your working style from the experience of doing such a major piece of writing and running your research project.

However, at some point you need to stop delving into your emotions and just get on with your writing. It's hard to do, but there'll be several occasions when you really have to force yourself to sit down and get on with some writing, editing or revisions. You've probably experienced this before, often at the eleventh hour just before a deadline, but you need to try to turn this 'last push' mentality into a more frequent strategy for getting work done.

Try setting yourself lots of mini-deadlines as you go along. You can ask your supervisor to help you with this if you need the threat of a tutor's irritation hanging over you. Don't expect your supervisor to be on your back hassling you when you fail to complete individual tasks as you go along, as she probably has several students to supervise.

Knowing when you need a break

Your productivity is likely to diminish as you get tired. If you find yourself going over and over the same passage of reading with nothing sinking in, take a break, even if just for a momentary stand up, stretch and slurp of water.

Working when you're really tired isn't a great idea. Your mind may be freed from some restrictions when you're a bit sleepy and some artists find their creativity flows more when they're tired, but for academic writing you need to attend to detail – a job that's easier when you're alert.

You may feel as if you're being productive, with the words flowing over the paper or screen, but often, work completed when people are tired is poor quality, as it hasn't been carefully considered. It's also pretty much impossible to proofread when you're tired as it's such a tedious task anyway and it's so easy for your mind to drift off and you may miss the very details you're trying to spot.

Some people swear that they work better when they've had little sleep, but this is often illusory. Perhaps you stay up most of the night and write a 2,000-word essay that gets a better mark than you anticipated as you know that it was rushed. But does this mean that you work best with that sort of pressure? You'll never know how much better you could have done if you devoted more time and effort to the task in hand.

It's perfectly possible that you suddenly have a sort of *second wind* just as you were planning to pack up and you find yourself writing furiously, desperate to capture and not forget your unexpected influx of ideas and moment of clarity. Just be sure to check the quality of your work when you're wide awake the next morning. A good idea is to highlight the section you've written in a second wind episode so you can easily identify it for careful review.

Just because you've managed to hand in work on time by working through the night in the past, doesn't mean it was the best quality work you could have produced. Even if this was manageable for a short essay, it's far less feasible for 10,000 words.

With a shorter essay, some people find it appropriate to think about their work for ages and research bit by bit. They then do the writing in one chunk or a couple of mammoth sessions. It's much more difficult to take this approach with a dissertation; you need to be writing as you go along.

You really need plenty of time for editing and reviewing your work and you need to be fresh in order to spot those minor errors that make the difference between well presented and sloppy.

If you're tired, you're far more likely to make errors such as failing to save a file, or saving your old file over your newer version, wiping hours of hard work at the touch of a button. If you must burn the midnight oil, take triple-extra-multi-super-care when backing up and saving files. (Also – save your frenzy of deleting old files until you've had a rest. It's best not to trust yourself to make serious decisions when you're tired.)

Chapter 17

Looking After Yourself

· ·

In This Chapter

▶ Maintaining optimum health

▶ Eating a decent diet

▶ Tackling emotional blockages and difficulties

▶ Winding down after handing in your dissertation

· ·

*Y*ou'll do well to consider your general well-being as you travel along your dissertation journey. Facing up to difficulties and being honest about how well you look after yourself are important when it comes to being able to cope with such an enormous project.

Managing your work is more difficult if you have a cold or you've got no energy. You can't guarantee good health, but you can maximise your possibility of staying well through adopting a healthy lifestyle. For information about a healthy workspace and safe use of computers, check out Chapter 16.

Enjoying Exercise

Undertaking a dissertation is a pretty sedentary activity so you need to make an effort to ensure that you take some exercise. Many benefits accrue from exercise such as reducing the risk of chronic disease, but the ones that are directly relevant to your dissertation performance are that exercise:

- ✔ Helps with your blood sugar levels (which need to be constant)
- ✔ Keeps your blood pressure at a safe level
- ✔ Boosts your immune system
- ✔ Increases self-confidence
- ✔ Can improve your mood
- ✔ Is useful to de-stress
- ✔ Can stimulate you and get you thinking

✔ Helps you get a good night's sleep

✔ Improves concentration and productivity

Exercising on a regular basis improves your cardiovascular system (which concerns the circulation of blood through your heart and blood vessels). If your heart and lungs are working well, you have increased energy.

 A workout at the gym or a brisk half-hour walk can help you calm down after a dreadful day. For most people, exercise reduces feelings of depression and anxiety.

Many people actually enjoy exercise. You may well already exercise regularly and know the benefits of this activity. If so, don't let your dissertation interfere with your regular exercise sessions, but do be aware that if you get very busy with your university work you may have to spend more time at the library and less on the sports field.

 If you represent the university, or play more serious sports, try to get a copy of your fixture schedule as early as possible so that you can work your study around your matches and training as effectively as possible.

 Don't overdo your exercise. Deciding out of the blue to run five miles a day before breakfast can take its toll, and going to extremes with the weight machines can put you at risk of injury. Take medical advice, listen to the gym staff (where appropriate) and undertake sensible, moderate, regular exercise.

Evidence suggests that regular exercise can increase your energy levels and have a positive effect on your sex life – but I can't possibly comment!

It's easy to find excuses not to exercise – most of us have used some of these:

✔ I have too much work

✔ I have family commitments

✔ I have to study right this minute

✔ I can't afford to join a gym

✔ There's nowhere decent to exercise near me

✔ It's not safe to go running at night

✔ The weather is rubbish – I can't go out in that!

The best way of overcoming these barriers is to make exercise a regular part of your everyday routine. Rather than setting aside a specific amount of time every day, however, you increase your exercise through accumulating activity throughout the day. Make it part of your routine to do the following:

✔ Brisk walking

✔ Vacuuming and other vigorous housework

✔ Walking up stairs instead of using lifts

✔ Taking the long route when walking around campus

✔ Gardening

✔ Walking up moving escalators

✔ Helping with DIY

✔ Walking the dog

The main point is just to try and get moving.

Think about the time of day that would suit you for exercise. Some people love to start their day with a burst of activity (plus you get it all over with and can feel smug all day), but others like to refresh themselves with a midday workout or prefer an evening session.

Your body experiences a natural dip in core temperature around six hours after you exercise. This can help you fall asleep a little better than usual, so time your workout carefully if you're having trouble getting to sleep.

Dealing With Your Diet

It probably comes as no surprise that I recommend you eat a healthy and balanced diet to help you maximise the quality of your work and to increase your stamina throughout the long process of your dissertation. This isn't a diet book, however, and so all I'll do here is highlight some of the concerns that arise if you fail to take care of your diet and mention some of the so-called 'brain superfoods' where there's some evidence that you may benefit from their effects.

The basics are (naturally) fruit and veg, some protein and carbs and just enough 'good fats' to deliver the essential vitamins and other nutrients you need for general good health. It's also vital to keep properly hydrated and water is the best fluid for this purpose. It's not just a case of what you eat, but how you eat it – your aim is to keep your blood sugar (glucose) levels stable.

If you can achieve a minimum of five portions of fruit and vegetables per day and stay properly hydrated (predominantly with water), you can pat yourself on the back for a healthy regime of food and drink.

If you don't eat healthily and regularly, you swing between sugar highs and lows (keep your diet high in fibre and eat protein and carbs together).

You need a balance of minerals and vitamins to keep well and the standard advice is that you can derive what you need from the following typical foods. If you eat reasonable portions of these, you shouldn't need any supplements at all:

- ✔ **Vitamin A:** Dairy products, green vegetables such as spinach and broccoli, peppers, tomato juice, and orange fruit and vegetables (mango, squash, carrots and sweet potatoes).

- ✔ **Vitamin D:** Oily fish (such as tuna, sardines, mackerel or salmon), dairy products and eggs. You also derive vitamin D from being exposed to sunlight, so try and get outside in daylight reasonably often!

- ✔ **Vitamin E:** Green veg like broccoli, Brussels sprouts and spinach. Also nuts, some soya products and eggs are good and try and cook your vegetables lightly as heat can affect the vitamin content. This 'fact' is disputed by some people, but soggy spinach isn't very appealing so there's no harm being extra careful.

- ✔ **Vitamin C:** Obviously the citrus fruits and juices are a great source as well as the 'superfood' blueberries. Other yummy foods on this list include kiwi fruit, strawberries, tomatoes and peppers.

- ✔ **Vitamin B:** Different B vitamins are found in various foods — B1 in whole grains, wholemeal bread and green leafy vegetables; B2 in eggs, milk, cheese and some meats (like liver); B3 is found in meats and nuts with lots of protein; B6 is in fish, chicken and cereals (wholegrains in general, not Co-Co Pops); B9 is in fruit; and B12 is in fish, dairy, meat and yeast extract, so Marmite on wholemeal toast is a super snack!

Sussing out supplements

For every piece of medical advice recommending food supplements, you find a warning about how overdoing it can be harmful.

Although most healthy adults don't need to add to their diet, some people do benefit from supplements. For example, vegans may require extra vitamins to make up for those that are usually obtained from meat and dairy, although these can usually be easily received from the standard dark green vegetables and some nuts and seeds (particularly sesame seeds, pumpkin seeds and almonds).

In years gone by, having a great vegan diet would mean expensive shopping in a local health food store, but you can now easily acquire brilliant products in mainstream supermarkets, such as tahini, tofu, soya milk and fortified fruit juices.

Another example is vitamin E which has been shown to help with mental function (also in relation to memory loss in the elderly). You can get enough vitamin E from a regular healthy diet. Other people who may benefit from supplements include:

- ✔ Women planning to get pregnant or in the early stages of pregnancy (need extra folic acid).

- ✔ People who have limited exposure to sunlight can benefit from additional vitamin D. (If you tend to stay mostly indoors or if you wear clothes that really cover you up, you may find vitamin D helpful.)

- ✔ Vegans and some vegetarians may appreciate additional vitamin B12.

- ✔ Those of you who are undergoing intense sports training.

- ✔ Elderly people and children (it's less likely they're doing a dissertation, but it's certainly not impossible).

- ✔ People who have been ill.

- ✔ Those on a weight-loss diet (although the advice is generally to increase fruit and veg rather than popping pills).

A common deficiency is that of iron (particularly prevalent among people who restrict their diets and also among women). Some studies show a link between iron and mental performance.

See your doctor if you're worried about your diet and need more detailed advice.

If you decide that you do need to take supplements, read the instructions with care and never exceed the recommended dose. Note that you'll be wasting your money if you don't take notice of the guidance as, if taken wrongly, all the goodness is flushed through your body and won't be absorbed. Various things interfere with nutrient absorption so:

- ✔ Take supplements with room temperature water
- ✔ Don't drink tea or coffee 15 minutes either side of taking the supplements
- ✔ Take with or after food as directed
- ✔ Don't take lots together as some interfere with one another

If you have known food allergies or intolerances, you should avoid your allergens in order to keep in tip-top condition.

Suddenly consuming massive amounts of vitamin E (or any other supplement) is NOT going to help you be more intelligent or write a better dissertation. It may actually make you unwell (especially if you have a condition affected by blood thinning).

Cutting down on the naughty stuff

Alcohol, caffeine and chocolate aren't inherently bad, but the way you consume them may be. Moderation in everything is good advice and this also holds true for these substances. Having a reasonably modest piece of chocolate or half a pint of beer as a reward for a day of hard work is fine and can even be very motivating, but if you think that you're overdoing it, try to rein in your consumption.

Caffeine is probably the most common issue for many students, especially as it can be used to pull an all-nighter when a deadline looms. It's best to try and stick to the guidance, or at least be aware of how much caffeine is contained in common drinks. Around 300 milligrams per day is usually the recommended limit. The following all contain about 300 milligrams of caffeine:

- ✔ About 3 mugs of instant coffee
- ✔ 2 cups of filter coffee
- ✔ 3 mugs of tea
- ✔ About 4 cans of cola
- ✔ Only 1 or 2 energy drinks

You also find caffeine in some medications, some chocolate bars, and (surprisingly) some green and herbal teas.

Too much caffeine can give you the jitters and may affect your ability to achieve a state of blissful, undisturbed, restorative sleep. However, abruptly giving up caffeine is a bad idea if you're addicted as you'll suffer from withdrawal headaches. Cut down and then cut it out. I suggest you try to develop a taste for decaffeinated products *before* you start your dissertation. Popular brands of tea and coffee all have decaffeinated versions nowadays and they're pretty reasonable.

Alcohol can be a real temptation for some students and in many cases social lives revolve around drinking and the student bar. Many universities are trying to improve the alcohol-free alternatives but until these really take a hold, the buzzy hub of your campus is quite likely to be the bar.

It's easy to drink more than you know is healthy and it's also easy to completely lose track of how much you drink. Most people underestimate how much they get through each week. A unit of alcohol is about half a pint of beer, a single serving of a spirit or half a glass of wine. You shouldn't really have more than two units a day if you're female or three if you're male.

Check out the BBC Health web pages that explain what a unit of alcohol is and show you the recommended intake levels: `http://www.bbc.co.uk/health/healthy_living/nutrition/healthy_alcohol.shtml`.

It's a sobering thought, but drinking too much has heaps of negative health effects, such as increased blood pressure, liver damage, weight gain, stomach problems and so on. Even if you're fighting fit and very healthy, I can assure you that a large alcohol intake won't help you write a brilliant dissertation.

Try keeping a drinking diary for two weeks. Write down any alcohol that passes your lips and the context in which you've been drinking. At the end of the fortnight, look at your patterns of behaviour. If you're drinking too much, think about ways to cut down, such as avoiding the bar at flashpoints in your day, or meeting friends in locations that don't serve alcohol.

See this BUPA site for tips on reducing your alcohol intake: `http://www.bupa.co.uk/health_information/html/healthy_living/lifestyle/alcohol/alcohol4.html`.

The National Health Service website is also helpful with the following links:

You can find an online test to assess your drinking habits at `www.nhs.uk/Tools/Pages/Alcoholcalculator.aspx?Tag=`, and you can find specific advice for students at `www.nhs.uk/Livewell/studenthealth/Pages/Smoking,alcoholanddrugs.aspx`. Health advice for all (including information about binge drinking, social drinking and hangover cures) is available from `www.nhs.uk/LiveWell/Alcohol/Pages/Alcoholhome.aspx`.

Alcohol can also affect your sleep patterns. You can fall into a deeper sleep initially, but it later becomes fitful and less recuperative.

I'd always advise anyone not to smoke, but it's not a great idea to try and give up an entrenched habit when you're in a situation that's likely to be stressful, such as writing your dissertation.

Sleeping, Relaxing and Setting Your Working Hours

Having eliminated your sleep enemies such as alcohol and caffeine, you should be better equipped for your rest periods. Your internal clock (also known as your circadian rhythm) is affected by light and by darkness and trying to keep this regular helps you sleep better.

You may prefer to work at certain times of the day, rather than others. This is often discussed by asking 'Are you an owl or a lark?', although the question isn't desperately useful since most people are actually indifferent. An owl would be more productive working later and not getting up early, whilst a lark would be an early riser and be back in bed around two hours before midnight. (Lots of research is being undertaken about this due to the increasing number of people required to work in shifts and so more information may be forthcoming soon.)

What you need to decide is when you are most alert and in the best state for writing. Rearrange your other activities around this, setting aside your alert time for your dissertation wherever possible.

Avoid having too much sleep as it has a negative effect on your sleep systems (and sometimes on the immune system). You need a certain amount of wakefulness and activity for healthy functioning.

What kind of things can help you relax?

✔ Reading something completely unconnected from your dissertation such as a novel or magazine

✔ Having a long, hot bubble bath

✔ Watching a favourite television programme (but limit your television to planned viewing so you don't end up losing a whole evening)

✔ Getting out of your home for a walk, cuppa in a local café (decaf of course) or popping in to see a friend

✔ Listening to a favourite radio programme (it's a good idea to download the programme so you can listen to what you wanted without being drawn into the programmes either side)

✔ Just sitting and staring out of the window (it's quite meditative)

✔ Having a chat with someone who's not in the least bit interested in your college work so you don't end up spending the whole conversation worrying about your work

The British Wheel of Yoga (bwy.org.uk) is the most well recognised organisation for yoga in the UK. They have some sleep exercises at www.yogaatwork.co.uk/sleep.htm.

If you're worried about your sleep patterns, see your GP of course, but also read the NHS advice at www.nhs.uk/Conditions/ Insomnia/Pages/Introduction.aspx?url=Pages/What- is-it.aspx. You can find some tips for general good health and good sleep at www.nhs.uk/Livewell/women4060/Pages/ Sleepclinic.aspx (it has 'women' in the address, but the tips are generally applicable to men).

Tackling Emotional Issues

It's not enough to eat healthily and get plenty of sleep. You have to deal with any kind of emotional blocks or barriers to successfully complete your dissertation. This section deals with pedestrian problems we all face, such as dealing with people commenting on your work and maintaining good relationships with your friends. I also consider how to tackle more complex problems that may catch you unawares.

Coping with criticism

One of the main roles of your tutor is to help you improve your work. If your work is completely perfect, there's little point having a supervisor in the first place. You have to accept that your supervisor uses his experience and background to help you increase your chances of getting a good grade. Your supervisor doesn't make points just to annoy you, but tries instead to help you.

When you get some feedback from your supervisor, keep the following in mind:

✔ Don't be disheartened if the whole page is riddled with comments and corrections – these can be more helpful than just getting a little mark in a corner of the page or no comments at all. At least you now have some suggestions as to how to improve your work.

✔ Your supervisor is likely to be correcting in a hurry and trying to give you the main points rather than full details. It's possible he may have missed something and so don't assume that everything that isn't highlighted is absolutely perfect.

✔ If your supervisor is pointing out where you have issues with grammar, or with facts, a lack of evidence, or contradiction, these are generally non-negotiable. If your supervisor disagrees with your opinion, it may be something you can take up as a discussion point. (Generally, tutors are quite happy for students to write things with which they disagree, as long as there's sufficient argument to support the student's conclusion and it's expressed logically and coherently.)

If your feedback is really negative, don't contact your supervisor in a kind of knee-jerk panic mode, demanding he explains everything he's said. Calmly read through the comments and try dispassionately to see whether what he's said seems reasonable and is something that you can apply. If you still think that his suggestions are unfair and perhaps too critical, find a sensible friend to talk it through with you and then decide what to do.

Getting your head out of the sand

The first step to solving a problem is recognising that it exists at all. Some people are able to put their worries to the back of their minds and carry on as if everything is fine. Most of us do this to some extent (it's a defence mechanism and a reasonable coping strategy) but if your problems are really mounting and you refuse to face up to them, you're sure to end up in trouble.

Listen to the people around you. You may, in a determined fashion, manage to convince yourself that everything is a-okay, but if several of your friends are trying to get you to show some awareness of the problem, stop and consider what they're saying.

Similarly, if your supervisor plainly states that you're falling behind, you need to take his comments seriously and ask him how you can improve the situation. Don't fob him off with bland platitudes saying that you're absolutely fine and you can manage if that's not true. Your tutor can't help you if he doesn't know that you have difficulties (supervisors may be clever, but they're not psychic).

Being nice to your support team

Think about who's on your support team and how you treat them – are you always as nice as you can be to the following people?

- ✔ University friends
- ✔ Non-university friends
- ✔ Family members
- ✔ Housemates
- ✔ Staff on your programme (administration, library, teaching)
- ✔ People at your work place

It's ironic that for most people, those closest to us bear the brunt of our bad moods, depressed moments and general irritation with the world. They're on the receiving end of our rants, tempers, meltdowns and panics.

It's a good idea to review regularly how you're treating the people closest to you. Without worrying too much about it all costing heaps of money, it's generally very appreciated if you remember to do them the occasional good turn. Remember to thank them for their help and support and buy them the odd glass of wine, bar of chocolate or cappuccino as a token of your appreciation of their long-suffering nature!

There's only so far that goodwill can take you. Do use the university support systems for study skills, IT support, careers advice, counselling, financial guidance and so on. However, your team of friends and family is there for your moral support and to keep you grounded.

Seeking help for more serious problems

If you get into a situation that you can't share with people closest to you or if you have problems that are so extensive that you need additional help, you have several people and services to whom you can turn:

✔ If you have a positive relationship with your GP, a good starting place for dealing with problems is to make an appointment for a chat.

✔ University counselling services are discreet and confidential and can be more useful than other (non-university) counselling services because the staff are used to dealing with students and are fully aware of the kinds of pressures under which you may be working. They also know how best to approach tutors and support staff if required.

✔ Your supervisor and the administration and support staff on your programme.

This isn't so helpful, however, if you feel you're being treated unfairly by people on the course. Before leaping to conclusions about being bullied or suffering discrimination, think carefully about your own reaction to certain situations. Record any incidents that you think show discriminatory behaviour and do this in a non-emotive fashion. Take information to someone you trust and ask them to help you evaluate it and consider the next steps.

It's great if you can help yourself when you're going through a difficult time.

Of the strategies noted here, some may be just right for you whilst others evince dismay, alarm, panic or humour. What matters is what suits you. If you feel better for it, who cares if someone else thinks that it's pointless or stupid?

✔ Relaxation techniques and exercise such as yoga and tai chi.

✔ The practice of meditation and visualisation techniques.

✔ One-to-one or one-to-two counselling and therapy (for example, focusing on relationships, using cognitive-behavioural methods and so on).

✔ Group therapies or support groups.

If you need help, the first place to look is your university. Posters should be dotted around the campus, you should have leaflets from the union and information online. If it doesn't have what you need, try a very useful website – the National Union of Students – who understand better than most about the pressures of studying: www.nus.org.uk/en/Student-Life/Your-study/Coping-with-study-related-stress/. You can find information about counselling in general at the National Health Service website: www.nhs.uk/Conditions/counselling/Pages/Introduction.aspx?url=Pages/what-is-it.aspx, and how the NHS supports

UK universities is explained at `www.student.counselling.co.uk/faq-m-3.html`, where you can find out how counselling can help students and get some reassurance about confidentiality. The section noted here shows you how to express your problems and explains what a counselling session is actually like: `www.student.counselling.co.uk/faq-4.html`.

The Samaritans are online and on the phone 24 hours every single day of the year: `www.samaritans.org`; 08457 90 90 90.

 Many complementary medicine techniques are controversial and have no evidence base that holds up under scientific scrutiny. Your GP and university medical services should be able to help you in ways that suit you. Don't let yourself be pressured into any kind of therapy that you feel is inappropriate.

 You may need a medical referral for some therapies and techniques.

Dealing with the unforeseen

The best preparation for coping with the unforeseen issues is to be as organised and clear as possible. If your plans are thorough and well considered, they're less likely to be derailed by some kind of disaster or problem.

Supervisors are human and do understand that illness, bereavement, relationship breakdown, having to care for another, financial woes and other concerns can seriously impede your ability to complete your work. Let your supervisor know that you have a difficulty that's affecting your work and if you don't want to go into detail, see the support staff and ask them to let your tutor know that it's a genuine concern, but is confidential.

 If you need additional time to complete, you need to request this through formal channels earlier rather than later. You may be required to provide evidence and so think about what constitutes reliable proof of the problem.

Taking Your Final Bow

It may seem unnecessary to have a section on completion – when you're done, you're done, right? Well, yes, in a way, but for some people it's more complicated than that and you need to be sure that you've considered the effects of handing in your work to avoid a continuation of stress once you've submitted your dissertation.

Knowing you've finished

It would seem that knowing when you've finished would be obvious, but in actual fact it can be more complicated than it first appears. If your limit is 10,000 words, do you simply stop writing when you reach 10,000? Of course not! Once you're near the prescribed word limit, your dissertation still requires an ongoing process of redrafting, editing and reworking.

You have a time limit for submission and you need to adhere to it, but be aware that all writers have to make a decision about when enough is enough and they must stop and move on to another task. Your redrafting and editing could actually last for weeks, months or even years as you try to get each word absolutely perfect. Of course you don't have years, as you need to meet your deadline, so you need to recognise when it's as good as it needs to be to satisfy you and your supervisor and the examiner. If your tutor is happy that you've listened to and acted upon advice and if you feel you have achieved an excellent standard, you can stop.

If you're in the very unusual position of having finished early, one of these two explanations is relevant:

- ✔ You've not actually done enough good-quality work and you need to really look through and see what needs to be completed properly.
- ✔ You're a very careful, well-prepared worker and now you're going to worry and fuss, possibly even starting to undo what is perfectly fine.

If it's the former, it's clear what you need to do. If it's the latter (and you have proofread twice), you need to accept that enough is enough and you should stop fiddling.

 If you find it difficult to stop fussing even if your work is really finished, speak to your supervisor about the possibility of handing it in before the due date so that it's beyond your reach and you can get on with something else.

Letting go after you finish

Once you've handed in your dissertation, you're done. Put it out of your mind and distract yourself. Most students have other coursework to occupy them, but if you don't, you need to find something to fill the sudden vacuum. Take a moment to congratulate yourself on completing the project – you've earned a celebratory cuppa, glass of wine, glossy magazine, packet of crisps, trip to the cinema or whatever floats your boat.

Don't revisit your dissertation and worry about things that are now beyond your control. Whether or not you need help with moving on, it's a great idea to review your dissertation experience. If you have a journal or kind of reflective portfolio, you can record these things, but if not, you can basically write yourself a letter (it's fun to seal it and mark 'for opening on *x* date' – choose a day in about three months when you've forgotten what it might be):

✔ Think through what you did and didn't enjoy about your dissertation topic.

✔ What you enjoyed/hated about the research methods you used.

✔ Anything you really regret doing/not doing.

✔ What features of the dissertation were exciting?

✔ What were the highs and lows?

✔ How would you feel if you were given the opportunity to do it again – what would you change and what would you keep the same?

✔ Which aspects of your relationships with others went well/ badly.

This is a cathartic activity, but other things may also help such as clearing up your workspace (put things away but don't have a ceremonial burning just yet) and moving away from anywhere that could allow you to reopen your files.

Winding down after submission

In order to have a relaxed hand-in experience, however boring it may be, the key (once again) is preparation. You may have some documentation to complete, such as a kind of cover sheet that goes on the front of your work and has a declaration that the work is all your own. Like most universities, where I work we have a sheet that the students complete with their details and the examiners write their comments on this sheet when they mark the work. If you do have this to complete, ensure that you collect it before the submission date, wherever possible, so you can complete it at your leisure and not in the potentially stressful situation of the hand-in room or admin office. If you do this, you're less likely to make mistakes and you have more time to check it over.

Now take a break. Enjoy yourself for a few days and revel in that feeling of satisfaction. You may find that you've forgotten you've finished it and it takes a few seconds each morning for you to remember that you're free! Relish the wave of relief that sweeps over you and notice that day-by-day you can start to put it behind you.

It's not really over 'til it's over and that means when you receive official confirmation that you've passed. If your supervisor has been confident of your success and you've honestly done all you've been asked properly, you can relax. If, alternatively, you're aware that your dissertation journey has been rather bumpy, be certain that you have all your notes and information to hand in case you need to make corrections or resubmit.

Dealing with failure

Well, it's not the outcome you wanted, but you may not be surprised that you didn't do very well. If you honestly know why you didn't pass, then you know what you need to do for the resubmission.

If you really can't imagine how you failed, you need to make an appointment to see your supervisor and also arrange to see the support services for extra help. You must collect your work so that you can see the comments that have been made.

Read through the comments with care and if you don't understand some of them or can't read them, make a note of where you're confused and raise these with your supervisor when you meet.

Try not to make the meeting immediate if you're very upset about your grade. There's no point shouting or crying; it's you that has to do the rewrite and you're only going to make it harder to get on with your work. You can cry and curse with your friends and insult your supervisor from the comfort of your sofa by all means, but don't forget that he's your source of help and so it's a good idea not to scream at him when you meet.

Be very honest. One example of an annoying attitude from students is resorting to promising they've tried really hard when they clearly have not. I have had students saying 'But this is the best work I've ever done. I just can't see where I went wrong' when we've been reviewing their work that lacked even capital letters and full stops. It's just not true that it's their best work.

If you rushed your dissertation and you regret it, but recognise that you rushed it, say so. At least the supervisor knows that you're probably capable of passing, but you need more time, another chance and a better attitude.

When you see your supervisor about failed work, have a plan of action prepared for the next submission to show you've been thinking about what needs to change.

The onus is on you to find out about any resubmission dates and details. If in doubt, check and check again.

If you think that you haven't been treated fairly, you can probably lodge an appeal. Universities have systems of checks and balances that normally involve any failed piece of work being marked by at least two different tutors. External examiners (from similar courses at other universities) also check through a sample of work to see if the standards are equable across the university system. Because of these measures, it's likely that your work has been moderated by different people and the grade you've been given has been agreed by a few qualified people.

If you launch an appeal or request for it to be re-marked, it's perfectly possible that the grade you have could be dropped to a lower level if the new markers feel that the first examiners were too lenient. So you need to be really sure that you're prepared for the possibility that your grade can go down if you request a re-mark.

In my experience, about a third of the work put in for re-marking achieves a higher grade and the rest remains unchanged (more often this is for essays than dissertations). When the mark is improved (or dropped) it's usually by no more than two or three per cent and rarely makes much difference. Occasionally it does change the classification of the work (for example, it drops from a 2i to a 2ii). On very rare occasions a massive mismatch occurs and then the paper could end up being marked by four or five people. I think I've seen this happen twice in a decade.

Taking the next steps

For many people the submission of an undergraduate dissertation was the final part of their academic career, but this is changing as increasing numbers of careers demand master's degree level qualifications as part of professional development. Since you've undertaken a degree, you're likely to be pursuing a professional job and even if this is in an unrelated field, you'd be well advised to hang on to your notes and data in case you find yourself wanting to develop some of your ideas at a later date in your studies.

Right now, it may seem absurd to you even to think about further writing and research, but if you have even the slightest inkling about it, keep hold of your notes. It's perfectly natural to be sick of it for now.

It's worth writing a letter or diary entry to yourself about the whole dissertation experience and putting it somewhere you'll remember to look when you embark on your next dissertation. It'll help you learn from your previous mistakes and stop you slipping into bad habits.

You may be keen as mustard to get cracking on the next degree, but stop for a moment and really think things through. Talk to your supervisor and friends (both on your course and some taking different courses) about what area you should study to help avoid you hurtling off on the wrong path, wasting time and energy. If you're really excited about further study, you can always capitalise on your enthusiasm by expanding your reading, especially keeping track of new research through following up leads from your thesis. You should also attend research seminars and offer to help out at conferences.

Many universities offer their alumni a reduced fee rate if they register for a higher degree with the university.

If you already have a place on a further degree, congratulations! Take a break of at least a few days before you get stuck into your work. If you're really interested now, you'll still be interested in a week's time. It's worth recharging thoroughly, as the next step is going to be at least as much work as the last one!

If your work is of outstanding quality (usually this means getting a grade of over 85 per cent), your supervisor may speak to you about publishing possibilities and encourage you to engage more fully with the world of academia. To do this seriously you'll have to take a further degree (or two), but you can dip your toe deeper into the scholarly ocean through these routes:

- ✔ Contacting journals and putting yourself forward to write book reviews.

- ✔ Offering to help organise conferences so you can attend for free or for a reduced rate.

- ✔ Joining your field's academic groups.

- ✔ Getting to know more about your field through reading and research or even applying for a post in research.

- ✔ Offering your services as a volunteer in a related area or organisation.

Working in an administrative or support department in a university can also help you understand how academia works and you can often get reduced rates on studying for a higher degree.

Part VI
The Part of Tens

'And this is the patron saint of studying.'

In this part...

*E*very *For Dummies* book has a Part of Tens, and this one is no exception. Here you find three chapters each containing ten brief nuggets of advice. I show you ten common mistakes to avoid, ten tried and trusted ways to make your dissertation a masterpiece and, finally, ten last-minute things to consider before you get your dissertation bound.

Chapter 18

Ten Pitfalls to Avoid

I've been supervising undergraduate dissertations for some years now and during that time I have seen students making the same old common errors when approaching their work – despite my pointed and friendly advice! In this chapter I give you a list of the ten most common pitfalls waiting to trip you up and how best to avoid them.

Avoiding the following pitfalls is going to help you enjoy a much smoother ride on your dissertation journey and a sure way of improving your chances of getting a good grade.

Not Contacting Your Supervisor Until the Eleventh Hour

Your supervisor is your main source of support when you're writing your dissertation – ignore your supervisor at your peril. Usually you're assigned to a supervisor early on in the first stages of your dissertation (or even in the preceding term). It's your responsibility to arrange a first meeting with your supervisor, so get in touch as soon as possible. Leaving contacting your supervisor until the eleventh hour is a potential disaster. You're going to lose out on invaluable support and advice, cutting down on the time she has to help you – and making her very cross indeed.

Don't have one meeting and then drop off the radar. Most supervisors aren't in the business of calling or emailing students – the responsibility lies on your shoulders – so make sure that you contact your tutor to arrange regular meeting times.

Assuming You've Covered Everything Without Checking

Some students make the big mistake of ignoring their university dissertation guidelines. If you've been seeing your supervisor regularly and acted on the suggestions I give in this book, you can't go wrong when writing your dissertation. If you've familiarised yourself with the details of your dissertation guidelines, checking them at each stage of your writing, you're sure of getting done everything you've been asked to do. Ignoring your dissertation guidelines and following your own sweet path is inevitably going to make a difference to your overall grade.

Students sometimes realise at the last minute that they've forgotten to do an important part of their dissertation such as the abstract or bibliography, so it pays to keep checking as you go along. And your final check is just as important. When you're near to your submission date, hop over to Chapter 20 to check that you've got any last-minute issues sorted.

Treating Your Dissertation Like an Essay

Avoid falling into the trap of telling yourself that your dissertation is going to be just like writing an essay, only a bit longer – well, a few thousand words longer. A dissertation is a much more structured piece of work than an essay and has to include a set number of elements as required by your university dissertation guidelines. When you're writing a dissertation, you have to include the following:

- Title page, Acknowledgements, Contents page
- Abstract and Introduction
- Literature review
- Research methodologies
- Bibliography or List of References
- Appendixes
- Binding

You must make sure that you're fully clued up on what's expected of you when writing your dissertation and that you're following all the instructions set out in your university dissertation guidelines. Students do sometimes fail on technicalities.

Adding Heaps of Appendixes

Don't assume that you're going to get extra marks for including all your research notes and photocopies of your favourite journal articles in the appendixes simply because you can't bear to leave the material out, and want the examiner to see how hard you've been working. You won't get extra marks – you're going to get marks deducted.

You may have been burning the midnight oil and have box files crammed full of fascinating data you generated that you can't find a good reason for including in the main body of your dissertation: such as illuminating chapters in books, brilliant quotations, great journal articles, the list is endless. Just because your supervisor has shown a great interest in your work, doesn't mean that the examiner is prepared to plough through a load of information that's merely on the fringe of your research question. Only include in your appendixes material that sheds a useful light on your research methodologies or background to your arguments. Your examiner is looking for succinct, tight argument, not examples of everything you've collected over the past year, making your dissertation the equivalent of an overstuffed shoe box!

Don't forget there's a difference between producing meaningful data, and churning out irrelevant data.

Ignoring Your Supervisor's Suggestions

You may sometimes feel that your supervisor never, ever stops. 'The importance of having a literature review', and 'What are you going to include in your research methodology section?' Your supervisor may try to persuade you to limit the data you're presenting or talk you into narrowing the focus of your research question. Bear in mind that your supervisor generally has good reasons for making such suggestions.

Think about it. Your supervisor more than anything wants you to pass, not fail. A successful student is just one more feather in the cap for a supervisor.

Listening to the advice of your friends may be more agreeable and privately you may be thinking that your dissertation is ground-breaking, exceptional and unique. Don't forget your supervisor has likely read more dissertations than you and your friends have had hot dinners. Maybe you just like to be different or you hate 'doing as you're told'? Just because your supervisor says that a dissertation on evolutionary theory really ought to mention Darwin, doesn't mean that she's necessarily right. Or, does it?

Rubbishing Your References

Producing an accurate record of all the references you've cited in your dissertation may not be your idea of a grand day out. Putting together your 'Bibliography' or 'List of References' can be long-winded, repetitive and fiddly. But the end result can be a wonderful way of gaining you easy marks.

A clear, accurate bibliography or list of references, presented alphabetically (or numerically) and properly formatted is the answer to an examiner's prayer. Some marking schedules have a specific set of points allocated to referencing and bibliographies but even where this is not the case, the quality of the referencing is definitely going to affect your final grade.

The purpose of your bibliography or list of references is to give your examiner all the information she needs to track the references down on the library shelves. Although you've read some great texts and discovered useful journal articles, if vital information is missing from the reference, making the item almost impossible to follow up, inevitably you're going to lose valuable credit for your research.

Don't trick yourself into assuming that nobody is likely to read your bibliography or list of references. Absolutely all examiners look through your bibliography or list of references to check out your sources, and an examiner expects your references to be cited with all the necessary details.

After years on the job, most examiners are eagle-eyed and can spot missing details by just glancing at a page.

Failing to Discuss Your Work

Don't make the mistake of cutting yourself off from friends and family while you're working on your dissertation. Get your friends and family involved by making them feel that they've got something useful to contribute. Of course, ultimately you're going to be working alone when writing up your research findings, but along the way it can benefit you greatly by engaging with other people and talking about your dissertation – both the content and the process.

Explaining your ideas to others helps you spot any weaknesses in your argument or gaps in your data. One of your friends or someone in your family can so often come up with a brilliant comment, helping you to clarify your thinking. By talking about what you're researching and writing, you get to see where your work may need improving, and being asked questions can help you to anticipate some of the discussions you're going to be having later with your supervisor.

When it comes to talking about the process of writing your dissertation, your friends and family are likely to come up with any number of tips for the actual writing, from the best time of day to get started – to the best time of day to switch off and join your friends in the pub.

Neglecting Good English

Your dissertation needs to be a credit to you – being written in good English and free from grammar and spelling mistakes. Fortunately spelling and grammar checkers are a boon for pointing out where your writing needs attention. Unfortunately, spelling and grammar checkers aren't foolproof and you still need to go through your work yourself picking up and correcting errors – sometimes even those words that the spellchecker okayed.

You need to present your ideas and arguments clearly and succinctly. Poor spelling and grammar can get in the way of what you're trying to say. Have a dictionary on your desk as well as a guide to English grammar, and use them. You also need to be aware of your audience and that the language you're using is geared to your level of reader. Communicating in text speak is fine on your mobile or sometimes even in emails. For example, I commonly receive emails that assume 'ev1 undst txt spk n use it 4 all msgs'. Yes, handy for text messaging but totally inappropriate in your dissertation.

Drawing Wild Conclusions from Limited Data

Often students fail to recognise the limitations of the data they're generating. Remember that you aren't expected to produce data that's going to rock the world. An undergraduate dissertation is supposed to be a useful contribution to your field of study, by examining the existing literature and showing that you've got to grips with current ideas – and then developing some aspect of your field of study in a thoughtful and scholarly fashion.

Using small samples gives you insufficient evidence to have a major impact on your field of study. However, the evidence you get from taking a small sample is sufficient for an undergraduate dissertation. You can't make grand conclusions from a small sample, but this isn't a problem when it comes to your dissertation; it's what your examiner expects. If looking at a small group is what you've been asked to do, your supervisor understands that producing large amounts of data is well-nigh impossible.

If you have great ideas for future studies, then doing an MA or PhD is your opportuniy for doing much more wide-ranging research and for making more of a splash. Keep your undergraduate dissertation in perspective.

Disregarding the Word Limit

Your examiner isn't going to sit there counting each word you've written while she's marking your dissertation. This doesn't mean that your examiner doesn't have a good idea of the total number of words you're using. After a few years of marking dissertations, most supervisors can judge from the size and weight of a dissertation if it's way longer or shorter than expected. Don't lead yourself into believing that not making use of your 10,000 word limit and producing a much shorter dissertation is going to be welcomed, because it's going to take less time to mark. You need to use up your word limit to show the depth and thoroughness that your dissertation requires. If your dissertation is physically thin, it's going to look suspiciously like you haven't done enough work.

Similarly, you're going to be mistaken in thinking that going over your word limit demonstrates depth of work or dedication. Being too wordy merely shows that you're unable to judge what's relevant and what's merely incidental.

When faced with marking either a short or a long dissertation, I get a kind of sinking feeling before even opening the front cover. In your dissertation you're usually required to provide a statement about the originality of your work and the number of words you're using. Each A4 page of text contains around 300 to 500 words and it doesn't take a lot of skill to get a good idea if the student's claim is way off the word limit.

Chapter 19

Ten Top Tips for Finishing Your Dissertation Successfully

In This Chapter

▶ Starting off on the right foot

▶ Getting the most out of your reading

▶ Sharing your concerns

---

*B*y following all the advice I offer in this book you have every chance of writing a successful dissertation. Here I'm picking out the ten best ways of making sure that your dissertation is finished successfully.

Stating Your Research Question Clearly

Putting down on paper the title of your research question is a sure way of focusing your mind on the research topic you've chosen. You may discover that your topic is simply too broad to make your research feasible – or the opposite, the topic you're choosing is too narrow to provide enough evidence to support your theories. In either case the advice of your supervisor is invaluable. Mostly, a supervisor spends a lot of his time trying to help a student focus on a narrower area of study than the one the student originally came up with. Your supervisor knows what he's talking about and is fully aware of how much work is involved and the resources available to answer your research question – encouraging you to tackle a small area of your field of study in depth and with a thorough approach. Having a clearly focused research question is going to help you achieve a higher mark than trying to work with a research question that's too wide-ranging and results in arguments that are correspondingly much less convincing.

Ask your supervisor to sign off your research question as early as possible so that you can get going on your task.

 As your ideas develop you may find that you need to amend the title of your research question slightly. Amending your original research question title is all part of the process of writing a dissertation. So try not to see your research question as fixed and unmovable.

Following Your Dissertation Guidelines

Throughout this book I stress the importance of referring to and sticking to your university dissertation guidelines at all times while writing your dissertation. Each university, module and course has specific rules that need to be followed when doing a dissertation. The advice I give in this book can only be general, you need to consult your own university dissertation guidelines for precise details.

Most universities provide a booklet and/or online access to information on what is expected of you when writing a dissertation. Your university or course may also offer information sessions where the details are clearly explained so that you're properly informed. It's up to you to access the information and get along to any meetings your university provides.

 If there's no generic help available, it's up to your supervisor to support you throughout. This is unusual, however, and so do check the information you have before running to your tutor with every single query that occurs to you. It's quite common for a tutor to send an email referring students to their programme, course or module handbook or to look for the answers to questions online.

You'll only annoy your tutor if you have lost your handbook and don't make the effort to collect a replacement. You want your tutor to be pleased to hear from you and keen to answer, but if you ask queries to which you should know the answers (such as library opening times or term dates) you might find they're not that forthcoming.

Planning Your Time Carefully

You usually have a full year ahead of you for writing your dissertation – but that time can fly by alarmingly fast. You need to plan how you're going to organise your time so that you finish your dissertation successfully.

The areas of your dissertation likely to take up large chunks of your time are compiling your bibliography, analysing your data and putting together your literature review. The tasks that may need reworking more than once are your abstract and composing your acknowledgements. But most of all you need to set aside enough time for revising, editing and proofreading. Only when you're completely satisfied with the result should you think of handing in your dissertation.

 Those apparent 'little jobs' can be incredibly frustrating – maddening even. Carrying out tasks that you find tedious is bad enough at the best of times, but can seem impossible when you're tired and pushed for time. Plan your time effectively.

 Try to stay calm. Work out how long you think you're going to need for the task – then double it (maybe even adding an extra hour or two for good measure). And if you do finish the task in your planned timescale, you've more than earned a nice cup of tea or a trip to the pub.

Taking Advantage of Your University Support Systems

Your university is more than likely to offer a range of support services aimed at helping students in times of need as well as giving help on more practical matters . Take advantage of these services. For example, your university library or learning resources centre has qualified staff who can show you how to structure your online searches to find the relevant information on your research topic. Your library can also organise inter-library loans for key items not held in your university library.

There'll be courses to help you learn how to use software and probably study skills sessions you can attend. There should also be on-line materials and support for you and maybe quizzes or reviews to help you identify your strengths so that you can work to your abilities and develop your areas of weakness or less experience.

You may already be thinking of applying for jobs and your careers service is the place to go for advice on interview techniques and ways of linking your dissertation topic to the requirements of the job. Your careers service is invaluable for helping you in identifying your skills and putting together your CV.

Make the support staff and the staff in admin your new best friends! Try not to come across as a pest, but frame your enquiries thoughtfully and firmly. If you do have a crisis later down the line, the support staff are likely to go out on a limb to help you or offer to get in touch with your supervisor on your behalf; the staff knowing how hardworking and serious you are about your studies.

Never lose sight that your supervisor is your chief support system – so if you have a difficulty that you can't resolve on your own, get in touch with your supervisor as early as you can.

Writing Rather Than Reading

I'm well aware that in this book I encourage you in reading widely around your chosen research topic. But there comes a time when you have to put away your reading and start writing. The danger is that the more you read, the less you feel you know, making it harder to put pen to paper (or finger to keyboard) – and realising that your topic is potentially huge and you're barely scratching the surface, even after three months of reading!

Be assured that your supervisor is going to point out pretty quickly if you've missed out reading the important texts.

Get down to writing earlier rather than later; you can always expand on what you've written by adding more source references as you go along. Whatever you write isn't going to go to waste – the passage you're writing may even end up in a different part of your work. But as you get into the swing of writing you're going to feel pleased with yourself that your dissertation is taking shape at last.

Choosing Your Research Methods Early

You've chosen your research topic, now you need to choose your research methods. Sorting out your research methods can take up more time than you think especially if you have to seek ethical clearance before getting started. If the research method you've chosen doesn't work out, at least by starting early you're giving yourself enough time to try another method. You also need to be getting on with your research to be sure of gathering enough data for your data analysis.

Think carefully through your research question and the best method of getting the sort of data you need. Don't waste valuable time writing a questionnaire and then giving up on it; writing an interview schedule and giving up on that; and ending up doing an observation! In your research methods chapter you need to point out any difficulties that your research method throws up (but without sounding negative), and then after following your research method shows how you're overcoming any negative aspects of the method you've chosen.

Getting Ethical Clearance

Getting ethical clearance before starting your research is vital. It's a disaster if you have to scrap your data from an observation, questionnaire or interview simply because you failed to obtain the correct kind of ethical authorisation and consent for your work.

Ask your supervisor sooner rather than later if you need to get ethical clearance before starting on your research topic. If you do, you need to make absolutely sure that your subjects fully understand the consequences of taking part and are happy to carry on.

Sorting out ethical clearance is your responsibility and you need to make sure of allowing yourself enough time to get any ethical aspects of your dissertation sorted.

Collecting Your Data Early

You're well advised to start gathering your data as soon as you can once your research question has been signed off by your supervisor. When you're carrying out your research project you can sometimes find yourself coming up against difficulties and barriers that you simply didn't expect to meet. Even experienced, professional researchers can't predict the hitches and complications they meet during their research – so getting started on collecting your data early is highly recommended.

Once you get started on your data collection, you may find that you need to revise your schedule because some interviews or questionnaires can take longer than you first expected.

Be polite and courteous to your subjects at all times. You never know when you may have to ask your subjects to do the same questionnaire or interview again in order to put facts right that you first recorded incorrectly.

Talking to People

Writing your dissertation can be a deeply personal experience, but your work's not top secret. You and your dissertation can greatly benefit from testing out your ideas on other people. Of course your supervisor is the best person to talk to, but plenty of other people can help out, although you're probably going to find that your supervisions are the best time for thrashing out specific ideas and issues.

Technical issues can often be resolved through checking out your university dissertation guidelines. You're then husbanding your time for discussing more meaty issues with your supervisor, tackling important theories and ideas, rather than spending time on more mundane matters.

Use your friends, family and fellow students as a sounding board for your ideas and theories, not forgetting to say that you're fully prepared to return the favour. Just talking about your research question helps to reinforce what you already know and highlights gaps in your understanding. You're also going to know from the person's confused expression when you're saying something illogical or stupid.

A study group or network of fellow students is a great place for thrashing out ideas.

Reading in Depth

Reading round your research topic is vastly important for getting a true picture of what's going on in your field of study. However, aim for quality over quantity. You're not expected to read absolutely everything ever published in your field. To make sure you're reading the important material you need to be discerning, spending time on reading acclaimed authors and really trying to get to grips with the ideas and theories being put forward.

If you're not sure what books or articles you should be reading, check with your supervisor. Your course materials may also be able to help if you see a particular author being mentioned frequently. (Chapter 6 offers some useful tips on reading effectively.)

Chapter 20

Ten Things to Check Before You Bind Your Dissertation

. . . .

In This Chapter

▶ Doing a final review of your work

▶ Spotting details you shouldn't overlook

▶ Appreciating that now isn't the time to make huge changes

. . . .

Watching Your Spelling and Grammar

You can sea hear how easy it is two right words that aren't put write by the computer your using. I've put six errors in the previous sentence and if you viewed that sentence in a word-processing program, none of them would have the wavy line that should pop up when there's a mistake. It takes human judgement to correct some blunders and there's nothing for it except to read the whole lot through.

If you can persuade a kind critical friend to help you out it can be extremely worthwhile, especially if she doesn't know much about the subject area. If this is the case, she could be more likely to pick up errors that you skate over.

 When you do run the spell check, make sure it's set to UK English otherwise you'll find you get non-standard spellings throughout your work.

Getting the Pagination Right

Numbering pages during the final stages of your work is fiddly and long-winded whichever way you set about it. When it comes to printing out, you can either combine the whole dissertation into one file and the numbers will go all the way from start to finish. Another way is to print each part and set the numbers as you go along. I prefer this method as it means you can make minor adjustments and if you make a mistake you can just print out a page here and there.

Either way, you need to check really carefully as the last thing you want is for a page to be missing, or repeated. It's really annoying to be in the flow of reading and turn a page only to find that something's awry.

Check with care and pay particular attention to how your contents page matches up with your text, especially if you've had to adjust a page or two.

If you make any changes, you'll have to go through the text and adjust any appendix page references as well.

Spelling Your Supervisor's Name Correctly

This seems almost silly, it's so obvious, but it's a common issue that students forget at the last minute. If you are required to put your name and that of your supervisor on the title page, just triple check that they're accurate. The same applies to your title and other course details.

A mistake in the title looks very sloppy and whilst the odd blob of liquid paper to correct a page number is not a big deal, it spoils what should be a clean, neat opening to your work. Don't go overboard — examiners aren't after elaborate coloured borders and sparkly paper, just go for clarity.

Proofreading Your Bibliography Painstakingly

Don't plan to do this task when you're feeling sleepy as it will pretty much finish you off! It's deadly dull, but needs to be done. Print out a draft (maybe even increase the font for this task if it helps – although don't forget that it'll affect the formatting) and get hold of a ruler. Line by line, check all the elements of each reference for consistency in commas, brackets, capital letters, colons, the use of '&' or 'and', and so on.

Once you've done the close check, get rid of the ruler and check the whole lot again, just for alphabetical order. Once that's completed, print out an additional draft in the correctly sized font to check for formatting issues and page breaks (try not to split references across pages).

If you can stomach it, leave it for a day or two and then look again for a final sweep. You'll be amazed how many minor things you'll have missed!

Avoiding Last-Minute Changes

Stay calm and don't panic. If you find a minor error somewhere, you can apply some liquid paper, or add a polite note to the examiner, but don't start pulling the whole thesis to pieces at the last minute, deciding your literature review is all wrong, for example. If you've done the proper checks, you should be fine. It will be far too disruptive to make major changes at the last minute.

Thanking Everyone Who Helped

You'll really regret it if you rush your acknowledgements and leave out someone close to your heart by mistake. Think it through, sleep on it and think it through again.

Anonymising Your Material

Take a very careful final look at your confidential material. Run a search on the actual names of every person and place you have tried to anonymise in case you've slipped up somewhere. Don't forget to thoroughly check all the appendixes as this is where the common mistakes are usually found.

Making Your Section Titles Clear

Even if you need to reprint the odd section, make sure you don't have a heading at the bottom of a page and the corresponding information is a page-turn away. It just serves to interrupt the flow of your work, making it unnecessarily complicated to read.

Double-Checking the Binding and Submission Details

Before shelling out your hard-earned cash on gold-tooled hard cloth bindings, you must check what's actually required. Generally, undergraduate work can be submitted in a comb binding with a plastic cover for durability.

Bind your dissertation appropriately! It's exasperating when a dissertation you're marking falls to pieces in your hands. This is especially frustrating when you're trying to mark on a train, or plane. Grrr!

It's pretty basic: You want your work to open easily, lie flat (preferably), be readable, have 'turnable' pages and be robust enough to cope with being shoved in the boot of a car, the post or a big box as it gets transported around between examiners' homes and offices or sent off to an external examiner in some distant university.

Working Out Your Journey to the Submission Place

Once you have it all planned out, give yourself two hours more than you think you need. Have with you the telephone number of a couple of friends and the administrative office in case you have a complete disaster and charge your phone fully before you set off with your work. Carry your work in a robust bag and keep it strapped to you (by putting it in a rucksack or shoulder bag) so you don't leave it on the bus or train.

Don't forget your electronic submission if this is also required.

Index

....

Symbol

* (asterisk), 131

• A •

• *Q* •

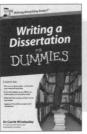
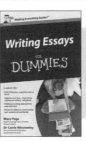

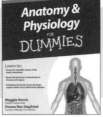

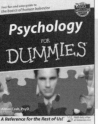

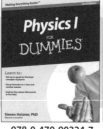

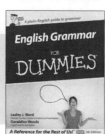
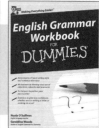

FOR DUMMIES

Making Everything Easier! ™

UK editions

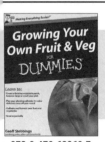

FOR DUMMIES

Making Everything Easier! ™

UK editions

SELF-HELP

978-0-470-66541-1

978-1-119-99264-6

978-0-470-66086-7

MUSIC

978-0-470-97799-6
UK Edition

978-0-470-66603-6
Lay-flat, UK Edition

978-0-470-66372-1
UK Edition

HISTORY

978-0-470-68792-5

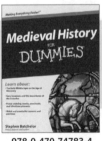

978-0-470-74783-4

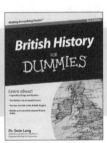

978-0-470-97819-1

Origami Kit For Dummies
978-0-470-75857-1

Overcoming Depression For Dummies
978-0-470-69430-5

Polish For Dummies
978-1-119-97959-3

Positive Psychology For Dummies
978-0-470-72136-0

PRINCE2 For Dummies, 2009 Edition
978-0-470-71025-8

Project Management For Dummies
978-0-470-71119-4

Renting Out Your Property For Dummies, 3rd Edition
978-1-119-97640-0

Ruby Union For Dummies, 3rd Edition
978-1-119-99092-5

Sage One For Dummies
978-1-119-95236-7

Self-Hypnosis For Dummies
978-0-470-66073-7

Starting & Running a Business Online For Dummies, 2nd Edition
978-1-119-99138-0

Storing and Preserving Garden Produce For Dummies
978-1-119-95156-8

Time Management For Dummies
978-0-470-77765-7

Training Your Brain For Dummies
978-0-470-97449-0

Work-Life Balance For Dummies
978-0-470-71380-8

Available wherever books are sold. For more information or to order direct go to www.wiley.com or call +44 (0) 1243 843291